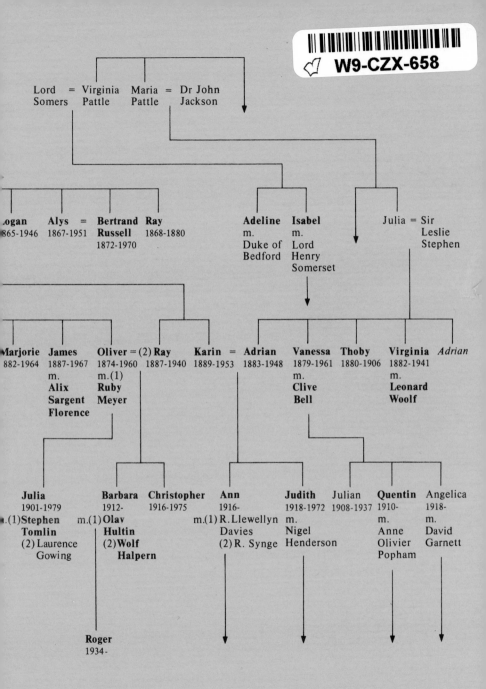

Lord = Virginia   Maria = Dr John
Somers Pattle   Pattle   Jackson

ogan   Alys =   Bertrand   Ray   Adeline   Isabel   Julia = Sir
865-1946   1867-1951 Russell   1868-1880   m.   m.   Leslie
                      1872-1970   Duke of   Lord   Stephen
                                                  Bedford   Henry
                                                            Somerset

Marjorie   James   Oliver = (2) Ray   Karin = Adrian   Vanessa   Thoby   Virginia   *Adrian*
882-1964   1887-1967 1874-1960   1887-1940 1889-1953 1883-1948 1879-1961 1880-1906 1882-1941
           m.   m.(1)   m.   m.
           Alix   Ruby   Clive   Leonard
           Sargent   Meyer   Bell   Woolf
           Florence

Julia   Barbara   Christopher   Ann   Judith   Julian   Quentin   Angelica
1901-1979   1912-   1916-1975   1916-   1918-1972   1908-1937 1910-   1918-
m.(1)Stephen m.(1)Olav   m.(1)R.Llewellyn m.   m.   m.
    Tomlin   Hultin   Davies   Nigel   Anne   David
 (2) Laurence   (2)Wolf   (2) R. Synge   Henderson   Olivier   Garnett
    Gowing   Halpern   Popham

                   Roger
                   1934-

REMARKABLE RELATIONS

Hannah Whitall Smith in 1893 (aged sixty-one)

REMARKABLE RELATIONS

The Story of the Pearsall Smith Family

by

BARBARA STRACHEY

LONDON
VICTOR GOLLANCZ LTD
1980

ISBN 0 575 02823 8

ACKNOWLEDGEMENTS

I am grateful for permission to use copyright material to: Constable & Co. Ltd (Logan Pearsall Smith, *Unforgotten Years* and *Reperusals and Re-collections*; Bernard Berenson, *Sketch for a Self Portrait*); Allen and Unwin Ltd (Bertrand Russell, *Autobiography*); Nisbet & Co. (H. W. Smith, *A Religious Rebel*); The Author's Literary Estate and the Hogarth Press (Virginia Woolf, *Letters*, vols I, II and III and *Diary*, vols I and II); Dr C. Anrep (N. Mariano, *Forty Years with Berenson*); J. T. Flexner and W. Flexner (H. T. Flexner, *A Quaker Childhood*); and Res-Lib Ltd 1980 (Bertrand Russell Archives, McMaster University).

The Frontispiece is from a crayon drawing of Hannah Whitall Smith at Friday's Hill, made in 1893 by Sir William Rothenstein. It is reproduced by courtesy of Sir John Rothenstein, CBE, KCSG, and Mr Michael Rothenstein, ARA.

All the photographs are taken from the author's collection.

Printed in Great Britain at
The Camelot Press Ltd, Southampton

Contents

Illustrations

Frontispiece

Hannah Whitall Smith in 1893
(*Crayon drawing by Sir William Rothenstein*)

Alys Russell campaigning for Women's Suffrage in 1910
Ray Costelloe, c. 1908
Karin Costelloe, c. 1908
Bernhard Berenson, 1909
Mary Berenson, c. 1914
I Tatti
Ray Costelloe, the Rev. Anna Shaw and Ellie Rendel in
    Buffalo, 1909
Hannah at Court Place, 1909
The Strachey family, c. 1893
Oliver Strachey, 1911
Mud House in 1936: Mary Berenson, Roger, Ray Strachey
Adrian Stephen, c. 1928
Virginia Woolf, Mud House, 1938 (photographed by the
    author)
Julia Strachey, c. 1911
Ray Strachey with her children, Christopher and Barbara,
    Mud House, 1928
Karin Stephen and her children, Ann and Judith, 1926
Ray Strachey canvassing in Chiswick and Brentford during
    the General Election of 1923
Nicky Mariano and Mary Berenson at I Tatti, 1929
Logan Pearsall Smith, c. 1931
Ray Strachey, 1940
Karin Stephen, 1927
Mary Berenson in old age with Roger, 1935
Bernard Berenson with Roger at I Tatti, 1935
Alys Russell in Wellington Square, 1948
Bertrand Russell in the 1940s

*A family tree showing the English Connections will be found on
the front endpaper and one showing the American Cousins on
the back endpaper.*

Preface

This book is based mainly on the vast and fascinating family archives which I have inherited. Some of Hannah Whitall Smith's letters have appeared under the title *A Religious Rebel* in 1949, edited by her son Logan Pearsall Smith, but there are still nearly 20,000 letters, as well as diaries, scrap books, photographs and other papers, including a large number of letters and journals by Bertrand Russell, which have never yet been published.

Some parts of the story told here have been told before, but a full picture has not always emerged. For instance Bertrand Russell's frank and masterly *Autobiography* still leaves his first wife's side of their marriage uncovered, and Alys Pearsall Smith's story is of considerable interest. Similarly, Mary Berenson's personality and her share in her husband's life and success have so far, I believe, been underrated. Those who knew her only during her later invalid years could have had little idea of what she was like in her prime.

Individually the members of this vigorous, close-knit and sometimes controversial family have appeared in various books in relation to various other people, but it is in their own right and as a family that I believe their story to be most interesting, and their characters most fully revealed. This is what I have tried to present.

A great many people and institutions have helped me in the preparation of this book, and I should like to thank them all. In the first place my cousin Ann Synge, for advice, hospitality and permission to use the papers of her mother, Karin Stephen; and also my other English cousin, Peg Stokes, and my American cousins Kim Smith Heatley, Nancy Nicholson, Margaret Collins and the late Drayton and Jane Smith for providing much invaluable material, hospitality and encouragement. I should also like to thank Professor Quentin Bell, Ronald Clark, Marjorie Housepian

Dobkin, Professor Richard Ellmann, Jonathan Gathorne-Hardy, Professor Laurence Gowing, Dr Brian Harrison, Jane Havell, Lady Ann Hill, Dr Richard Kenin, Dr Artem Lozynsky, Dr Luisa Vertova Nicolson, the late Benedict Nicolson, the Rev. J. C. Pollock, the late Countess Russell, Gordon Waterfield, and the staffs of the Hampshire Record Office and the Sussex University Library.

I am particularly grateful to Professor John Slater of Toronto University and above all to Kenneth Blackwell, Archivist of the Russell Archives at McMaster University, Hamilton, Ontario, for the patience, kindness and generosity with which they have helped me over the Russell material, and for the authorization of their Archives Permission Committee, who control the copyright of Russell's unpublished papers, to quote so freely from them. They do not, of course, necessarily agree with what I say or imply. I am deeply grateful, too, to all those connected with the Berenson Archives: Dr Cecil Anrep, for authorizing access and allowing me to make quotations; Professor Craig Smyth of the Harvard University Centre for Italian Renaissance Studies (which used to be the Villa I Tatti) where the archives are kept; his helpful staff, and in particular Signora Fiorella Gioffredi Superbi, who looks after the papers. I wish to express my gratitude to Charles Feinberg for over twenty years of friendship and generous help over the Whitman connection; to the Canaday Library at Bryn Mawr College for allowing me to work there and consult the Carey Thomas papers at a very inconvenient time, and to Miss Lucy West for her assistance; to Dean Keller in the Department of Special Collections in the Library of Kent State University, Ohio, for hospitality and help with the Logan Pearsall Smith papers in their possession; to Mrs Igor Vinogradoff who let me read and quote from Logan Pearsall Smith's hitherto unpublished letters to her father, Philip Morrell, and to quote letters from her mother, Lady Ottoline Morrell, to Bertrand Russell; to the Humanities Research Centre, University of Texas at Austin, and their research librarian, Miss Ellen Dunlap, for generously letting me consult and quote from their wealth of material; to Professor J. S. Kent, for very kindly checking the early chapters; to Lord Dacre (Professor

Hugh Trevor-Roper) for allowing me to quote from two of Logan Pearsall Smith's letters to him; to John Russell for generously allowing me to use Logan Pearsall Smith material of which he holds copyright; to Miss Gertrude Traubel for granting permission to quote from Horace Traubel's *With Walt Whitman in Camden*; and to the Library of Congress, Washington DC, and the Houghton Library, Harvard University, for permission to use material from their collections of Logan Pearsall Smith's papers. Last but not least I want to thank Professor Ernest Samuels and his wife Jayne, whose co-operation and friendship have been a continual support and encouragement.

I would like to emphasize that any opinions expressed in this book are in no way to be imputed to those who have helped me, but are either my own or those of the characters quoted.

Oxford
1979

Foreword

HANNAH WHITALL SMITH, wife of Robert Pearsall Smith, was born into the Quaker community of Philadelphia in 1832, and died in England in 1911. She was a remarkable woman, deeply loved and as deeply disliked. Her two sons-in-law, Bernard Berenson and Bertrand Russell, who both became famous men and lived to be over ninety, agreed in presenting a very uncomplimentary picture of their mother-in-law. Russell, who married and deserted her younger daughter, Alys, considered her heartless, dishonest and scheming, and came to think that his wife was altogether too like her mother. Berenson, while less outspoken than Russell, found Hannah crude and uncultured and resented the influence she retained on his wife Mary.

Both daughters, however, and their brother Logan Pearsall Smith admired, loved and trusted her, and so did one of her granddaughters, my mother Ray Strachey. Hannah was a fierce feminist, and an adoring mother. She was an even more adoring grandmother, providing a home for Ray and Karin when their mother ran away from her first husband, Frank Costelloe, with Berenson. Ray, her favourite, grew up to follow in her feminist footsteps and married a brother of Lytton Strachey, while Karin, who was not quite so admiring, became one of the first Freudian psychoanalysts and married the brother of Virginia Woolf.

They were a family of writers; even Alys, the least literary of them, won a *succès d'estime* in her old age as a broadcaster, and was at work on her memoirs when she died. All the others published books; some of them, notably Logan and Ray, many books. Hannah herself wrote mainly on religious subjects, and her best-known work in that field, *The Christian's Secret of a Happy Life*, became a classic and is still in print, but it was as a letter writer that she excelled. She wrote daily to her close family; first to her mother and sisters, then to her daughters and granddaughters; less often to her husband and son; and almost all the letters were returned and preserved. The daughters and granddaughters were brought up to write daily letters, and this habit was carried on almost without a break until the Second World War. A high proportion of these letters are extremely readable: lively, humorous and perceptive, they provide a vivid and continuous picture of their own and their friends' lives.

Hannah arrived in England—a wrong-way immigrant—in the 1880s; a radical, shrewd and uninhibited observer, she wrote home to Philadelphia not only family news but long monthly circulars of political and social comment. It was, of course, an age of letter writing, without telephones or speedy transport, but even so, the quantity, the quality, and the survival of so full a correspondence is remarkable. There are over 20,000 letters in the archive I have inherited, including some 6,000 from Hannah, a selection of which were published by Logan under the title *A Religious Rebel*, and more than 6,500 from Mary Berenson. There are also numerous diaries, unpublished autobiographies and biographies (finished and unfinished) and quantities of scrapbooks and photographs, in addition to the vast Russell and Berenson archives which are now in scholarly hands in Canada and Florence. Unfortunately neither Ray's nor Karin's husbands could be persuaded that letter writing was a desirable occupation, so their records are deplorably inadequate.

I could not investigate this treasure fully until I retired from the BBC, but I always determined to do so one day, and to try to produce a coherent portrait of the family and its story. The lives of the family illustrate a number of varied and fascinating themes, such as the impact of Evangelical philanthropy on the Quietism of the mid-nineteenth-century Quakers, the way it developed into political feminism, and the surprising scope and freedom which could be achieved by intelligent and enterprising women— American women in particular—within the social constraints of the late Victorian era. The letters also show how small was the "intellectual world" of England at that date, and the surprisingly close way in which so many of its members were connected. Lastly the adventures of the younger generation give a clear idea of the excitement of the battle for women's suffrage, and the birth of Freudian psychoanalysis.

I find that I am not exempt from the family weakness for writing about itself, but I think that the letters tell a story, and present characters, that will interest others.

One of the most noticeable characteristics of the family was its matriarchal nature. Descent ran, without question, from mother to daughter, and being the eldest daughter of the eldest daughter of the eldest daughter, I was always aware of being considered the "heir" to the family tradition. Family names were necessarily changed in each generation (sometimes more than once), but the women thought of themselves as "Whitall Women", taking their designation and their nature from Hannah herself.

Logan Pearsall Smith, the only boy in the family to survive, took an ambivalent view of what he called "these vehement, powerful Penthesilean* females". In his essays, *Reperusals and Re-collections*, he wrote about Ann Cooper Whitall, a formidable ancestress who was a heroine of the American War of Independence, and who kept a censorious and ill-spelt diary. Refusing with militant Quaker disapproval to countenance the fact that a battle was actually taking place around her farm at Red Bank, New Jersey, only when a cannon ball tore through the room in which she was working did she move her spinning-wheel down to the cellar. Every now and then, Logan maintained, the "Cooper Snap", which Ann Cooper had imported into the placid Whitall family, broke out again in one of her female descendants—of whom Logan's mother, Hannah Whitall Smith, and his cousin Carey Thomas, for many years President of Bryn Mawr College, were notable examples.

Logan ended his essay thus: "Even now, in the American or English nurseries of her descendants, Ann Whitall seems to stir in some cradle, and her plangent voice makes itself heard. The husband of a niece of mine once told me that after his marriage he found that his wife was an Ogress, was the daughter and granddaughter of Ogresses, and had become the mother of a fourth of the species."

* Penthesilea was an Amazon queen.

Part I

PARENTS

THE HERETICS

Hannah and Robert

IT IS DIFFICULT today to picture to oneself the quiet, prosperous, virtuous and narrow-minded life that was lived by the community of strict Orthodox Quakers in Philadelphia over a hundred years ago. Both Hannah Whitall and Robert Pearsall Smith, the man she married in 1851, at the age of nineteen, were "birthright" Quakers of that city, but whereas most of their neighbours and relatives took the values and prejudices of their little community for granted, Hannah and Robert were to burst out and build a very different kind of life.

Hannah was something of a rebel from the first. Truly religious girls, among the Quakers at that time, were expected, when their piety reached a certain level, to adopt a highly unfashionable kind of headgear called a "Sugarscoop Bonnet". Hannah dreaded the idea, and though her dearest friends succumbed and even her betrothed urged her to make a gesture and adopt it on her wedding day, she could not bring herself to do what she considered ridiculous, even for the sake of religion. Men, too, "went Plain", but Hannah was not impressed by this either. Of Dillwyn Smith, who was to become a first cousin by marriage, she noted:

> One time in Yearly Meeting in Baltimore he believed it was required of him to take off his pantaloons in a public meeting, and put them on again wrong side out, to turn his vest in the same way as his coat, all of which he did, out in a public meeting, and tried even to turn his boots, but in this couldn't succeed. Then with his clothes all turned inside out, he walked up the middle aisle, stopped at the gallery, turned around to the meeting and said that as he was turned inside out, so would their hearts have to be turned.

It was not that she doubted the importance of religion; all through her life religion remained her deepest and most absorbing interest, the one topic of abiding fascination and romance. Combined with her practical intelligence and an irrepressible lurking sense of humour, this led her to pursue Salvation with unabated enthusiasm in many strange places, though she herself remained unshakeably sensible and well balanced.

She was the eldest child in an unusually loving family, with a delightful father, John Mickle Whitall, who had started life as a sea captain. He was also a very strict Quaker, and his refusal to remove his hat to the owner, to swear at his crew, or to carry arms to protect his ship against pirates in the China Seas might well have cost him his job. But he had flourished and when he gave up the sea he became a prosperous glass merchant.

Robert's family were also of good Quaker stock, but more "bookish" with more pretensions to social status, and less simple piety. Robert's father, John Jay Smith, was indeed an "Unbeliever" though he achieved a gratifying conversion in old age. Robert himself was extremely pious and earnest; handsome, charming, perhaps a little lacking in business sense and, like all his family, too preoccupied with his own health, but for all that, an excellent match for Hannah.

She tried her best to assume a proper demeanour and learn to share his interests. "RPS says he never passes five minutes without considering what will be the right and most improving way of spending it," she noted admiringly in her diary, and: "RPS spent an evening here and we had some very serious conversation about our future prospects in life—that we may set out humbly and suitably to our situation in life and to the stand we hope to take in society. I think we both of us feel life to be very solemn and earnest."

On one point she was absolutely determined, and luckily Robert agreed with her: it was essential to improve her education. The Quakers had always held that God spoke directly to each individual soul, male or female. Elders and preachers were as often women as men, and no Friend would dare to question his wife's actions if she claimed that the Spirit had moved her in some specific "concern". Thus they enjoyed a degree of equality between the sexes highly uncommon elsewhere at that date. Nevertheless, even among Quakers, Robert was unusual in this respect. Hannah's two sisters married within the community, but neither of their husbands would have approved the degree of freedom which Hannah was able to take for granted, then and later.

Robert and Hannah were married in November 1851, and moved into their new home near Robert's parents in the Philadelphia suburb of Germantown. Hannah was "intensely, extravagantly happy", but not altogether reconciled to her new duties, and she noted: "I have an inward dislike to housekeeping, but this I *must* overcome. I must be thorough in everything, shrink from no unpleasant tasks, be managing, prudent, economical. This is *really* my duty and must be done. . . . Still, one of my duties to myself is to spend all my leisure time in earnest study."

She became pregnant almost immediately, and the resulting physical distress, the first she had ever suffered, depressed her greatly. Just after her twentieth birthday she wrote in her diary: "I cannot hide from myself the fact that I am unhappy. . . . I am too young to be married. The cares of life have crushed all the joyousness out of my spirits." After the birth of her daughter Nellie the worst of the despair passed, but she felt very frustrated. "Rebellious still," she wrote. "Impatient because now are overthrown all my fond hopes of a life of study—of becoming a thoroughly educated woman. . . . Greek and Mathematics I must now lay aside, and for the present most of my reading. Well, I suppose I can do it, and still be a good and useful woman. But it is a great trial."

It was not, perhaps, as bad as all that. In later life Hannah wrote "Ridiculous" against this entry, and said in her autobiography: "I believe my diary was my safety valve, for . . . after writing there the most tragic and despairing records I would . . . go off to bed quite happily . . . and wake up the next morning full of the joys of a new day."

By February 1854, only eighteen months later, she was pregnant again, and blamed Robert severely:

I am very unhappy now. That trial of my womanhood which
to me is so very bitter has come upon me again. . . . It is all the
more heavy a trial because my husband agreed with me in
thinking that I am too young for such cares and such suffering
and he promised I should not again be so tried at least until I was
twenty-five. . . . Well, it is a woman's lot, and I must try to
become resigned and bear it in patience and silence.

Hannah did not take easily to motherhood, which was strange
in view of the rapture it was to bring her later, but the son who
was born in August, and called Frank, was almost no trouble, and
she was soon back in good spirits.

Her family and friends expected that now, with two children,
she would settle down to the sober social and domestic life of her
Quaker circle, but Hannah was determined to be "as splendid as
she might be" and get herself a real education somehow. "Of
course I must expect censure and disapproval from every side in
trying to act out my convictions of life's true purpose for
women," she wrote in her diary. "I am grieved that my parents
understand me so little. But I cannot think it right to give up my
independence of character even for them, though I love them
so truly."

As Robert was busy with the publishing business in which his
father had set him up, she carried on by herself, taking Greek
lessons and reading doggedly, if without much plan: history,
philosophy, Browning (whom she greatly enjoyed, though she
found Elizabeth Barrett Browning unspeakably coarse), Matthew
Arnold. It may not have amounted to a thorough education, but
what she did manage to do was to make a crack in the Quaker
shell that had enclosed her world, to glimpse the possibility of
other values and other standards.

At one stage she had the ambitious idea that it might be possible
for her to go to college, in spite of her family responsibilities, and
Robert agreed she should have a master to prepare her for the
junior class at Haverford. She no longer grudged the time she
spent with her children; she had begun to realize what an utter
delight they were going to be to her, and she was determined to

pass on to them the happy childhood her own parents had "tucked under her jacket". But the plans for a formal education foundered among the housekeeping duties. And on Christmas Day 1857 there was a dreadful blow, when her daughter Nellie died, aged five, after a short attack of bronchitis.

This was Hannah's first encounter with death and loss, and though she tried desperately hard to reconcile herself, she was terribly unhappy, the more so as she was thrown into an unsure and chaotic spiritual state. The loss of a daughter was particularly bitter because Hannah always preferred girls to boys. She was devotedly fond of Frank, but she felt in her heart that a son could never be so richly satisfying to her as a daughter might be— indeed that a boy could never really be as valuable and interesting a human being as a girl—and it was not until Mary was born in 1864 that Hannah's maternal feelings were really satisfied. Meanwhile, in her grief for Nellie, she turned more eagerly than ever to the search for religious truth.

Robert's temperament was very different from hers. He was a man of unstable character but warm affections, moved far more by emotions than by intellect. He was not troubled by Hannah's increasing hunger to know the Truth, but was far more concerned to respond to the powerful religious feelings that arose in him, and to pass these on to other souls. In addition to his publishing he had now embarked on a number of religious and charitable works, but it was already clear that his main talent was for preaching. He was also beginning to entertain more and more religious friends in his own house—travelling preachers, men and women of other denominations, or those in search of spiritual help, such as one young Presbyterian whose cries of "Oh my Unbelief" were so loud as to resound through the house. This hospitality, which reached alarming proportions during his later, more expansive periods, sometimes gave Hannah great rewards in inspiration and pious conversation, but sometimes it brought guests whom she could not like or welcome. The rolls of dollar bills with which Robert was liable to speed the holy guests on their way could often ill be spared, and these incursions always meant work and worry. In later life she used to say that "Robert stood at the corner of the street and rang a bell to call in every disreputable religious tramp that was in hearing."

Their new friends, however, began to open their eyes to all sorts of Evangelical practices, such as Bible Study, salaried preachers, baptism and hymn-singing, all of which were still stubbornly rejected by the Quakers, but which gave Robert and Hannah new leads on the exciting trail of Salvation.

They were neither of them prepared to keep quiet about their new discoveries, and Hannah in particular was anything but tactful. She read the Bible for the first time as a source of doctrine, and found with rapture that she could believe what it told her. One of her new friends, a Plymouth Brother, explained to her that this was "Conversion", and she started metaphorically battering all her friends on the head with the Good News. "Certainly I could not keep it to myself. . . I began to buttonhole everybody, pulling them into corners and behind doors to tell them the wonderful and delightful things I had discovered in the Bible."

She must have been a disturbing influence, and it was no wonder that she met with disapproval. She and Robert became more and more critical of what they regarded as the ridiculous bigotry of the Quakers. Robert's father, John Jay Smith, himself no bigot and a shrewd business man, had started a cemetery called Laurel Hill, to be a more beautiful and worthier resting place for the dead than the crowded, unmarked and often water-logged Quaker burial grounds in the city, and had transferred his baby daughter there in 1837. It was particularly hurtful to Hannah, whose own daughter now also lay at Laurel Hill, to know that the place was considered offensive to Friends. She and Robert began to feel that they might have to leave the community, but it was a bitter thought and they kept postponing the final step. They searched on, and in 1859 were "finding much comfort in attending a weekly meeting at the house of a most excellent Methodist brother", where they heard a great deal of talk of the call to Holiness.

For Hannah, to hear of some new religious benefit was to plunge headlong towards it. She was never willing to be outdone in any spiritual experience, and yet she never pretended she had received it if she had not done so. Robert, the ideal soil for the seeds of ecstasy, was perpetually being drowned in floods of glory, but Hannah, to her lasting sorrow, felt none of this. Hers was not an easily aroused nature, and try as she might, she never experienced what all those "dedicated saints" told her they were feeling, and this cast her down mightily.

The Methodists were to have a great and abiding influence on both her and Robert. They were induced to go to one of the many Camp Meetings then being held all over the country, and there Robert was recognized at once as a soul-stirring preacher. Hannah, too, was persuaded to take part, though she was not yet confident enough to preach herself.

On their return they finally resigned their Quaker membership, as they felt the need to be baptized. This was the last straw for the Friends. It was made clear to Hannah that she was no longer welcome, even in her parents' house. "I have had a sad, sad day," she wrote to her sister Sally. "I found during my visit last week that I was not welcome to anyone . . . and made up my mind that it should be my last visit. This, I confess, saddened me a great deal; I had not *dreamed* that the fact that I had left the Society of Friends on conscientious grounds would cause any real alienation from my earthly father's house."

Her two brothers-in-law, William Nicholson who had married Sally, and Dr James Thomas who had married Mary, also refused to have her in their houses, but the continued love and loyalty of the sisters wore them down by degrees, and they finally relented. Nor was her father's house closed to her for long. Hannah's heresies became in the end a somewhat despairing family joke, and her friends, too, could not keep up their disapproval in face of her cheerful mockery. "I tell them their prayers often get answered upside down," she wrote to Sally about some ladies who disapproved of her. "They met *every day* one summer to pray that *I* might not become 'Broad Church' and I kept on getting broader and broader, and finally they got broad themselves."

Robert finally joined the Presbyterians, but Hannah could not follow him in this as she found their views against the preaching of women unacceptable. It was the Plymouth Brethren who had first introduced her to Bible Study, and so it was to them that she attached herself after her baptism. She learned the doctrine of Justification by Faith, and for some time she stayed with them. However it soon became clear that the Plymouth Brethren would not be able to satisfy her permanently. She found their meetings an increasing struggle with worldly pride: "My objections . . . were very naughty ones," she wrote in her diary, "principally because they were mostly poor and in a position of life inferior to my own." More important, however, was their extreme Calvinism. The Brethren at whose feet she was sitting were extremely stern about "Election". Some, they held, were elected to Salvation —and as Hannah drily commented, "We, of course, were among those elected to Salvation and for this we were taught to be profoundly grateful"—while others were elected to Reprobation. She struggled to believe this, but found it totally contrary to all she had found in the Bible. She was overcome with despair at the thought of so much sin, often due to circumstances entirely outside the control of the sinner. A loving God, she reasoned, must be incapable of granting Salvation to some and denying it to others. Finally, after much agony of mind, she became convinced that every human being, without exception, was destined to salvation, and her heart was at rest.

This belief, the Doctrine of Restitution as it was called at that time, got her into even more trouble, this time with the Brethren as well as the Friends; but she had begun rather to glory in "Persecution" and allowed nothing to hinder her.

It all culminated in a great revelation which she described as the Motherliness of God, claiming that her own feelings of love and delight in her children had "taught me more of what are God's feelings towards his children than anything else in the Universe. . . . If one looks at what one calls the lower creation, one will see that every animal teaches us this supreme duty of self-sacrifice on the part of the mother. The tiger mother will suffer herself to be killed rather than that harm should come to her offspring."

It was not, perhaps, fortuitous that the animal Hannah chose to illustrate her thesis was the tiger. One day a celebrated preacher

from Boston came to visit the Smiths, and conversation at breakfast turned, as it must so frequently have done, to the subject of
Restitution. The preacher, hoping to convince Hannah that God
was not quite so foolishly loving as she supposed, declared that
there were some sins a daughter could commit which a mother
could never forgive. Hannah described the ensuing scene:

> It was more than I could endure to hear both mothers, and the
> God who made mothers, so maligned, and although the speaker
> was my guest, I broke forth into a perfect passion of indignation
> and, declaring that I would not sit at table with anyone who
> held such libellous views of God, I burst into tears and left the
> room, and entirely refused to see my guest again.

This was an early example of what came to be known throughout
the family as Hannah's "steamroller manner", something once
encountered, never forgotten.

When the Civil War broke out, business became so bad that
Robert's publishing concern was effectively ruined. The Smiths
were forced to give up their nurse, let their house, and go into a
cheap boarding house for the winter in order to save money.
Strangely enough, Hannah was less deeply stirred by the great
issues and struggles of the war than she was later in life by far more
distant conflicts. The Quakers, of course, did not sanction fighting,
but there were some echoes even within the community. Robert's
elder brother Lloyd, a sceptic like his father, took a gun to
Gettysburg and came home safely, while Robert and his younger
brother Horace went nursing in Harrisburg. Hannah, however,
did not take part in any way, nor was she an active worker for
Abolition, though she adhered of course to the Quaker view that
slavery was wrong. At this time of her life her attention was
entirely absorbed by the pressing problem of how to resist private
temptation, and it was this problem—not perhaps one of a very
severe kind, in view of their sheltered lives—which drew both
Hannah and Robert towards the "Holiness" revival and the search
for a "foolproof" method of avoiding sin.

SEARCH

Hannah

IN FEBRUARY 1864, after a nine-year gap, Mary was born and at last Hannah had a daughter again. From the first she almost worshipped the child. "Such enjoyment I am sure no one ever took out of a child. I sit and look at her in a sort of rapt ecstasy till I could, and often do, cry for very joy." But almost at once her happy world was turned upside down. It was arranged between her father and her husband that Robert, who was in a bad financial way, should be taken into the family firm. He was to be manager of the Whitall-Tatum glass factory at Millville, New Jersey, and the little family would have to move there immediately.

Millville was a very small place, where almost no one lived at that time, except the glassworkers and a few traders. It was a train journey away from Philadelphia, which held Hannah's dearly-loved family, all her religious friends and interests, and her charitable work. She wrote to her sister Mary: "Millville is doleful. Dirty, weedy, cobwebby, littered, bilious . . . but my *greatest* privation I feel to be the utter absence of any religious fellowship for *me*."

Almost worse, to her, was that it had all been settled by men, without a word to her, and she had been presented with a *fait accompli*. She had thought she had found a husband who really treated her as an equal. No doubt, even now, he was more thoughtless than tyrannical—Robert was always acting on impulse—and this was a most excellent opportunity for him to wipe out his debts and start in a new and more successful business; but to Hannah it was still a heavy cross.

However, there was plenty to do setting the house in order and looking after the children. It was lonely for Frank without any of his many cousins nearby, but Hannah managed to borrow her sister Sally's son, Whitall Nicholson, to share Frank's tutor. Sally had some doubts about the wisdom of entrusting her eldest boy to the apparently casual discipline in Hannah's "Liberty Hall", but Hannah replied: "I do not think Whitall runs any more risks here than at home . . . and Frank has so little of an adventurous spirit in him that there is no encouragement." She seems to have thought the two boys very unenterprising, and not nearly as much fun as a girl would have been, so she contrived to persuade Sally to send her daughter Bessie for visits too.

Hannah used to call Bessie "Sunbeam" and highly approved of her, but her favourite among her nieces was Carey Thomas, the eldest daughter of Hannah's sister Mary. Carey was a tomboy who was convinced that she was able to outdo any boy of her age in riding, climbing, racing or anything else, and a convinced and outspoken feminist from her earliest childhood. She was determined to achieve, as she triumphantly did achieve, the first-rate education her much-admired aunt had had to forgo, and was always up in arms at any instances of injustice to women.

When Hannah got home after arranging for all these delightful guests, she found that Robert, too, had started to entertain visitors.

Well! [she complained to Sally] I came home and found the house inhabited by a Baptist clergyman and his little daughter, a child of ten. I can tell thee it was, and is, a trial, for I see no prospect of their going. . . . Robert is enthusiastic over him because he preaches such a pure gospel . . . but . . . I *cannot* enjoy close contact with such people.

Hannah was still nursing a grudge against Robert. She was pregnant again, and though this was now a delight to her, it did no good to her temper. The baby was born in October 1865 and called Lloyd Logan. From the beginning he seems to have been a difficult child. When he was only four months old Hannah wrote: "Logan and I had our first regular battle today and he came off conqueror, tho' I don't think he knew it. I whipped him until he was actually black and blue and until I really *couldn't* whip him any more and he never gave up one single inch. His obstinacy is really alarming."

Mary was certainly preferred. Every letter Hannah wrote was full of her beauty, her charm, her intelligence, and her sense of fun. Robert was becoming her slave; Frank, old enough not to feel jealous, was devoted to her, and so was Charlotte, the German nurse who gave her the nickname "Mariechen" which she kept all her life. She could hardly avoid being spoiled, but she was not entirely without discipline. "Her insubordination was irrepressible," Hannah wrote to her mother, "and she finds every night need to pray 'Please Heavenly Father make me obedient so that the stick mayden't [sic] whip me.'" She clearly got a share, even if not an equal one, of those early whippings. As Hannah got more experienced with her children and threw off other people's advice, she gave up physical punishment altogether and learned to manage them to her own satisfaction—if not always to that of outsiders—by praise, indulgence and bribery instead.

In July 1867 a fourth child was born and named Alice (later spelt Alys), and a year later yet another girl, called Rachel, or Ray, followed.

Throughout this period, when Hannah was blissfully occupied with her growing nursery, she was far from abandoning her religious adventures. She tried to start a little Quaker Meeting in Millville, which, not surprisingly, turned out too heretical to be approved, and she searched the Scriptures to support her strong feeling that she was called upon to preach.

It was a barren spot for her labours. "There is little *pure* gospel preached in the whole town I am afraid. The Presbyterian minister doesn't know whether he is a Christian himself, and the Methodists are dreadful." Nevertheless it was to the Methodists, with their excitable ways, their gloryholes and mourning benches, their singing and groaning, so different from the familiar quiet ways of Quaker worship, that she and Robert were finally drawn.

Many of the workmen at the factory were Methodists, and Robert and Hannah began to invite them to the house for religious conversation and Bible readings. Hannah's dressmaker, too, would tell her about their beliefs, and Hannah began to attend

a

c

b

d

a) Hannah Whitall, 1851 (aged
nineteen)
c) Logan Smith, 1874 (aged nine)

b) Robert Pearsall Smith, 1875
d) Alys Smith, 1879 (aged twelve)

a

c

b

d

a) Mary Smith, 1880 (aged sixteen)
b) Logan Pearsall Smith, 1886 (aged twenty-one)
c) Grace Thomas, Alys Pearsall Smith and Madge Whitall at Bryn Mawr, 1885
d) Carey Thomas, 1886

their meetings and to feel, once again, that a revelation of the real truth was hers. Nor, of course, could she refrain from passing it on. "Everyone who came within range of my influence," she said herself, "was obliged to listen to my story." When her cousin came to stay for a few days of godly conversation, she greeted her on the doorstep with the words: "Oh, Carrie! I have something wonderful to tell you, we must not lose a minute before we begin."

The great object of all their struggles was now Sanctification; the first blessing, that of Justification or forgiveness, they had already achieved by their conversion and faith. What was needed now was an experience described as the Baptism of the Spirit by which they would know that they had reached Sanctification or continuing freedom from sin.

Robert and Hannah both fought for this in their different ways. They took to attending Methodist Holiness Meetings, determined to get whatever there was to be got in the way of blessings. At her first such visit Hannah found that she had forgotten her handkerchief, but never having shed any tears in a meeting before she was not troubled. "But at this meeting," she wrote, "the fountains of my being seemed to be broken up, and floods of delicious tears poured from my eyes. I was reduced to great straits and was obliged surreptitiously to lift up my dress and use my white underskirt to dry my tears. I have never since been to any meeting without at least two handkerchiefs safely tucked away in my pocket, although I have never since been so overwhelmed with emotion as that time."

She continued to enjoy the meetings rapturously. "I count them among the most entrancing times of my life," she wrote when she was seventy. "To this day the sight of a camp chair or of a tent under the trees always brings back to me something of that old sense of supreme happiness that used to fill every hour of those delicious Camp Meetings." She did achieve the certainty she had been seeking, though in her own way. "A knowledge of truth was all the blessing I ever received; and although at first I was somewhat disappointed, I came in time to see that a knowledge of truth was all the blessing I needed."

Robert, as usual, went about matters in a much more emotional way. On one occasion, he told Hannah, he was shaken from head to foot "by what seemed like a magnetic thrill of heavenly delight, and floods of glory seemed to pour through him." His final Sanctification occurred on a train. "One day, in a railway carriage, I for the first time saw in the Scripture what the Blood of Christ had done for me. . . . The next night found me preaching to the sailors at our seaside home, and I have been at it ever since."

Hannah's happiness was crowned in 1868, when the firm suddenly decided to move Robert back to the head office in Philadelphia. Although she was given no advance warning of this move, the outcome was so welcome that she made no complaints. Four years' absence had brought Hannah forgiveness for her heresies and reconciliation with her parents. This was a great joy to her, as all through her life her love for the Whitall clan was extremely strong. John Whitall, a very loving and generous father, now offered Robert and Hannah the house next door to his, 1315 Filbert Street. Hannah feared it might be too close, and that the children might disturb her mother. "I am afraid both the children and I will suffer from my nervous dread of her being troubled by them . . . but there is one unmanageable member of my family, and that is Robert. Thee knows that he always *will* have Bible Classes and meetings wherever he goes, and at these there is always singing. Does thee suppose father and mother will care?"

When it came to singing it was not merely the noise that was at issue, but also the ingrained Quaker distrust of music. There were many "worldly" things that Hannah would have to conceal from her mother, including her sewing machine, one of the first in the community, and an organ she bought for Frank. An organ was considered marginally less depraved than a piano, but even so, it had to be hidden in an upstairs room where Mary Whitall was unlikely to penetrate.

They did move in finally, and all was well. The babies continued to be delicious. "Alice . . . is so fat that she has to waddle just like a duck and reminds me of old Aunt Ann Scattergood cut down small. . . . She is the very personification of a fat, old,

comfortable country Friend, with about an acre of face." Logan
was still giving trouble, but Hannah was beginning to learn how
to deal with him. "He seems, more than any of the other children,
to need the tender loving care of a near relation. His disposition
is so peculiar that I feel an increasing dislike to leaving him much
under the care of servants. . . . Love seems to be the open sesame
of his character and I find I can often *kiss* him good when other
means fail."

Frank was growing up. He was now nearly fifteen and his
parents decided to let him work for the winter in the Philadelphia
office of Whitall-Tatum, before finding a suitable college for him
in the following year. He was a quiet, biddable boy, suffering
from weak eyesight, but cheerful and natural. Unlike Mary and
Logan he never reacted against piety, but was swept up into the
dramatic world Robert and Hannah inhabited. He managed to
attain what he called in his diary "a real experience of consecra-
tion" when he went to Haverford the following year, but both
parents were liable to descend upon him at any moment, to
preach to "the fellows", and he was given the nickname of
"Frankie Smith, the prayer meeting genius".

In 1871 he began to fall in love with the daughter of Hannah's
old teacher and dearest friend, Anna Shipley. All seemed to be
going well, but in July 1872, when he was eighteen, Frank fell
ill with typhoid, and within a week he was dead.

Hannah had begun to find in the boy a real companion, and
even to some extent a confidant. She was desolate, but tried hard,
as she did with any death, to dwell on his new happiness in
Heaven. "If all we believe about the other life is *really true*," she
wrote to Anna Shipley, "how can we do anything but rejoice
as one and another of our loved ones is taken to its blessedness."

Robert was more vulnerable. Already some years before he had
gone through a period of depression, and this had now reappeared.
For some months he had been in an extremely disturbed condition, going through "spells", as Hannah called them, when he
would reproach her hysterically for not loving him in the way he
needed to be loved, and as he loved her; of being cold, un-
emotional and wholly unsympathetic to his own nature. This was

combined with great restlessness, depression, frenzied activity and sleeplessness, and their relationship became very strained.

Frank's death was too much for him, and he had a full-scale nervous breakdown. It was decided that Hannah should take him, and all the children too, to a hydropathic Sanatorium at Clifton Springs, N.Y., run by a Dr Foster, which was recommended to them as "a sweet Christian home for invalids".

At first she was very lonely.

> Robert is miserable [she wrote home] . . . worse than he has ever been, I think, and this is *very* depressing. Dr Foster says it is chiefly owing to his liver, and he has directed his attention chiefly to that, with the result thus far of making him worse. Some nights he scarcely sleeps at all, and he says that he suffers untold agonies. My very heart aches for him, and yet I can do nothing to relieve him.

Life at the Clinic became more agreeable as Hannah began to make friends with other visiting ladies, and Robert began to improve at last. The doctor was a great comfort. "Dr Foster believes as much in praying as in using remedies and he prays with Robert nearly every day, wonderful prayers, Robert says. . . . Dr Foster has taught me something which is *deeply* interesting— but I cannot put it in a letter."

Dr Foster's teaching was indeed remarkable, and she described it many years later, in her papers on Fanaticism.* One of the other ladies reported to her that Dr Foster seemed to have "some secrets of the divine life thee and I ought to know". So the two ladies persuaded him to divulge them.

> Never shall I forget that interview [wrote Hannah]. He began by telling us that "The Baptism of the Holy Spirit" was a physical thing, felt by delightful thrills going through you from head to foot . . . and that this had been revealed to him in the following manner. He had been praying to the Lord to give him the Baptism . . . and he found that whenever he prayed

* *Group Movements of the Past*, ed. Ray Strachey (1934).

especially earnestly he had physical thrills which he had thought belonged to earthly passions. He blamed himself exceedingly for this, and thought what a sensual man he must be, that in his most sacred moments such feelings should come. . . . One day . . . an inward voice seemed to say "These sensations you so much condemn are really the divine touch of the Holy Spirit in your body." . . . Immediately, he said, he began to receive them with thankfulness and the result was that they had become so continuous that there was scarcely a moment in his life without them. . . . My friend and I had not dared to say a word while this revelation was being made to us, and when Dr Foster left us we sat for a long while in dumbfounded silence.

The Doctor was preaching the fulfilment of the Union between Christ and his people as the Bridegroom and the Bride, as typified in the Song of Solomon—a delusion that spread widely, if secretly, in those days of psychological ignorance and religious fervour. Hannah later became one of the first of her contemporaries to document some of these curious bypaths of human behaviour. Although deeply shocked, the ladies were, as she said later, "utterly ignorant of the wiles of the devil"; they had "such absolute confidence in the holiness of this saint of God . . . that they felt they dared not reject the doctrine without further prayer and consideration".

Hannah could not quite bring herself to approve, however much she pondered, though neither did she entirely condemn. Robert, it appeared later, had no such doubts. Meanwhile the news was passed around in whispers. By Christmas Hannah and a partially recovered Robert were home again.

TRIUMPH AND DISASTER

Robert

No SOONER HAD Robert got home than he began to show signs of relapse. He was as nervous and sleepless as ever, and on top of everything else he started a religious periodical called *The Christian's Pathway to Power*, pestering Hannah into contributing regularly but writing most of it himself. Hannah, now pregnant again at forty-one, was driven to the verge of a breakdown herself.

After much discussion and consultation it was decided that Robert must be removed from his work, his religious activities, and his family, until he could recover his peace of mind. He was released from the business for a year, and money was found for him to go to Egypt and take a soothing trip up the Nile. He sailed for England in February 1873, but instead of travelling on to Cairo, he stayed in London and started religious work there.

England was fairly palpitating with Revivalism in the '70s, and the skilled and experienced American preachers, such as Moody and Sankey, who had been practising their art for years on their side of the Atlantic, found the English fields ripe for harvesting. Robert was inevitably caught up. He had an advantage over other revivalists in that he was handsome, well mannered, and far more "gentlemanly" than most. He appealed not only to mass audiences but to earnest men of means, pious noblemen and evangelically minded clergymen. Sponsors came forward with alacrity, and "Breakfasts" were held to introduce him.

Meanwhile Hannah had relieved her grief by writing a memoir of Frank, publishing it under the title *The Record of a Happy Life*. No sooner did it appear in America than she began to receive a flood of letters from readers who had found the story uplifting and consoling. Robert decided to prepare an English version, but this brought him into sharp conflict with Hannah. He had rushed ahead, as usual, and with the assistance of one of his attendant "deaconesses" had made a large number of wholly unacceptable alterations in Hannah's text, one of which was to remove all use of the Quaker "Thee". This roused the tigress in Hannah: "I think thee can hardly know just how it would feel to have one of thy books, and especially one so sacred and precious to thee, treated in this summary way without even being consulted about it. I hardly feel as if I could bear to see one of your edition myself, and I *cannot* bear to have them circulated here. And you will have to yield to me in this."

Robert, however, was beyond her control. She wrote again and again begging him to stop overworking and rest: "[The doctor] told me I must *command* thee to stop instantly. I replied that I had long ago made up my mind never to waste my commands where I knew absolutely they would be utterly disobeyed." Despite her pregnancy, Robert continued to flood her with emotional appeals until she was near despair:

Thy last private letter gave me a heartache, as they always do, and some sleepless hours in the night. Thee says it is only *friendship* that I feel and that there is a far deeper love behind it. I suppose thee must be right, but I do not understand it. I cannot comprehend any love different from that which I feel, and I do not think I *want* to. It does not seem to make *thee* happy nor to enable thee to make *me* happy, and I believe I will not strain myself seeking after something that I cannot even conceive of. . . . Oh please do take me *as I am*, and not insist upon my being unnatural and strained. I do not feel as if I *could* endure any more of the strain of the last two years.

She was worried, too, about money, though she put a good face on it and confided to Robert's sister: "I wonder whether those breakfasts do not cost a great deal. However, I reckon *we* can't help him giving them; and if only he has a good time and gets well I shall not care about money. I should never be afraid but what I could support myself if the worst came to the worst."

As it became clear that Robert was taking his new life as a

full-time preacher very seriously indeed, she tried to reconcile
herself to the idea:

> It surely seems as if thee ought to be altogether on the Lord's
> work, if we look at the results when thee is so engaged, and I
> think *thee* has always felt a sort of secret call to it. But I confess
> I have never been willing before. Now, however, I feel an
> entire consent of my whole will, if it really is the Lord's mind
> . . . the only thing is thy debts—they would have to be paid—
> how much are they?

She achieved a degree of resignation, if not total enthusiasm: "I
cannot influence thee, I cannot please thee, I cannot, try as I may,
be the sort of wife thee wants; and unless the Lord undertakes
for me there is no hope."

The child was born dead, and she could not help feeling that
the strain she had been under might have helped to bring this
about. "I suppose I used up all my vitality in the Lord's work,"
she wrote to her friend Anna, "and in bearing the burdens
necessarily laid upon me by my dear husband's state of health,
and there was not enough left for the baby. It has been an inex-
pressible disappointment to me and I do not care to dwell
upon it."

The last two painful years had given Hannah increased strength.
She had acquired a faith never to be shaken, which gave a be-
guiling stamp of certainty to all her preaching. Nevertheless her
most marked characteristic was her inquiring mind. She would
listen, throughout her life, with warm and untiring interest, to
any tale of spiritual eccentricity or personal trouble, and as a
result more and more were brought to her. At first she was often
blind to the dangers involved, and it took her much time and
more sorrow before she learned to recognize the follies and
fanaticisms of the human race, and to give wholesome and
tolerant, if not always acceptable, advice. Now she wrote again
to Robert about Dr Foster's revelation: "There does seem to be
a truth in it, and I feel as if it would be a great means of restoration
to health to thee if thee could get fully into it. Do try."

Advice, it would seem, that Robert was already following:

What thee tells me [she wrote] of the petting of thy kind young deaconesses and thy enjoyment of it, is only another proof of the radical differences in our natures; *I* could not endure it. There is not one person on the face of the earth whom I could *bear* to have tuck me up and fuss over me after I was in bed, not even my mother, dearly as I love her. And yet I can believe it is to thee a real pleasure.

But as the evidence accumulated, Hannah began to be disillusioned with the doctrine. An emotional friend called Sarah F. Smiley opened her eyes:

When I told her of my experiences at the water cure [Hannah wrote later] she seized upon it . . . putting herself under the teaching of the doctor there, hoping that she might learn his strange secrets. The result was that she went into the wildest extravagances. . . . Among other things she felt it her duty to ask him to stand naked before her, and also to do the same thing herself before him. To what other lengths she went I have never known. . . . She really believed that Christ had often come to her at night when in bed, as the real Bridegroom, and had actually had a bridegroom's connection with her. She taught this doctrine to a choice circle of friends and even tried by personal contact to produce in them those physical thrills which she believed were the actual contact of the Holy Ghost.

This was too much for Hannah's common sense, but Robert was still enthusiastic. One of his first English disciples, a lady called Lizzie Lumb, wrote him a series of remarkable letters between 1873 and 1875, describing the gratifying results of her "Betrothal with Christ": "The thrill commences in the love nerves, with a great throbbing, as though a heart beat there, and rises to the regions of the chest, with a thrill and sweet confusion of union," and later, "Most earnestly do I thank you for revealing such treasures to me, as you have in this mystery of the heavenly marriage."

Since Hannah did not have a new baby to look after, Robert insisted that she come over and join him with the children; she finally felt that it was her duty to give in, and agreed to sail in the New Year of 1874.

As was always to be the case, she was disastrously seasick on the voyage, but on arrival regained her spirits sufficiently to deliver a first judgment on the English way of life, particularly condemning the ghastly cold of the bedrooms. It was not all depressing, however. "There are several noblemen among Robert's friends who come here quite familiarly. And I am glad to find that they are not one whit more elegant than the circle I am accustomed to in America. I feel at perfect ease with them." She had never before met a Lord, nor lived in a society where such distinctions were an everyday fact of life. As a child she had devoured a forbidden novel by Grace Aguilar called *The Earl's Daughter*, and the romantic childish image, which she never entirely threw off, contrasted oddly with her down-to-earth observations of what Earls and their daughters were really like.

She admitted later that if she were to be English she would want to belong to the aristocracy, though she went on: "My independent spirit would revolt, I fear, at the idea of anyone Lording or Ladying it over me." It seems a not unreasonable preference in the intensely stratified and snobbish society of Victorian England.

Robert and Hannah were at first accepted by the aristocratic and upper middle class Evangelical world on their religious merits, and their class was ignored as irrelevant, but this world ruthlessly rejected them when Robert's shortcomings became apparent. Outside the orthodox Evangelical fold, however, they made a more personal and permanent place for themselves. As Americans, they could not be "placed" on sight, like English people; they had good looks, good manners and an adequate cultural background, and the less conventional members of the privileged classes, at least, were able to accept them without social strain. Hannah's behaviour with the Lords and Ladies she met, then and later, was far from subservient, as that of an English snob would have been; she made a number of lifelong friends among them, but she never lost her half-romantic, half-mocking feeling that there was something "different" about them. "Look," she would say to a fellow American, "there is an Earl on that sofa"—in the same tone as one might say: "Look, there is a giraffe under that tree."

One of the first and most lasting of her friendships was with Georgina Cowper Temple, later (when her husband was given a peerage) Lady Mount Temple. Her husband William was a very sweet-natured, generous and religious man about whose family there had been some scandal. His mother, Lady Cowper, a sister of Lord Melbourne, married Lord Palmerston, then Prime Minister, on the death of her first husband. However, it was widely assumed that their connection had begun nearly thirty years before, and that William was in fact Palmerston's son. On Palmerston's death William inherited Broadlands, his beautiful house in Hampshire, and added the family name of Temple to his own.

Georgina was wonderfully generous and virtuous, and if she was also wonderfully vague and woolly-minded, none of her many friends held it against her. Hannah and Georgina met at a luncheon party given to introduce Hannah to the English religious world and to test her orthodoxy. Lady Mount Temple described the scene:

> She [Hannah] happened to have seen a funeral in the street, and as she spoke of it we all put on the conventional look of sadness. "Oh," she said, "I always give thanks when I meet a funeral, for the brother or sister delivered from the trials and pains of this mortal state." How wonderful, I thought, and could not help exclaiming: "Is it possible? Do you give thanks for everybody's deliverance?" I was indeed an enfant terrible. She was among a party of Evangelicals at a time when the universal hope was deemed a heresy; she was on her trial. She owns that she went through a few moments of conflict, but truth prevailed, and looking up with her bright glance, she said, "Yes, for everybody; for I trust in the love of God."

As Hannah remembered, Lady Mount Temple then came across and gave her "a most loving kiss", with an invitation to hold a series of meetings at Broadlands in July 1874.

Here, in a singularly beautiful setting, with the house's pillared portico overlooking green lawns and superb tree-shaded riverside walks, was held the first of the three great conventions under Robert's direction, which were to have lasting results in the Evangelical world, as well as in Robert's and Hannah's lives.

Robert did not claim to belong to any particular sect; he did not try to convert unbelievers; his call was to a state of Holiness in those who already believed, whatever their creed. The great appeal made by him and Hannah lay in the apparent simplicity and efficiency of the methods they advocated for the conquest of sin.

About two hundred people came to the first Broadlands meeting, forty or fifty staying in the house, undergraduates camping in the park, and the rest boarding in the neighbouring villages. Meetings were held under the beech trees in the lovely summer weather, and round any corner, according to Robert, one might come upon a select group on their knees, praying or searching the Scriptures. Hannah's preaching was as great a success as Robert's. One of the guests wrote:

> She was to me the most inspiring and unusual figure. In her speech there was a freshness, directness and force of expression, with singular facility of illustration, that were very captivating, while what she said was so reasonable and practical as to be almost irresistible . . . such vivid animation, such intense joyous vitality, such a striking glance, such racy forcible speech, I do not remember in another.

It was agreed that another larger and more public meeting should be held as soon as possible, and that Robert, whose tact and eloquence were widely extolled, should direct this, too. Oxford was suggested, as plenty of accommodation was available outside the University term, and although this meant moving extremely fast, the Oxford Convention opened just a month later.

Hannah continued to be worried by Robert's workload. At

Oxford his day started at 7 and ran through without a break to 9.15 at night, and he preached three times a day. Hannah held a daily meeting for ladies—though gentlemen were not excluded, and many were present at her Scripture lessons. Some eight hundred to a thousand people attended the Convention, and the success was overwhelming. There were many foreign pastors, including French and Germans, said to be meeting in Christian amity for the first time since the Franco-Prussian War, as well as evangelical English clergy. One of these, Canon Harford Battersby, was converted by Robert's eloquence, and went on to start the Keswick Evangelical Movement, which is still active in many parts of the world today.

Robert's sensitivity enabled him to tread unerringly through what might easily have been a quicksand of rival prejudices. As was customary, his addresses were full of small homely stories, often concerning railway journeys, which seemed to stimulate his religious feelings, and although purportedly about himself, they often contained a large element of the fictional. There were also revealing, if guarded, references to that belief in Christ the Bridegroom which Hannah was coming so to distrust.

The Convention drew to a triumphant close, and it was agreed that another, bigger still if possible, should be held in Brighton the following year. And so Robert and Hannah returned to Philadelphia for the winter, once more in close harmony, he to write the report of the Oxford Convention and she to assemble the articles she had written for Robert's periodical *The Pathway* into book form. It was published as *The Christian's Secret of a Happy Life*, and was to become a religious classic. It has been translated into a great many languages, European, Asian and African; has so far sold well over two million copies; is still in print, and now available in paperback. It was to draw her into a long career of writing, correspondence and counselling.

Early in 1875 Robert sailed for England again, to confirm the arrangements for the Brighton meetings. He found that the members of the committee—particularly Mr Stevenson Blackwood—were uneasy about Hannah. It was bad enough for a woman to preach; many, in particular the Germans, found it extremely shocking; but for her to preach Restitution, or the denial of Hell, was dangerously heretical, and a possible stumbling block for the faithful.

Hannah was not very reassuring when Robert wrote to tell her of this. "I quite enjoy the thought of your pow-wow over me," she wrote back cheerfully, "and of Blackwood's condolences with thee on the possession of such a dangerous article as a heretical, preaching wife. . . . I do not in the least mind being a heretic. In fact I think it rather suits my cast of mind." And as the controversy went on she wrote:

I do not intend to be endorsed by anybody. I *must* have freedom to hold my own views; and as I have not the least desire to preach unless the Lord wants me to, He shall be my only backer. And they might as well know this first as last. I intend to carry my own donkey in my own way, and if they don't like my way they can . . . walk in another road. . . . As for thee, poor fellow who can't steer clear, I *do* sympathize with thee. But I guess we can manage.

Peace was finally restored, and Robert set off on a preaching tour of Europe in the early spring. At Broadlands and Oxford, the continental pastors had urged him to preach in their churches, and he was far from reluctant. Germany was almost as ripe for evangelization as England. He had received most flattering invitations, not only from his own friends and disciples but from men of high religious repute and standing, including the Berlin Court Preacher, the Rev. Mr Baur. The Imperial sanction was given to his visit, and the great Garrisonkirche in Berlin was put at his disposal. That Robert spoke nothing but English deterred no one. Indeed the fact that he spoke through an interpreter, except for the phrase *"Jesus rettet uns jetzt"*—"Jesus saves us NOW" —seemed to act as a further attraction. He travelled through France, Belgium, Holland, Germany and Switzerland, preaching wherever he went, drawing bigger and bigger crowds as his fame went before him. In Germany, as in England, the effects of his mission can still be traced a century later.

It was not surprising that Robert should return to England in early May in a somewhat intoxicated state, crying out, according to Logan, "All Europe is at my feet!"

Hannah now joined him, and things seemed less uncivilized to her: "England looks *very* familiar. Today is the old familiar cloudy sky, and the smoke is just as prevalent as ever and the beautiful trees and grass just as green. The people are very *Englishy*, but look like old friends this time, and I do not seem to see anything at all foreign." The children and their nurse had been warmly invited to stay for the whole summer with the Barclays, a wealthy Quaker family, at Monkhams, their home in Essex. Logan was sent to a school for boys whose parents were serving in India, while the girls shared the Barclay children's governess and tutors. Hannah joined Robert in London, where they found much to enrapture them:

We went off early to breakfast with Mr Gladstone. . . . It was *deeply* interesting. First of all we began on Temperance, upon which subject I delivered my soul and about which Gladstone spoke *delightfully*. But we soon got onto the *one* subject, and Robert talked for about an hour, telling about the work and explaining the doctrine preached which is producing such wonderful results. Robert did it very interestingly and Gladstone listened with the deepest attention and evidently understood the subject clearly, and seemed to think it was just the thing needed to vivify the church. . . . He kept putting in little ejaculations such as "Yes, Yes, that is what is sorely needed" or "Yes, alas, such a backsliding condition is only too true of many of us" and other like expressions.

And so, on the crest of a wave, to the great Brighton Convention on 29 May 1875. Brighton had provided the Town Hall, the Corn Exchange, the magnificent Dome, and the whole main suite of the Prince Regent's Royal Pavilion, free of charge, as well as a number of private rooms for smaller meetings. But even so it was not enough. Eight thousand people came, and all the big meetings, especially Hannah's Bible Readings, had to be held twice over to accommodate the overflow. £2,000 was raised to pay the expenses; congratulatory telegrams from Moody and Sankey, who were holding the final meeting of their tour in the Haymarket Opera House, were read out, and cables were received from across the Atlantic to say that another 8,000 people were praying for the Convention there.

Hannah wrote home:

Just as at Oxford, a great wave of blessing seemed to sweep all before it. . . . We stayed with Fowell Buxton . . . his wife is Mrs Barclay's sister Rachel, and they have eleven children. They are a most delightful family and certainly did exercise the most *royal* hospitality. They gave Robert leave to invite any friends he pleased to meals. I warned them of the rashness of such a permission to *him*, but they persisted, and the result was enough to have appalled an ordinary man. Robert would come in to dinner with thirty, forty and even fifty foreign pastors, and the rush and crowd were something wonderful. Altogether Mrs Buxton paid for 1317 meals during those ten days, and it was all done with such princely hospitality as made it delightful.

By 11 June it was all over, and they returned to the Barclays. Robert was to rest there, writing the report of the Convention, before going on to Keswick to lead Canon Harford Battersby's first meeting. Hannah, with Mary and some friends, went off for a fortnight's trip to Switzerland. When they reached Dover on the way home, the storm broke.

This morning [we] left at 7 for Calais expecting to be at Monk-hams . . . at 8 or 9 [she wrote to her parents from Dover]. But just as we were seated in the train ready to start, the boy from the telegraph office came along shouting "Telegram for Mrs Pearsall Smith" and I received the following from Mr Barclay. "Mr S. ill in Paris at the Hotel Louvre. We think you should return to him at once. All conferences given up." You cannot imagine my perplexity knowing as I thought I did, that he had no possible call to Paris, and ought, indeed to have been at

Keswick at the Conference. It is nearly two hours since we sent our telegram to him at Paris, but as yet no answer has come and there is nothing to be done but wait.

Finally she decided to send the eleven-year-old Mary on to the Barclays with her friend, and herself returned by the night boat to Paris.

In her absence, during the few days following the Brighton Conference, it had leaked out that Robert had been preaching—and, it was said, practising—those doctrines of Dr Foster's which Hannah's friend Sarah Smiley had so enthusiastically promoted. The sponsoring committee, including Mr Blackwood, informed Robert that he must immediately cease all preaching. They put out a somewhat disingenuous statement saying that he had had a fall from a horse some years previously "followed by congestion of the brain and long-continued distressing nervous symptoms".

Robert was entirely shattered. He fled to join Hannah in Switzerland but got no further than Paris, and there collapsed. Hannah put up a loyal front of cheerful good sense. "He is thoroughly convinced," she wrote to her parents from Paris, "that he *must* not go on with his work, and I have persuaded him that it is a plain indication from his Heavenly Father that he is to go home to America and renounce his business for the present. And to my great joy, he is willing to do so." As soon as he was well enough, they crossed the channel again, Hannah collected the children from Monkhams, and they took refuge in a remote cottage in North Wales while waiting for the boat home.

Meanwhile rumours were, of course, spreading among the faithful. The Keswick Conference was almost wrecked by Robert's defection, but the organizers finally decided to carry on, and the meeting, purged of his heresies, became a yearly event which continues to this day.

The rumours reached the newspapers in the end, and the committee put out another statement reading:

Some weeks after the Brighton Convention it came to our knowledge that the individual referred to had on some occasions, in personal conversation, inculcated doctrines which were most unscriptural and dangerous. We also found that there had been conduct which, although we were convinced that it was free of all evil intention, was yet such as to render action necessary on our part. We therefore requested him to abstain at once from all public work, and when the circumstances were represented to him in their true light, he entirely acquiesced in the propriety of this course.

Many critics assumed that Robert's error was that of Antinomianism—the belief that he who was saved was above the moral law—then a particular bugbear of all who distrusted the "enthusiasm" of the Holiness movement. In fact the real heresy was not named, though there can be no doubt as to its nature. In later years Hannah called it "the subtle doctrine concerning the physical manifestation of the Holy Spirit which led my dear husband astray", and in old age she finally admitted that it always ended in free love, or something very near it.

Hannah blamed Blackwood and, whatever her private opinion, maintained dutifully that the whole business was a cruel libel, and her husband perfectly innocent. When she got back to Philadelphia she wrote to one of her English friends:

> I need not tell thee, I am sure, that my dear husband is entirely innocent of the vile charges against him. Their only foundation consists in his tender fatherly ways with a lady whom he was seeking to help spiritually. . . . She had been used to being very free with him in the presence of others, looking upon him, as he thought, as a father, even going up to him once after one of my Bible lessons and kissing him in the entry before the company passing out, which surprised him very much. The consequence was that he never thought of offending her, nor of any harm whatsoever, when in an interview that *she* had requested, he put his arm around her and in a very fatherly way soothed her as he tried to help her in her spiritual difficulties. It was a *thunderclap* when he found that uneasiness was felt . . . I can tell *thee* that the lady was Miss Hattie Hamilton, who

wrote *How to enter into Rest*. As to the doctrine . . . Robert
thought it was a very precious truth at the time, but he has
been led to think since that it *must* be a delusion.

Conceivably her energy in Robert's defence may have covered a
remembrance that she too had once advocated, if not practised,
the same delusion.

A COMMONPLACE LIFE

Hannah

ROBERT'S LOYAL FRIENDS, both in England and America, still believed in his innocence, but he was a broken man. A year after the disaster Hannah wrote to her friend Mrs Barclay:

> It makes my heart ache to look at my dear husband and think of the blight that has fallen on him. You think that I make a mistake to say that his life is blasted. You would not say this if you knew him. A more sensitive, tender-hearted, generous man never lived, and this blow has sorely crushed him in every tender spot. . . . He often says to me that his life is one long agony . . . it could not be otherwise; and I have not the faintest hope that he will ever recover from it. There *are* storms which uproot and overturn even the stateliest trees, and what wonder then if the weaker ones are utterly prostrated by them. . . . My life is full of the dear children's interests and of the sweet cares for my husband and parents. A *commonplace* life is, I am sure, the most desirable for a woman.

This was not to be allowed, however. Dr Cullis, a religious friend, was determined to reinstate Robert, and despite all protests laid on a Camp Meeting for him in the summer of 1876. They both found it "a wearisome performance", though Robert's preaching seemed to have all its old power. Hannah described one curious manifestation to her sister: "Boole got a great Baptism during the meeting, the unmentionable kind, and was so completely carried away by it, poor fellow, that he came near to making love to me, and actually did get into a deep and spiritual flirtation with a lady there who had left her husband because of his ill usage."

Although the meeting achieved its public purpose, there was

still something seriously wrong with Robert's religious life. He was morbidly sensitive about the repercussions of the English scandal and given to what Hannah regarded as equally morbid introspection. "Do give up this introverting process," she wrote to him a year after the meeting, "and seek for the manifestation of Christ in thy soul." But as the years passed his doubts grew, until his faith had entirely gone. By 1881 Hannah had abandoned the effort to conceal his backsliding:

> Aunt Rebecca Collins was in the car yesterday, and asked me most confidentially about thy "views". It was very embarrassing, and thee positively must give me liberty to tell the truth, for I cannot lie even for thee. I made the most of thy heart disease etc. etc., and she was greatly relieved. But why thee should mind people knowing the simple facts I cannot see. . . . Alas, poor human nature. But as human nature goes, thee, dearest, is a pretty good specimen of it, even if the unsanctified part of thee *has* got the better of thee, so I will send thee lots of love.

Hannah was made of sterner stuff. She soon recovered from her initial desire for a "commonplace life" and was away once more, exploring any fascinating fanaticism that came her way. Once more she summoned cousin Carrie: "We have wonderful times in our house now. Come and get stirred up."

In 1877 she was off to another Camp Meeting, enlisting Robert's support:

> I believe Heavenly Father loves and honours the fanatics most. I want thee to promise not to whisper a word about thy perplexities while I am there. It is a ticklish seat on the top of a greased pole and the least push one way or the other might upset me. But if I can have ladies in my tent before whom I am compelled to sit steady I can get along I hope.

She kept her balance on the greased pole and went on eagerly with her religious researches. "The ladies . . . at our house this spring have that *quaking* under the power of the Spirit that gave the early Friends the name of Quakers. Mrs Ashmead and Mrs Bond both *quake* wonderfully at times. And yet neither of them are at all remarkable for any depth of natural character." But she herself seemed to be confined to what she called "a sort of *dead level* arrangement . . . the glamour of fanaticism *will not* get into my life, do what I may".

She never stopped trying, however, even with a group of whom she said: "What with their seven judgments, their two resurrections and their rebuilding of Babylon and their two witnesses, and their time, and times and half a time, there is such a complicated arrangement of affairs altogether that one's best comprehension can hardly unravel it."

She made another effort to give up reading fiction. All her life she had swung between the feeling that fiction was a harmless recreation and an equally strong feeling that it was a snare of the Devil. As she said to her friend Anna Shipley, "It seems as if one *needed* now and then the recreation of some other reading than religious, and yet whenever I do it, it always seems to bring a cloud spiritually." Now, however, it looked as though she had found the perfect substitute, in her "dear fanatics". For one whole summer she was fascinated by a strange group which had taken the house next door, and which included a highly respected Methodist minister called Lansing and two middle-aged sisters who claimed they lived, moment by moment, under the detailed guidance of the Divine Spirit. "Their story is a perfect romance," she wrote to cousin Carrie. "Nobody needs the excitement of a theatre or novels who lives this interior life of walking with God, for the curtain rises every day upon tragedies and comedies and inconceivable romances." She defended these people until she heard that two hitherto perfectly respectable young women in Boston had been made pregnant by Lansing, who persuaded them that he had been chosen by God to father a chosen race.

But she was soon off again on another colourful trail, reporting to her sister Mary:

I must add a line about the Second Coming developments. . . . On top of the "Purple Man" and his followers comes another prophet on the same subject . . . to deliver the most solemn warning that Phila[delphia] has ever received. . . . I agree with thee that the Purple Man *is* hard put to it to bring all the past millions of people back to this earth. That sounds to me like the most utter nonsense.

The amusement with which she described the fanatics she met should not obscure the fact that she was very serious in her quest. She longed for a mystical experience of God, and her adventurous nature could not help hoping that the bold claims of the "prophets" and "saints" would one day lead her to the reality she was seeking.

Her passionate interest acted like a magnet, and drew deluded and desperate people—almost all women—from far and wide to confide in her. Most of these women suffered from unhappy married lives. "Only the other day," Hannah told Anna Shipley in 1882, "I looked at a row of them who happened to be sitting together, and every one of them, *I* knew, though no one else did, had husbands who made their lives, as far as the earthly side of it goes, one long torture."

All the terrible tales she heard, and delighted to believe, gradually hardened her heart—never very soft towards husbands, or indeed men of any kind—until the very word "husband" aroused an automatic reaction of disapproval and disgust. She was still fond of Robert, though she was far from blind to his weaknesses. Her comments over these years were never unkind, but they were, perhaps, more bracing than sympathetic.

In addition to her search for religious experience Hannah gave further Bible readings, later published in book form both in England and in America, and was extremely active in philanthropic work. She helped to hold Temperance meetings for drunkards in Philadelphia, and was much annoyed when they were turned away. "Joshua does not like having them come to his coffee house, so we are obliged to move our meeting. For to *stop* the work would be wicked. Yesterday *sixty* of those men rose for prayer and *twenty* were converted." Certainly they seemed to be getting results. "At Murphy's this morning I found such a lovely looking young fellow who signed the Pledge there although he was drunk. . . . He said so pitifully: 'I don't want only to sign the Pledge, I want to be *good*.' The children were all dreadfully interested."

Prison visiting was the next thing:

On First Day morning Mrs Bond and Logan and I went with Elizabeth Comstock, the Friend's preacher, to the Penitentiary. We stood at the end of one of those long corridors and preached to the rows of cells with their doors a little way open. . . . We sang a good deal, and the prisoners joined in, and thee cannot imagine how touching it was to hear their voices sounding out of those dismal cells. . . . I asked Logan to let me tell about his conversions, as *his* share in the work, and with a great deal of blushing he consented. It interested the poor prisoners very much and afterwards . . . a good many of them said they wanted to see "that little boy" and they wished he had preached to them.

She was also working hard for the Women's Christian Temperance Union, and its remarkable leader, her friend Frances Willard. This movement, which started in a spontaneous crusade in the ever-enthusiastic Middle West, with women kneeling outside saloons and successfully "praying" them into closing, had now become fully organized. Founded when the men's organization refused to let women hold office, the movement grew with the realization of the appalling social conditions which were part caused and part anaesthetized by heavy drinking; it was now nation-wide, and was later to enrol more than half a million members throughout the world. Today it seems naïve and even impertinent, with its Battle Songs and Pledges, its credulity and piety, and its simplistic belief that drink was the root of all evil. But it represented something new and vitally important: the first move of American women into properly organized social work, and the training in political action it provided soon showed women the need for the vote, and for participation in decision-making in all fields.

All this was meat and drink to Hannah, and she attended all their Conventions (each one "the grandest I have had yet") and became the President of her local branch and National Superintendent of Bible Study. She was also writing a life of her father, worrying over women far away ("the awful condition of women in India is perfectly heart-rending"), travelling to Annual Meeting of the Quakers, with whom she had become more or less reconciled, and to summer Camp Meetings all over the East and South, and finally, by 1882 (much to the disapproval of her sister Mary, who advocated a more devious and "feminine" approach) speaking at Women's Suffrage meetings. She sent her daughter Mary the reports of her first speech on Women's Suffrage:

> I am thoroughly roused on the subject for I have had so many cases of grievous oppression of men over their wives lately that my blood boils with indignation. And before thee is married I want to have thy position as the equal of thy husband settled on a legal basis. The moment one looks into the subject at all it seems utterly incomprehensible how we women *could* have endured it as patiently as we have. Literally and truly up to within a few years women have been simple *slaves*. And some women say they like it! Ugh! It is one of the worst vices of slavery that its victims are contented with their lot.

In spite of all these absorbing outside interests, Hannah's first pleasure, as well as her "manifest duty" throughout these years was her family.

The Whitalls had always been an unusually affectionate family, and John Whitall, in particular, was most dearly loved by all his children and grandchildren. All their lives, Hannah's children remembered their happy childhood with loving gratitude, and the most vivid of their memories were of the kind of treats most parents would not have encouraged—an excursion when they were tiny just to stand under a waterfall; a trip to the meat market to revel in the sheep's eyes and the gory mess of pigs' intestines; running out in the rain at their grandfather's farm to catch frogs for killing, and eating their hind legs; enormous bonfires, and permission to ride and sail and hunt entirely on their own. It was only when her daughters grew up and began to attract potential husbands that Hannah began to fret over them.

While all the children enjoyed the summers on the farm, some of the others found Hannah's tigerish defence of her own brood both alarming and, at times, unfair. She felt that nothing was too good for them, and nobody, not even her well-loved family, must be allowed to get in their way with anything they owned or desired. Her niece Carey wrote: "Aunt Hannah is the most completely honest woman, grand and noble in many ways . . . only deluded in two things, her slavish devotion and real selfishness for her children and her Christianity."

John Whitall had two mild strokes while Hannah and Robert were in England, and on her return home Hannah devoted much of her time to looking after him. He was gradually failing, and New Year's Day 1877 saw the last of the huge family gatherings where the children used to sing a specially written song of greeting for him, as they all lined up, the smallest first, and filed into the dining room to give him the present they had clubbed together to buy. There were twenty-three grandchildren, ranging from twenty-one years old to a few months, at that last gathering. In June that year he died in his sleep.

In less than three years Mary Whitall followed her husband, and a year after that the last of the older generation, Robert's father, John Jay Smith, died too. There were four surviving Smith children: Lloyd, the eldest, the one who had fought at Gettysburg and who looked after the library left to Philadelphia by their ancestor, James Logan; Horace, with whom Robert had much in common and who came to suffer from the same over-excitement alternating with depression; Robert himself, and their unmarried sister Lizzie, known to the children as Aunt Lill.

When John Jay died there was no undue mourning. Hannah reluctantly made Mary drop the idea of a party that had been planned, for fear of gossip, but her comment was astringent to the point of "Plain Speech": "As father says, no other family would do it, and people do not know how little we cared for poor grandpa."

The distribution of the older generation's money, together with the increasing prosperity of the Whitall-Tatum glassworks, brought Robert and his family real wealth. When Hannah's mother died they decided to leave the Filbert Street house and move back to Germantown, near brother Jim Whitall and the Smith relatives, and they took a large house on Germantown Avenue. There they kept horses for the children, and a phaeton and pair, in which Robert delighted to drive to work every day, and take his friends for spins in the City park. Hannah had adequate staff to look after the house and the children during her many excursions, and the whole family was able to take ambitious summer trips every year. Against this increasingly luxurious, if not notably elegant, background, Hannah watched in her "passion of motherhood" over her three precious daughters, and her strange handsome son.

Logan was a problem in many ways: introverted and reticent in a world of ebullient female extroverts; a lazy letter writer (a strange phenomenon in that family); and a late developer in all intellectual matters, only learning to read when he was ten. He was mainly interested in dogs, shooting and sport. He was a delicate child, and suffered severely from recurrent malaria. To avoid this, he was sent to Atlantic City, to Clifton Springs, to the Adirondacks, and finally in 1879, only three years after General Custer's defeat at Little Big Horn, to stay with Governor Hoyt, with whom Robert had made friends, out West in Wyoming Territory. Though only thirteen, he travelled there on his own and rode out of Fort Laramie with the Governor's military escort, with whom he was photographed, to attend an Indian pow-wow.

The malaria appeared to have been cured, but Hannah still did not trust the Philadelphia climate, and Logan was sent off with his sister Alys and several of his cousins to a school in Providence, Rhode Island. "It is a great advantage to him to be in the middle of such a nice band of girls," Hannah wrote, "and I find that they all have quite an idea of taking him in hand in a very *cousinly* way."

At this school Alys and Logan caught mild doses of scarlet

fever. Whether through carelessness or ignorance, they were sent home too soon, and they passed the disease on to their youngest sister, Ray, who died of it in 1880, at eleven years of age. Including the stillborn baby in 1873, this was the fourth child Robert and Hannah had lost. Hannah drew on her religion with her usual fortitude, but this last loss left her for many years, if not for ever, with a deep feeling of insecurity about her remaining children, and a corresponding conviction that all children should be given everything they wanted. She wrote to her sister Sally: "I can always bring Robert round by talking about the probability that the children will die. . . . Thy children don't die, or at least have not yet. Losing one child makes parents very indulgent to those who are left, I think generally."

Whether for this reason or not, Robert was a most loving and indulgent father. In particular he adored Mary, his "Poll" as he called her, and she soon learned how to wind him round her finger. Mary, in the true family tradition, was already keeping a diary at twelve, in 1876, and it shows her to have been both precocious and dashing. She used to ride in the park, and flirt innocently but enthusiastically with all the young men of Germantown, or so it seemed. Every week she and her hordes of cousins used to meet for a social evening in one family house or another. Twenty or thirty of them would sit in the "parlor", in a great circle, talking and laughing and flirting and playing games, and Mary would map it all out carefully in her diary afterwards, to show who sat next to whom.

Alys described Mary's effect on a less scintillating sister:

I felt my hopeless inferiority [to her] . . . (not knowing that I might one day grow to be even better looking) and decided that my only merit and attraction must be in an unselfish character. So when we went to pick bilberries I secretly put all mine into my sister's cup, or if at home she sent me to buy a quarter of a pound of chocolate for 10 cents, I would add to it 5 cents of my own to get a better quality. I became a terrible prig, and my unselfishness, rather ostentatiously displayed, has always dogged my actions, until I suddenly felt free, at 79,

when I came to live alone, to be as selfish as I liked. But I have
never really liked it, such are the habits of a lifetime, and I am
still obliged to subordinate my likes and dislikes to those of
other people.

Hannah began to worry that all this riotous fun, however
desirable in itself, might prevent Mary from getting that education which she still believed that girls must have—"at bayonet
point" if necessary—and Mary, who was an intelligent girl and
liked to study, agreed. So off she went to boarding school,
pursued by a swarm of letters from Hannah, advocating
warmer winter clothes and longer sleep at night, with much
sage moral advice, and enthusiastic sympathy with schoolgirl
"smashes".

Meanwhile the family had taken to a new kind of "fun", and
were spending their summers camping in the wilderness. The
first year, 1878, they went to the Adirondacks and took Carey
Thomas with them. Carey was the only one of Hannah's family
to equal her fierce feminism and her passionate desire for education. Carey's mother, despite her own sweeter and more yielding
character, approved of her ambitions, but her father was conventionally opposed to any idea of college for women. He was
finally won over, and Carey went both to Cornell and to
university in Europe for two years.

Hannah, of course, encouraged Carey with all her might, and
showed her the diary she had written during her early married
years, with its laments for lost opportunities and resentment at
too early childbearing. Carey took all this even more deeply to
heart, perhaps, than Hannah herself. She won the first *Summa
cum laude* to be granted to a woman at Zürich University, and
was appointed first Dean and then President of Bryn Mawr
College, where she became something of a legend. She also
remained unmarried, whereas Hannah concluded in old age:
"Daughters are wonderful luxuries, they are well worth a bad
husband, at least mine are."

Carey and the children loved camping, but Hannah confessed
to her mother:

How do I like this sort of life? I do not like it at all. I can't sleep comfortably . . . four thick in a bed is rather too much even altho' I have had Alys fenced off with stakes. . . . Then I cannot eat in a muss, nor do I like to get along without bread. I do not care for boating, nor fishing, nor hunting, and sitting on a log does become monotonous after a while. It certainly is not the life for me. But if the rest enjoy themselves that is all I ask, and I can get along.

In 1880 they were more ambitious, and went to Colorado and the Yosemite, and finally on to San Francisco. As a treat for Hannah they stopped over in Salt Lake City just long enough for her to pay a call on one of the widows of Brigham Young, the Mormon leader, who told her that she had been "sealed for eternity to Joseph Smith, and after his death had been sealed in time to Brigham Young. And she seemed to think it was a wonderful advantage they possessed over us Gentiles that they were *sure*, by the sealing process, of having a husband throughout eternity." Not, one would imagine, a necessary ingredient of eternal bliss in Hannah's eyes.

The children adored camping, and all the adventures that went with it, so—as the girls had to be chaperoned—Hannah went with them every year, despite all the discomforts. Each year at the end of the trip she swore that she would never do it again, but each year she was there again as before. The children had no idea of her feelings, and it was not until they read her letters after her death that they discovered what a trial it had been to her.

Part II

CHILDREN

PRECIOUS DAUGHTER

Mary

MARY HAD GROWN up into a tall handsome girl with black eye-brows and a firm chin. She had inherited many qualities from her father, as she well knew, including his extravagance, his enjoy-ment of his own emotions, his mercurial temperament and his hypochondria. She enjoyed camping as much as Hannah hated it, but in 1880 the sophisticated charms of San Francisco appealed to her even more. All through her life she was to note down and remember with greedy pleasure the good food she ate and the places where it was obtainable, and this year she wrote to her cousin Albanus Smith:

> Potage Paysanne, Hors d'Oeuvres, Brochettes de volaille à la maître d'hôtel; poisson: Boiled salmon (fresh); meat: chicken and venison; vegetables: potatoes, peas, cauliflower, asparagus. Dessert: pie, meringue à la crème, ice cream, cake, candy, coffee with cream. There were a great many other things, but that is what I took.

The following year, when she was seventeen, she went to Smith College, where she enjoyed life as much as ever. She made two close friends there, a beautiful blond girl called Evelyn Nordhoff, whose brother Walter married her cousin Saidee Whitall, and whom Mary loved dearly until she died in her early thirties in 1898, and a delicate, earnest girl called Florence Dike. She enjoyed flirting with all the young men she met—Bandersnatches, as they were called by the family, from Lewis Carroll's *Hunting of the Snark*—although this was not referred to in her letters home.

The arts, with the exception of some literature, had always been a closed book to Hannah, as to all Orthodox Quakers of her day, but now that her children were beginning to show interest she did her best to keep an open mind. She went to a lecture by Oscar Wilde, but was not impressed. "Oscar Wilde is a 'sell'," she wrote to Mary, "he looks like two radishes set up on their thin ends. He does now and then say a fine thing about art, just about what I would say about religion. But his manner is so poor, and his style so excessively 'Rosa Matilda' that I believe everybody is disgusted —Logan did not get *one* idea from him." Logan himself wrote to Mary: "Poor Oscar Wilde has had a hard time with the college students in America. I don't believe girls would treat him in the way he was treated by the Rochester seniors." And he added: "Is thee aesthetic?"

Mary replied jovially:

I haven't the time to be "aesthetic", and besides, what's the use in Germantown? [Many years later Logan wrote "TRUE" in the margin here.] I should like well enough if all the family were aesthetic, and I was, naturally, but I am far too busy to make the family aesthetic, *even if* I could! Imagine mother in an old gold dress waving a peacock feather fan. . . . No, mother is far grander and nobler as she is, than if she spent her time on such things.

However, Logan's aesthetic sense was definitely burgeoning. "Now that they are dividing grandpa's things", he wrote to Mary, "I wish someone with taste was at home to get nice things, but particularly old things, of which grandpa had so many. . . . My judgment has no weight with the family, but thine has." Mary replied: "I confess that I haven't very much taste for old things really, tho' I like well enough to have them in the family. I like to know about things, but I don't care so much to have them. I think it is very nice that thee does, however, and perhaps when we are both older thee will teach me to prize relics."

Logan was now at Haverford, feeling much more sophisticated than most of his classmates. "There is a great field for young Americans here," he wrote to Mary at the end of the year. "Our trouble has been, I think, that as soon as any of our people have

got decently civilized they have immediately skipped over to
Europe and have left us here in darkness. . . . I think we should
bend all our energies to converting the Philistines instead of
running from them."

He was growing up fast, and developing a definite character
and tastes of his own. He was nicknamed "Ye Cynic" by the
family, while Mary was known as "Gummy", after Dickens's
Mrs Gummidge, because of her constant complaints about her
health, and Alys became "Lurella" or "Loo" after the heroine of a
favourite novel by Howells. Logan and Mary wrote to each other
regularly during their college years, and Mary took a good deal of
trouble to advise him about his reading. "If I were in thy place,"
she advised in 1882, "and wanted to exercise the love that I am
sure is latent in thy mind for poetry, I would begin with the *Lays
of Ancient Rome* by Macaulay. . . . But of course thy taste will
enlarge and expand. I have passed through the youthful senti-
mental stage, and I haven't got into the real one yet."

She was not far off, however. At that time the poetry of Walt
Whitman was considered barbaric and even indecent in its
emphasis on physical passion, whether or not those who disapproved were aware of Whitman's homosexual bent. When,
therefore, one of Mary's tutors recommended *Leaves of Grass*, it
was with considerable reservations. "Miss Sanborn lent me Walt
Whitman," Mary told her mother in May 1882. "There are
perfectly *disgusting* parts, but she warned me of them, so I was
preserved from them." Nevertheless she found "something sublime in it, it is so fearfully reckless and courageous and honest".
Her friend Florence and Miss Sanborn warned her never to speak
a word about Whitman, "for he is *dreadful* in parts—the parts I
fortunately knew enough to skip . . . so don't mention my having
read him." Hannah's reaction was not unexpected. "Walt
Whitman must be perfectly horrid as a man. His—what do you
call it? not poetry certainly, is idiotic. Do not waste a minute
on him."

But in the autumn Mary began to reread the poems, and her
first nervous fear of what people might think melted away into
admiration. The "Poet of Camden" then lived at his brother's

home just across the river from Philadelphia, and when Mary
arrived home at Christmas her father greeted her at the railway
station with the words: "Poll, Walt Whitman is coming to lunch
tomorrow." For Mary's sake, Robert had innocently ventured to
invite him to a meal and a drive in Fairmont Park, and the poet
had agreed to come. As she recalled four years later:

My poor father little dreamt what a bombshell he was introducing into the quiet and respectable Quaker community in
which we lived, for he had never read a line of Whitman's
poems! I knew in my guilty heart that I ought to have warned
him—but even I, with my keen impressions of the first shock of
the plunge into his poems, did not dream of the "tempest in a
teacup" that would be roused by the entry of this prophet into
his own country.

Mary was surprised to find Whitman living in "a smallish brick
house which I can describe in no other way than by calling it
'genteel' . . . a more incongruous apartment could not be
imagined for the poet of the 'barbaric yawp'."

Whitman spent three days with the Smiths at Christmas, and
returned for the New Year. He made immediate and lasting
friends with all the family except Hannah. The children, particularly Mary, he found delightful, though as Mary remembered
many years later, he used to sit in the hall outside the dining room
when he had finished the little he ate. "Once when I went out to
him and asked him to come in again, he said 'No, Mary, I love to
hear you laugh, but I don't care about your conversation.'"

Mary was deeply moved by the visit, and described it in her
diary:

He is 63 years old but seems much older, for he walks very
slowly, leaning on a cane, and his hair is silvery white. . . . He
is very receptive of new ideas and is remarkably teachable. . . .
He called me "his dear friend Mary" and told me that I understood him entirely in his writings. He said it was a great pleasure
to him, for someone had told him that he had not written for

women, only for men, and it had nearly broken his heart. One afternoon all of us were sitting round the open fire . . . and conversation turned to God. Mother asked him what his idea of God was. "Mary, you tell them," he said. Then as best I could, I told them that while God was unknowable to us, yet to Mr Whitman *everything* in life came direct from God. And that this was not only perceived by the intellect but was directly known through the feelings. That a great peace was in his mind about God. "And I say to mankind, be not curious about God. No array of terms can say how much I am at peace about God and about death". After a few minutes silence, he smiled at me and said that nothing in a long while had *comforted* him so much as what I had just said.

Back at Smith, Mary wrote most enthusiastically to Logan: "Somehow I feel of late a new interest in things, even the commonest. . . . Everything and everybody is interesting. The immediate cause is W.W. . . . I relieve my mind to thee. . . . Aunt Sarah and other people write me such dreadful letters that I dare not talk about him much—or at all . . . and so I am continually in a state of repression."

The Germantown family and friends had been making a great fuss about the indecency of Walt Whitman, and Hannah passed it all on to Mary:

If thee knew more of men and their overpowering passions thee would understand how inflammatory such things as W.W. has written must necessarily be to many men, in fact to most. . . . A girl's reputation cannot be too carefully guarded, and if the report were to get around that thee admired Walt Whitman's poetry so much, some young men at least would think it was those dreadful parts thee liked and would stamp thee as impure at once.

It was strange to see the heretic Hannah so much influenced by her conventional surroundings.

Robert, who had now read "some of the worst places",

composed a letter to Whitman, telling him that he did not want to see him again, but cautiously sent the letter to Mary first for her opinion. Mary's reply—and she was not yet nineteen—gave good grounds for the love and admiration Whitman came to feel for her:

> I hope thee will not send this letter to our dear old friend. Thee has expressed to him plainly enough already what thee thinks, and I believe it would hurt him too much. He is old—leave him the pleasure of remembering those happy days and the warm appreciation which he received which has been most comforting to his heart. . . . If thee doesn't want to see him again—there is no need to tell him so at any rate, and spoil his new pleasure. . . . Emerson argued long and earnestly with him to omit certain portions of *Leaves of Grass*—but when he found Walt Whitman firm in his own opinion, he invited him home to dinner, honouring and loving the man, in spite of what he considered his mistakes. Well, it may not do for us to be [as] liberal as Emerson, we are not Emersons. However Walt Whitman is received nearly everywhere in as much "Society" as he cares about. Aunt Sarah may object—but what sort of a Liberty Hall would we have if we followed her advice? Of course thee and mother are at liberty to decide just what you think best. For my part the presence of that lovely spirit in our house is a thing I shall never cease to be thankful for.

Robert destroyed the letter, and became a warm and valued friend of the poet.

By the middle of February, Mary was delighted to hear that her father had invited him to stay again. She had inspired Logan with her enthusiasm and he wrote to her:

> I have indulged in a little W.W. today. . . . As thee said, it is *fixing*. . . . Yesterday I was in town and . . . there was the old gentleman himself looking very natural and lovable. . . . He told me that thee and I were the only young people that understood him, and said he was going to send thee things. . . .

When I see him I never think of him as a grand poet, but simply as a dear old man.

He continued, with an echo of his father's Santification days: "I first got interested in poetry coming up in the train from Atlantic City, in about an hour my ideas on many subjects were entirely changed, especially the way I looked at vulgar and stupid people. Now they seem beautiful souls temporarily in uninviting attire." Alas, this was not a point of view he was able to preserve in later life.

There was one approving voice for Whitman in the family, that of Hannah's beloved niece, Carey Thomas, who wrote to her mother:

I am struck dumb at the thought that Aunt Hannah is entertaining Walt Whitman. . . . *I*, of course, should be charmed to entertain him; but to think that one of *you* should receive in your house the man who has written more grossly indecent things than perhaps any other man whose books are printed in this open manner—this consoles me for many things. . . . I remember yet how he phrased Rossetti's line, which was so objected to that he omitted it in later editions, "monstrous maidenhood intolerable". Because I disagree with him "from in out" on this point would none the less make me anxious to meet him. He is our greatest living genius. Tell me if they like him as a man. Do approve of Aunt Hannah's having him.

Mary Thomas sent this letter to Hannah, who in due course passed it on to her daughter, adding:

My objection to W.W. is not that he writes on these subjects, but that he writes in such a *brutal* way, making a woman's use for man just the brutal gratification for man's lusts . . . and to say that a pure maiden is 'monstrous maidenhood intolerable' is to me so revolting that I *cannot* feel anything but disgust for the man who should say it.

Mary's view of sex was less prejudiced than her mother's, and she wrote back:

Thee writes in a spirit of *loathing* of what God had made natural in men, and in women too, which thee calls "brutal lust". . . . It is only the abuse thee ought to loathe, the want of self-control. . . . Thee says I know nothing about men. I trust at least that their minds are not all taken up with it—I *know* they are not . . . I guess thee would say "Ugh" at the thought of any young man feeling what to me seems a most natural desire to be near a girl whom he likes, to hold her hand, to put his arm around her—I should be sorry to be forced to loathe so many of my friends.

And so Hannah yielded. "It is a trial to me, but I believe in liberty. And as I sometimes want people you do not like, I must give you the same liberty I want for myself." She also said: "I love thee, my precious, with an untellable mother love, and thee may know this wherever and whatever happens. Moreover I am *on thy side* against the whole world, and even against myself, if this last could be possible; which however I do not think is, for thy side *is* my side always, I guess." And in later life, however much she disapproved of her daughter's beliefs or behaviour, Hannah kept this promise to the letter.

Whitman came to Germantown Avenue many times after this. He enjoyed the company, the conversation (when it was not too youthful), the comfort and the good food.

They always treated me with peculiar consideration [he told Horace Traubel], made the home so much mine . . . its servants at my beck and call if I had wished it—the overflowing table which contained everything but a tipple (you know the Smiths were opposed to all tippling)—yes, everything but a tipple, which by the way, some of us would now and then slip out and get round the corner.

He genuinely liked Robert, and described him as an agnostic, "a man more or less of the world—fond of horses, good living, believing in goods—yet seeing more, too than that". For Hannah, as one might have expected, he had little understanding or liking. "She takes her doctrine, if she don't take her whisky, very straight, the sort of get under my feet religion which gives hell out to the crowd and saves heaven to the few." An ironic description, in view of the trouble Hannah had got into for insisting that Heaven was, in fact, for everyone.

Whitman was fond of all three children. Mary, above all, he called his "staunchest living woman friend", and "bright particular star", adding that she was "very radical indeed, almost along with the anarchists". Logan was "a good boy", and Alys "the most American—the most democratic—best calculated to measure *Leaves of Grass*. . . . Oh! she is handsome too—the finest specimen of womanhood I know, almost." He was perhaps misled by Alys's beauty into thinking her more poetically receptive than she really was, for she wrote many years later: "I used to go from college every Saturday morning to visit him in his Camden house, across the Delaware river. I didn't then appreciate or even much enjoy his poetry, and I was such a puritanical prig that I cut out many passages from the copy of *Leaves of Grass* he gave me."

At Smith college Mary was chasing other alluring hares, too: Herbert Spencer, for instance. Hannah was terrified that this would destroy her faith, and wrote: "I fear thee is on the road that will lead thee into the sad and dreary and unhappy and unscientific haven of agnosticism. Is it *necessary* for thee to read Herbert Spencer? . . . Thy father gave place to the doubt and has lost all sense of perception of God. . . . Do, my precious daughter, hold on here. It is a far more dangerous place than thee thinks." Mary replied placatingly:

I see the danger of weakly drifting into a belief in nothing in particular and everything comfortable in general—and that is where papa is, I think—I wouldn't say he had "weakly drifted" there, because it is probably a reaction with him. . . . Dear mother *don't* write as if I were on a "fearful precipice". I *honestly don't think I am.* . . . I do believe Spencer will not do me any harm. He is dreadfully illogical, and often contradicts himself.

Mary's closest friend was still Florence Dike, and during the summer vacation of that year, 1883, they went off together to one of the last sessions of the Concord School of Philosophy. Mary later described the trip:

We were the only people there under sixty, I think, except William James, who came to lecture on "The Stream of Consciousness" (afterwards embodied in *Psychology*). But I can guarantee no-one was more serious than we in our efforts to assimilate "Transcendentalism". We saw Emerson, but he was already passing into the solitude of old age, and the only impression we gained was of quiet, aloof, unworldly spirituality. But we diligently read his essays aloud to each other, especially the one on the "Oversoul". . . .

I spoke of William James, and recall now how during one of his lectures, when old Miss Peabody [the educationalist and pupil of Emerson] in a round muslin hat, fastened by an elastic under her fat chin, and a wide-spreading dress-sacque, was taking a nap on the platform, Prof. James drew what he called the 'Stream of Consciousness" on the blackboard, and began putting little crosses around it, to indicate "the external world", "personality" and I know not what. One of these crosses he called "The Infinite" and the word roused the sleeping old Transcendentalist from her slumbers. She straightened her hat with one fat hand, and extended the other towards the lecturer with a silencing gesture—and then said impressively: "The Infinite; we should all strive to rest upon the bosom of the Infinite,"—and so saying, relapsed again into sleep. Prof. James at that instant caught sight of us stifling our laughter in a pew at the back of the hall, and for one brief instant our eyes met his in indescribable amusement.

William James was to become a very good friend of the Smiths. He had a great admiration for Hannah's "healthy-souled" and realistic attitude to religion, and called her "the Mother of Pragmatism".

The Smiths were definitely going up in the world. Around this time Robert decided to dignify the name of Smith by adding to it his mother's maiden name, Pearsall, a practice followed in turn by his children. Hannah, however, preferred her own maiden name, and remained Hannah Whitall Smith, which made for some confusion later on in England, where wives were expected to drop their own names entirely on marriage. Their financial position, with the ever-increasing prosperity of Whitall-Tatum, had now become comfortable enough for Robert to indulge his generosity freely. This generosity was one of his most engaging character- istics, but from time to time it seemed to become an uncontrol- lable urge. Hannah did not approve of many of his gifts, but to her satisfaction, he was very generous to the feminists, and he also subscribed lavishly to the Women's Christian Temperance Union.

Early in 1883, however, he rashly invested the considerable sum of $50,000 in the Sierra Grande silver mines. In his open-handed way he also provided Walt Whitman with 200 of these shares— enough, it was reckoned, to yield an income of $50 a month. As usual, he had been more optimistic than wise. Hannah wrote to her sister Sally in July: "The mine, I fear, is a dead failure. Mr Smith is in the *depths* about it. He invested so heavily that the loss is really serious and we all have to economize most uncomfort- ably. No-one knows what is the matter, and it seems as if there must be a great cheating somewhere." Whitman's stock failed with the rest, and only brought in nine diminishing dividends before becoming worthless.

Around this time a serious rift developed between Hannah and Robert. Whitman remarked on it to Traubel, six years later. "There was some trouble in the family . . . some infelicity; for some years Pearsall and Mrs Smith had no words—no relations— with each other." Logan, after his father's death, referred to thirty years of congenial married life, out of a total of forty-seven. This may have been due to Hannah's growing exasperation at Robert's extravagance, or to her inevitable loss of respect for him after the way he reacted to the disaster of 1875, but it seems probable that there was also some specific marital misdemeanour, of which no record survives.

Hannah remained impeccably dutiful, sympathetic and loyal in all outward ways, but though they made up their differences, she came to have less and less patience with his faults as they grew older. Robert was a kind and good father, as she freely admitted, but he was also lamentably weak, self-centred and self-indulgent. His religious beliefs had gradually dwindled into an interest in Psychical Research, and he was fading into a comfort-loving, health-obsessed, elderly bore.

Meanwhile he was forced to stop the WCTU subvention. "I told Mrs Hunt," Hannah wrote to him, "that the Temperance women must not expect any more money from thee, as in thy desire to help the cause thee had gone into a mine which had failed. She said it was a dreadful disappointment . . . she had found *the man* at last, the one man in the world who knew how to appreciate the WCTU and was willing to give them money. And now alas!"

Hannah tried to instil the need for economy into Mary, but this was no easy task. When Robert told Mary about the mine she answered gaily:

I will try to be very careful about unnecessary expenses . . . I got my summer dresses before I knew that the mines were as the flower of the field, when we were all feeling rich and building castles in Spain. However it is not so bad after all, since it is all my summer outfit and my best Fall dress combined and is only $113.00. I feel quite in the humour of saving money altho' I suppose I don't know very much about it nor what it really means. I am not quite sure to whom to apply for lessons—not thee I guess!

Luckily the lean period did not last long, though in 1883 they had to take their summer holiday in Maine, instead of the more distant Yosemite. Hannah found the camping as trying as ever and reported to her sisters: "The groans I have . . . repressed at various

times during this trip would have furnished ... enough for
several series of revival meetings, I verily believe. ... My stiff
knees and other accessories of old age make it too tiresome for
even me to enjoy."

There was to be just one more camping trip the following year.
Thereafter her children would drag her to ruined temples and
picture galleries instead of mountain trails and camps.

NUPTIAL FLIGHT

Mary and Frank

DURING THE WINTER of 1883 all sorts of fascinating plans were in the air. Mary was hoping to go to the newly opened Harvard Annex (later to become Radcliffe), while Logan went to Harvard itself, or, even more exciting, to go to England with her cousin Saidee Whitall, to study at Oxford or Cambridge. Meanwhile she was at home "frivolling" as she called it, vainly trying to study on her own, and working for a kindergarten teacher's diploma.

Hannah was becoming alarmed at the flirtatious nature of some of Mary's "frivols", but Mary continued unperturbed. In February she went off for a holiday in Atlantic City with cousin Saidee and reported that they were "bandersnatched" by a young man who carried their bags. Hannah at once began to fret, and Mary replied: "It kills me with laughter to think that my unwary term 'bandersnatched' raised a second thought in anyone's mind. . . . There is not a single young man of any kind or description in Atlantic City, as far as we have discovered. (I hope this won't suggest to anybody that we have been *looking* for them! We haven't.)"

Full of the thought of the cultural treats in store, she now gave Logan some sisterly advice on how to deal with parents:

Mother has devised a much keener scheme than the Harvard one. It is this—it is this. Papa doesn't want thee to go to Harvard. So that a year abroad would be a happy compromise for him. Heretofore he has not been willing to hear of thy spending a year abroad after leaving college. "Business" he has always said. But now that thee has Harvard to hang over his head he will let thee have a full year abroad. That of course would be quite as nice as Harvard . . . and then think of the

delightful little expeditions ... London with the Art Galleries
—Paris—Switzerland! ! ! And the people we would get to
know. ... If thee is keen thee will let the Harvard scheme go,
on condition of having a year abroad after thee has taken thy
degree. Say "abroad", not England, for it strikes papa more
favourably.

Meanwhile one of Mary's college friends, Edith Carpenter, had
come to stay at Christmas, and she and Mary's cousin Bond
Thomas had promptly become engaged, provoking a typical
comment from Hannah to her sister: "Oh Mary, these children!
What sparks and tinder they are! I begin to be afraid to see a pair
of trousers even hanging up in a store!"

In 1884 the annual meeting of the British Association for the
Advancement of Science was held for the first time in Montreal,
and some of the visiting Englishmen went on to attend the meetings of the American Association of Science in Philadelphia. It was
a very hot September, and some of them stayed with local
families. Mary described it all to a friend:

It was a most interesting and delightful week. I spent all my
days in the city, melting from one long lecture to another, with
occasional interludes for ice cream and soda. We had all the
horses out every evening and drove all over the country. ... I
can still see the cavalcade in my mind's eye—Father attired in a
light and airy costume of Japanese silk driving the pair, with
three "Scientists" all attired in linen dusters (as it was so hot)
admiring the "fine night" and the "view". Then followed
Saidee ... with two more linen-dustery Scientists, and then
your humble servant ... making a hollow pretence of knowledge of Electricity or Physics or Philosophy.

She took three of the visitors out to call on Walt Whitman, and
among them was Frank Costelloe, an Irish barrister from London
and student of philosophy. Costelloe, a shortish bearded man,
nearly ten years older than Mary, was greatly attracted to her, and
she to him. They talked much and frankly, and one day Mary

took him for a drive. As she recalled some five years later, she told him about the mentally unstable inheritance of the Smiths, which Robert would recite in a gloomy litany whenever he had one of his "nervous spells", and how she feared she was fated to "follow in my father's miserable footsteps." Frank did not put much weight on it, and persuaded her to put her fears aside. He claimed that the foundations of the world were the four cornerstones of God, Duty, Freewill and Immortality, and being a Catholic and a lawyer, he offered to prove this to her, which appealed to her hunger for philosophical certitude.

After the visitors left, Mary settled into Harvard Annex, sharing lodgings with Logan, who had managed even better than Mary had hoped and had been allowed a year at Harvard as well as a year in Europe before starting in the family firm. Though she did not tell her parents, Mary was writing to Frank Costelloe. They went on exchanging letters throughout the autumn, and finally Frank proposed and was accepted by cable. Mary said nothing to anyone until she went home for Christmas.

She was enjoying Harvard as much as she had hoped. She wrote later:

> I was convinced that the only serious study for serious people was philosophy . . . and spent most of my effort on that subject getting infected with the philosophy of Berkeley (which in fact I have not had the mental energy to entirely shake off) and being led by Professor Palmer, whose sole female pupil I was, to become a Hegelian. (I have almost forgotten now what it was, but I remember a great sense of elation and enlightenment.)

She and Logan were also eagerly pursuing "Culture". Of one lecture by Edmund Gosse she said: "When he mentioned the sacred word 'Botticelli', I remember looking at my brother with eyes brimming with emotion and saying 'Oh Logan, we are at the very heart of things!'"

One day she took a trip down to Baltimore to stay with the Thomas cousins, and gave a talk to nearly a hundred ladies on her philosophy of life. Helen Thomas, who was thirteen at the time, described it in her book *A Quaker Childhood*:

> Tall, golden-haired and lovely, she seemed not in the least disturbed either by the size or the age of her audience as she announced her subject: "The Duty of Self-Development"... I had heard many tales of Mary's fascination, but I was totally unprepared for the reality. Her radiant beauty and a kind of vital force I felt emanating from her bowled me over... Mary was preaching ... the duty of developing one's own gifts: "If after giving it a fair trial, any particular task continues to be disagreeable, we can be sure it is not the right task for us."

Aunt Mary Thomas was not quite so hypnotized as her daughter and felt it necessary to add a warning note against allowing pleasure in a course of action to be one's only guide. She also asked Hannah to prevent Mary from spreading her dangerous gospel among the Baltimore cousins.

Mary did not find it difficult to put up a smokescreen to distract her parents from her love affair. When one of her cousins got engaged, she wrote disingenuously to her mother: "Who will be next? Thee is the only [mother] in the family yet spared. May it long continue to be the case until our fair Lurella chooses some fascinating baldhead.... Logan announced tonight that getting married young always seemed to him almost like dying young. He will probably be the first to go off!"

Another diversion she employed was to make use of the attentions of her philosophy tutor, writing to her mother: "Prof. Palmer has been very kind to me since we came back ... he is one of the most fluent and interesting talkers among the professors." Hannah, alerted by such praise, invited him for a visit of inspection at Christmas, and Mary wrote to her father: "Mr Palmer is very anxious to meet thee and mother (the parents of such a brilliant student ! ! ! (sarcastic marks)) and asked me to send thee his thanks for the invitation.... He has been very kind to me and I am glad to think thee and mother will know him. I like and admire him so much."

By now Hannah thought their engagement was imminent and prepared an alarming document, which she addressed to Professor Palmer, giving her specifications for the man who might be permitted to marry her daughter. It was headed "On the Authority of a Husband", and began:

I believe motherhood is more of a passion with me than with most women. And I often think I must feel just as a lioness feels when her cubs are in danger. Therefore you will understand, I am sure, why I write as I am now going to do. . . . I have discovered that husbands . . . are very jealous of their "rights" and are unwilling to allow any freedom of action or development to their wives. . . . They are *masters* in short, and wish their wives to be slaves. . . . I believe there ought to be an equal partnership in all property or incomes that accrue to them jointly after marriage and that each partner should have an equal authority in the disposing of it . . . each one, however, to retain the personal control of any inherited property. I believe the mode of living and all the details of life, whether large or small, should be the *joint* arrangement, and that neither should override the other, but each should wait for a mutual conviction. In short I believe in a *perfect equality* between husband and wife as between man and man. . . .

There was a great deal more in the same vein, and she concluded: "I am convinced that most of the misery in married life arises from the fact that, unconsciously perhaps, the soul of the woman is chafing against the *tyranny of sex*." In view of the fact that Mary had already accepted another man's proposal, it is to be hoped that this document was never actually sent to Professor Palmer.

Hannah was soon to think that, by comparison at any rate, he would have been eminently acceptable. She wrote to Mary after the Professor's Christmas visit: "From the first moment I fell in love with him, and even the thought of thy marrying him, to my great surprise, looked pleasant and comfortable to me." But it was not to be. The news about Frank was broken to them over the holidays. It was difficult for Hannah to welcome any man as a husband for her precious daughter, but that the one chosen was not only a foreigner but also a Roman Catholic, and even, she feared, of a somewhat lower social class, was hard indeed. A spate of protesting letters followed Mary back to college:

Only when thee is older will thee be able to understand what a *thunderclap* it was to find that our almost idolized daughter had become involved in a love affair with an utter stranger and a Roman Catholic, before we had dreamed of such a possibility. . . . The horror of his religion only grows upon me more and more the more I look into it. I have mailed thee a perfectly authentic account of a girl's stay in a nunnery in Charleston . . . [it] will give thee a true picture of one important phase of Roman Catholic religion. . . . Find out whether [Mr C.] really is a Jesuit or not. Do not fail to ask this, as we shall want to read about it before we go over. Also again I ask thee for the name of his birthplace and where his father's farm was. I have asked thee very often for this.

There was a strong prejudice against Catholics in Hannah's circles—Irish Catholics most of all—but Mary thought little of it and was quite prepared to be converted if Frank could convince her. Frank had been perfectly open about his background, which was scarcely as alarming as Hannah made out. He lived in London, and was a barrister with Radical political ambitions. His father had been of Irish tenant-farmer stock, and had married his landlord's daughter, thereafter becoming a surveyor in Glasgow. Frank had been a very clever boy and had won scholarships first to Glasgow University and then to Oxford, where he shared a Balliol Exhibition with the young Asquith. He studied Classics and Philosophy, and did extremely well, becoming a particular favourite of the formidable Master of Balliol, Dr Jowett.

The details he sent somewhat reassured Robert and Hannah. Furthermore it was abundantly clear that Mary was not to be shaken, so Hannah began to put a good face on things. "We are getting very good accounts of Mr Costelloe," she wrote to sister

Sally in April, "and I am beginning to hope that he may not be bad after all." They now planned to take the whole family, including their cousin Madge Whitall, Alys's great friend, to Europe for the summer, and hoped to take a closer look at Frank before establishing Logan somewhere in Germany for the winter. Hannah gradually became calmer, but to her friend Priscilla Mounsey she admitted her doubts: "I never had anything that was so hard to trust for. For I do not want my daughters to marry at all. I think marriage is a *frightful risk*; and I do not like men."

They sailed on 24 June 1885, Hannah seasick as usual, and they were met by Frank at Southampton. Quite soon it became apparent that Hannah had no hope of delaying the engagement. She wrote to her sister: "I find that it is a foregone conclusion that [Mary] is to marry Mr C., and *soon*, and the certainty of it brings over me all that it will mean of separation and loss to me. . . . To lose her is like losing the sunlight . . . for it will be losing her to have her live in England, this ocean is an awful barrier."

Meanwhile they all settled down for the moment in London, where Robert "blossomed out into a complete English rig, and looks like a Duke at the very least", Hannah said. He found none of the embarrassment he had dreaded in returning to England after the débâcle. On the contrary, he seemed "to have renewed his youth in the most wonderful manner in this air, which always *has* suited him. And he is very happy meeting so many of his old friends, who are lavish in their kindness. I believe *he* would not mind living here, but *I* should." Hannah herself was as heretical as ever. She met her old friends Richenda Barclay and Priscilla Mounsey and complained to her sister Sally:

They are both dreadfully religious and want me to be preaching and praying to them all the time. And they are not "Broad" and that is *most* embarrassing, as thee knows. . . . Altogether I am used up with them to that degree that I can hardly endure it. . . . I do think Evangelical people are too disagreeable for anything. If I have to be much in London I shall just have to announce my heresies and cut loose from the whole lot.

It was finally decided that Mary and Frank should be married in September, so that Alys and Madge could enjoy the occasion before they had to return to Philadelphia to start college. The wedding was held in Oxford, and as a great honour Dr Jowett invited them to hold the wedding breakfast in Balliol Hall—the first time, it was said, that such a thing had happened. Mary and Hannah paid a brief visit to Paris, where a sumptuous wedding dress was made, though the dressmakers "were overwhelmed with astonishment at Mary because she doesn't wear corsets and insists on her clothes being loose".

Hannah described the wedding day to the family: "All the arrangements, which had necessarily been very hurried, were most satisfactorily accomplished. . . . One thing which pleased me, and that was that Mary did not have to promise to obey. . . . Mary looked lovely and was radiant with happiness. Alys who sat by her, declares that she ate right straight through the menu from beginning to end." The menu still exists, and this would certainly have been a considerable feat, but the letter Mary wrote to her friends about her feelings after the ceremony implies that she might have achieved it. "The curious sensation came over me . . . of being either a girl in a book or the fat lady at the Dime Museum—but it passed in due time and when we got to the Library, where the Reception was held, I was Gummy Smith—no Gummy Costelloe—once more, and I even felt, I blush to say, decidedly hungry while we were waiting for breakfast."

Hannah went on in a more lyrical vein:

I did not shed a single tear and smiled and was cheerful all through. Robert engaged a band to play in the gallery during the déjeuner, because he thought as the people were largely strangers to one another it would make it less embarrassing. At the close we had three speeches—the Master, Mr Jowett, a most distinguished scholar, proposed the health of the bride—in lemonade—and made a very flattering speech about Mr Costelloe. . . . He referred to Mary very prettily and quoted a latin sentence which he said meant when translated "There she is, look at her". Poor Frank had to respond, as this is the English custom. . . . Robert followed him in quite a nice little speech, ending with a warning to all parents with daughters not to entertain young men from other countries at Scientific Conventions.

Frank and Mary had to rush off to catch the four o'clock train to London and a night train on to Scotland, because Frank was standing for Parliament as a Gladstonian Home Ruler in November, and was due to make a speech in Glasgow the next night. Hannah took Alys and Madge back to Philadelphia, and arranged to return immediately to help settle Mary into her new home, which her parents had lavishly contributed to furnish.

THE UPROOTING

Hannah and Family

ALYS AND HER cousins Madge Whitall and Grace Thomas were enrolled for the opening year of Bryn Mawr College in the autumn of 1885. Grace's sister Carey was Dean of Studies in the new college, and she made it her life work to ensure and preserve the highest academic standards there. Carey had hoped to be made the first President, but she was only twenty-seven, and though her scholarship and energy were admired she was un-proved in any administrative capacity, and the post was given to Dr James Rhoads, a prominent Philadelphia Friend. It was inconceivable to Hannah that a mere man should be preferred to such a woman as her niece, but Dr Rhoads proved to be a sensible administrator, who co-operated fruitfully with Carey in her academic plans. In 1894 Carey succeeded him, and became in the course of time almost as legendary a figure in the College as Dr Jowett had been at Balliol.

Though Alys was prettier than Mary, with blue eyes and curly brown hair, she was neither as brilliant nor as self-confident as her sister, and she was nervous of the stiff entrance examination. She duly passed, however, and recalled in later life:

I enjoyed my four years at Bryn Mawr very much. . . . [Carey] lectured in English composition, . . . and was particularly good on the logic and sequence of sentences. Her correction of an essay on Browning I wrote for her was: "This writer seems unacquainted with any but the simplest form of sentence." It has been a stimulus to me ever since to write longer sentences. . . . Woodrow Wilson was one of our professors, very young and in his first post, I believe, and I attended some of his historical lectures. But he didn't succeed in interesting me in history, and indeed made no impression on me. I learnt more

from a little German professor who tried to impress me by
proposing to me in the train one day.

Hannah settled the girls into their quarters and hurried straight
back to Mary. She reached London to find that Frank had lost his
election—he had not really expected to win, though Mary had
been more hopeful—and that Mary was already pregnant. They
were moving into their new home at 40 Grosvenor Road, in
Westminster overlooking the Thames, living in one room and
cooking their meals over an open grate while the workmen
finished the decorations. Mary had a miscarriage in the midst of
the turmoil, but Hannah coped with everything.

In January 1886, as soon as she was better, Mary went off with
Frank and Logan to visit Frank's strange "aesthete" friend, Eric
Stenbock,★ at his estate on the gulf of Finland. Mary wrote to her
friends:

> Count Stenbock—who is taken direct with all his extravag-
> ances, recklessness and brilliancy from one of Ouida's novels—
> took us to a different place for each meal, and sometimes to two
> different places for one meal. . . . Our strict adherence to
> Temperance principles amused and angered him, and made him
> drink enough wine for us all. But as he has already graduated on
> absinthe and opium, wine cannot affect his nerves in the
> slightest. He is a most curious study. Altho' he lives to amuse
> himself—with his extravagant meals, his poetry, games and all
> the imaginable devices for entertainment, he isn't really amused
> by them, and is clever enough to know that he isn't. . . . Count
> Stenbock has his own rooms furnished in the most aesthetic
> style, with a lamp burning before a Buddha and an Eros—and
> his other gods disposed in various places. When he was at
> Oxford, he said, he and one of his friends (who is now insane)
> used to try a new religion every week.

It was certainly a change from Germantown.

★ Count Eric Stenbock 1860–95, a strange Estonian aristocrat with an
English mother; poet, eccentric, drunkard and drug taker. Frank had met him
at Oxford, and befriended him.

While she was away, Hannah was off on a round of visits, renewing her acquaintance with Lord Mount Temple's nephew, a rather different kind of aristocrat:

[Mr Cowper] dresses like a country farmer and wears his trousers turned up at the bottom most of the time, which I understand is the "swell" thing to do. I suppose the idea is that being so grand in themselves they do not need the help of fine clothes to set them off, as common mortals do. . . . I was amused at one thing: he said that a man was foolish to keep lots of property he never saw, and that one could be comfortable with *only two thousand* acres round his house.

Robert was also enjoying himself, and had worked out a new scheme for international copyright. His father had made quite a lot of money in his time by pirating English books cheaply when there was no English copyright in America, and possibly Robert felt vicarious pangs of conscience. Hannah reported: "Robert is having quite a 'boom' with his copyright business, and has been made an Honorary Member of the Literary Club of London, which is a great honour. There is to be a dinner for him next Third Day at the Club. He is quite a lion."

When Mary got back and the house was finally finished, Hannah had more time for her own interests, and she explored boldly in all directions. Her viewpoint on English politics was fresh and often shrewd, and her comments were perceptive. She wrote in February 1886:

Last Monday the unemployed workmen of London had a demonstration at Trafalgar Square, and I attended it (not however as one of the *unemployed*). It was an immense crowd and they were addressed by some violent and so-called "social democrats" who seemed ready for anything that would bring about a revolution. One of the speakers said "If we cannot get bread we must have blood", and again "If they do not give us what we ask we will meet here next time to sack the West End baker shops." I went in and out among the crowds freely and without molestation and made very close observations, and I must say I saw very little earnestness or determination of any kind. The men seemed out for a frolic and joking and laughing was the order of the day. . . . There were lots of young men from 18 to 21 who were up to all sorts of tricks, and when the meeting broke up these rowdies . . . rioted through one or two of the West End streets breaking windows and "looting" the shops. No-one thinks it was the bona-fide working men at all who did this rioting but only the rowdies who always hang about on the skirts of the crowd. But it frightened London out of all its senses for a day or two. I never saw such a frightened lot of people. I went shopping the next day and had it all to myself pretty much. The shops were all barricaded, and nobody was out shopping but me and London seemed paralyzed. And there was not the slightest sign of rioting anywhere.

A few days later she got a glimpse of the other side of the affair:

On Tuesday Mary and I went to a Hunt! I have always wanted to see an English Hunt that I might know how to picture it when I should read about it. . . . A good many horses went down on the train with us, also their owners. . . . Mary and I sat in the same carriage with a young lady all attired for the Hunt in waistcoat, cravat, and round hat, with her riding dress on and her whip in her hand. There were two or three gentlemen with her, and we soon found from their conversation that she was the sister of Lord Randolph Churchill. . . . It was very interesting to hear his sister and her friends discussing "Randolph" and his plans for the Irish. One of the men appeared to be the owner of one of the houses that had suffered during the riots, and he said the ignominy of it was almost worse than the damage; that he would not have minded half so much if his windows had been broken by genuine stones, but that to have legs of mutton and loaves of bread dashed through one's drawing room windows was a little much.

Mary had hoped to settle down and acquire a real philosophical education from her husband, but she found herself instead being swept into the maelstrom of politics and philanthropy. "There are so many things to do in London," she complained, "that it is almost impossible to avoid doing too much. A good many philanthropical people one meets are too busy to have any home life at all, or even to make real friends. It is very unwise to live so, and yet I can perfectly understand it, because idleness seems wicked where there is so much to be done."

She had developed a genuine gift for public speaking, and was trying very hard to live Frank's life and adopt his religion, but neither was entirely congenial to her, and frustrations were already creeping in. "For a wonder", she wrote in 1887, "Frank did not have to sit up all night to work, so after he came home at ten we actually had a chance to talk." She was beginning to realize that he was not as perfect as she had imagined; that he was more polemical than intellectual, and quite hopelessly careless and unpunctual.

Alys, who was far more pious and filial than Mary, was writing letters from Bryn Mawr, to which Hannah replied with streams of motherly advice:

Thee is a precious daughter, darling, to be willing to stay single for me. But I do not want thee to pray against falling in love, for thee might get someone who would be as lovely to me as to thee, and to have thee married and settled near me with a real nice fellow with a darling set of grandchildren growing up around me would be what I should like better than keeping thee single. . . . Only I am glad thee doesn't like Englishmen. The more I see of them the less *I* like them. They have no manners for one thing, and they *are* arbitrary, say what you will.

In the spring of 1886, Robert and Hannah took the opportunity of Logan's stay in Germany to start off on a real Grand Tour. Hannah stopped over in Brussels first, for some Temperance meetings, and not even a wild snowstorm could quench her eagerness to see all. In Berlin she joined Logan, who did his best to convert her to Good Music and Old Masters. "The music was very fine, Logan said, and it did sound very nice, but my inward ear for music has never been opened yet, and I confess I did not particularly enjoy it. Logan says it is an evolution I shall have to get in Heaven. And I suppose I must if I am to enjoy the harps there." As to the pictures she was even more emphatic:

> I may as well tell the truth at once and say that *I do not like them*! I am sure if any modern painter were to paint such poor pictures now, he would be hooted out of the profession. . . . I think, of course, they were wonderful considering how long ago they were painted etc., but that is not the orthodox style of praise, I know, so I do not hope to build any reputation.

Unlike her sister Mary Thomas who, said Logan, had "gathered up her skirts and marched through the Louvre looking neither to the right nor to the left," Hannah went on dutifully trying to like Old Masters throughout the trip, but without much success:

> I saw the Sistine Madonna of Raphael. I am thankful to say that I liked it. . . . Logan is a staunch adherent of the Old Masters, and I believe he feels it necessary to keep a close watch over me for fear I will make some awful remark displaying my ignorance to the people around. Not one Madonna have I yet seen who seems to know how to hold her baby at all. They all hold him off in the most awkward and unnatural manner until I fairly ache sometimes to take him in my arms and give him one real good mother hug.

Robert joined them in Vienna. Hannah found, as she expected, that she strongly disliked both Germany and Austria, as she considered their treatment of women boorish. However, she failed to find as many opportunities for righteous rage as she would have wished, and complained: "I have not even had the satisfaction of boiling over with indignation at seeing a woman and a cow hitched together pulling a cart, with the man walking alongside driving them."

Constantinople was another matter. She was fascinated by the strangeness and colour, and though—naturally—her "heart ached for the Turkish women" as she floated past the Seraglio, she was delighted when she went calling "in a Sedan chair lined with yellow silk and felt like a Harem woman". She even praised Turkish clothes.

> Their women *do not lace*, and they *wear short skirts* and I feel as if in these respects they were centuries ahead of us. I wonder if it will be possible to introduce our ideas of women's position and at the same time keep those two vital points of hygiene undisturbed. It *ought* to be, but alas! with civilization comes conventionality always, and I am very much afraid that when the faces of the Turkish women are uncovered, their waists will begin to be squeezed and their skirts to trail.

When they got back to London they found that Frank was very anxious to accept the invitation of the Swindon Liberals to stand for them as a Home Rule candidate in the coming General Election. Hannah, despite her continuing fear that he held "that hateful notion of the authority of husbands", persuaded Robert to finance him. "Frank", she wrote to her husband, "thinks he would be *sure* to get in on this Irish question, and the Gladstone party want him. But the question of the money stands in his way . . . what would thee think of helping him some? It *would* be a comfort to have him in Parliament, would it not?" However, in spite of Robert's help, Frank was not elected. "I am not sorry that Frank lost it," wrote Hannah, "for I do not think he is rich enough yet to be able rightly to afford it. Mary is secretly glad too, I believe, for she says she would never see Frank at all."

In September 1886 Hannah and Robert went back to Philadelphia, though with no great enthusiasm, taking Alys and Logan with them. Logan was now to leave the nest, as he was starting work in the New York warehouse of the family glassworks. "We were all eager," reported Hannah, "to know how Logan liked his first introduction to business life. He seemed quite to enjoy it." He was more frank in a letter to Mary:

> The most startling fact in regard to my menage is that breakfast is at 7.15 in the morning. When you have recovered from that shock to your nerves I will go on to say that the business hours are from 8 to 6.15, with half an hour for lunch. Over the business itself I will draw a veil—I tell the family that I enjoy it which, tho' not exactly an accurate statement of Fact, is a most consoling Thought for them.

He wrote later that what he most disliked about the business was the stifling and tyrannical atmosphere. "Every one of the employees lived in instant fear of dismissal, and in the hope of profiting by the disgrace of others. A heavy blustering bully was the tyrant of the warehouse." His malaise was strengthened by his growing urge to try his hand at writing. He wrote a number of short stories (which he later admitted to have been very bad) in the manner of Henry James, and remained deeply affected by the spirit of Walt Whitman. To Alys he wrote: "I am living in dread of catching some emotion or other. What I fear is a literary ambition of some kind—did thee ever know that our father, mother, uncle, grandfather, great and great-great-great ditto all wrote books—& all poor ones, too, except perhaps mother's which I have never read? It is kind of depressing to think of."

Over in England Mary was pregnant again, and Hannah was thrown into a perfect frenzy of maternal solicitude. Letters poured across the Atlantic urging her to take care of her health, to go to bed early, not to work too hard and not to let Frank oppress her, until Mary was driven to protest both on her own account and on Frank's. "I have no doubt I have been an old fidget about thy health," Hannah admitted in October, "but I really am convinced at last that thee and Frank both are fully alive to the importance of it, so I will not bother you any more." She rather spoiled the effect, however, by adding at once: "But now darling, thee must be careful not to make the mistake of laying off the care of thy health upon my shoulders when I am by, and feeling therefore free to do careless things because I do not protest against them."

Mary also complained that Hannah was too critical of Frank, and that she appeared to dislike him.

Thee is mistaken [she replied] in thinking I dislike him. I really like him very much. . . . If there seems a little constraint in my manner it arises from the fact that I cannot talk freely before him or with him on account of his "knock-down" manner of arguing. . . . No doubt this is very foolish, but somehow one does not like to be knocked flat at the very outset of an argument. . . . You are both wrong in thinking I object to marriage *per se*. I do not. . . . What I object to is the present usual relation of the sexes in marriage, by which the man is considered, and considers himself, *master*. From this *my whole soul revolts* and until this is righted I cannot encourage any woman to enter into this legal slavery.

A month or so later there was more friction. In answer to a complaint from Mary that she felt uneducated beside Frank, she wrote:

As to thy ignorance, darling, that comes of marrying too young. Had thee had Frank's extra ten years of study, with the opportunities thee would have had, and thy natural talents, I am sure thee would have been up to him. . . . Thee might have had a student's career, it was what I had planned for thee, but thee chose instead to marry; and a married woman who undertakes to keep house and have children . . . cannot expect to study. I am afraid thee will have to put up with thy ignorance and make thy wits stand thee in place of knowledge, as I have had to. . . . Perhaps if thee can keep thy daughter from marrying too young thee and I may be able to see our dreams fulfilled in her.

However Hannah was even fiercer in defence of Mary than she was in attack, There was an outstanding example of her "steam-roller manner" during the Christmas gathering at sister Mary's house in Baltimore in 1886. Helen Thomas, the youngest daughter, described it:

Edith★ was leaning . . . over the table towards Aunt Hannah. "I do not mean that Mary is intentionally cruel," I heard her say, "but she does lead men on to fall in love with her. An atmosphere of adoration seems necessary for her happiness." Absorbed in analysing her friend, Edith quite failed to notice that Aunt Hannah had grown pale with anger, for after a moment's pause she went on, "Mary finds a new love affair stimulating. She is very much like Goethe in temperament." "How dare you say such a thing to me, Edith," Aunt Hannah's voice rang out, silencing all conversation down the table. "You call yourself Mary's friend and you compare her to Goethe, the most notoriously immoral man who ever lived. . . . Mary is an angel of goodness. She cannot help it if men fall in love with her, but she uses her power only for their good." . . . The tears were streaming down Edith's face . . . she pushed back her chair and rushed from the room, Alys and Grace after her.

Hannah wrote a full account of the scene to Mary, protesting that since she considered Goethe to have been

a most wickedly immoral man, and cruelly heartless besides, to the victims of his brutal passions, this analogy between thee and him was simply *intolerable* to me, especially as it was made at the dinner table. . . . I told Edith afterwards that she must excuse me, but that thee was the apple of my eye, and that it would grieve me unspeakably to think that *thee* could approve of Goethe's conduct, or that people should think thee could.

Early in the new year Hannah began to worry about Robert's extravagance again. She complained to Mary:

He . . . is buying things and giving away money right and left. He has bought a house in Arch Street for $25,000 without ever

★ Edith Carpenter, who was now married to Bond Thomas.

consulting me, and is going to a great deal of expense in fitting it out for the Laurel Hill Board. It *may* be a good investment as property is going up in that neighbourhood, and anyway it will, I hope, lock his money up so that he cannot speculate with it. But whether good or not, I am powerless, for if we have the least difference of opinion on money matters, he gets a nervous spasm.

However, Logan and Alys were now old enough to help, and Robert did not feel it necessary to have a nervous spell when they tackled him. "I got Alys and Logan to talk to him," Hannah told Mary, "as he will not let me say a word . . . and he took it in very good part." The crisis was over for the time being.

That summer the family (with the exception of Logan, who was still at work in New York) crossed over to England again, as Hannah was determined to be there for the birth of Mary's baby. The child was born on 4 June 1887, a large and healthy girl, who was named Rachel, after the sister who had died young and the Smith grandmother, Rachel Pearsall. Mary had a very bad time, and Frank won qualified approval from Hannah. "Frank . . . never left Mary a minute through all her dreadful suffering," she wrote to cousin Carrie. "Husbands ought always to do this. Nurse says they ought to be pinned to the wall beside the bed and *made* to stay."
Logan wrote Mary a typical letter of congratulation:

I object to infants on principle, which is hardly the appropriate thing to say here I am afraid, altho' it is true, but still my hatred of the race doesn't go so far as to keep me from sending a blessing to welcome my niece. . . . In a nice letter I got from thee not long ago thee expressed some views on French art which I must some day do my best to eradicate from thy mind —but dear me, how useless to talk to thee of art now, one might as well talk metaphysics to a horse.

The Smiths, disporting themselves once more in aristocratic

circles, found life in London more delightful than ever, and by the end of the summer Hannah wrote home:

> There certainly *is* a charm about the English upper classes that is indescribable, and I confess I *do* enjoy them exceedingly. For one thing they are far more like Americans than the classes below them. I am quite convinced that we Americans are in a further state of evolution than the English. . . . To be an American seems to be a certain passport to their favour. They seem to look upon us all as belonging to the aristocracy. . . . I would rather live in London, I believe, than in any other place in the world, dearly as I love America and the people in it.

When they sailed for home at the end of August, she told her English friend, Priscilla: "It is very hard for me to leave Mary here . . . and it nearly breaks my heart. I do not see how I can live on the other side of the ocean from her, I am seriously thinking of getting R. to come over here and live, for I believe he would like it, but we must wait and see what Alys does, for I cannot leave her."

As soon as they arrived they were met by a new development: Logan had decided to give up business and take to a literary career. Hannah warmly approved: "In my secret heart," she wrote, "[I] felt glad of his decision, although it *does* seem a shame to let such a sure chance of fortune slip through his fingers. Still, if the boy has genius it would be a far worse shame to extinguish it in the Glass business . . . so I encouraged Logan and we awaited with eagerness father's decision."

Alys described the scene:

> After dinner we settled ourselves in Papa's room for a long talk. We naturally discussed business for a while and Logan worked upon all our feelings by telling us some stories of Albert Tatum's meanness. One story in particular of the way Albert had insulted one of his clerks, a grey-headed man of over fifty, particularly roused our indignation, and Papa exclaimed: "No man can or ought to stand such things unless he has a wife and

family to support". "Which I have not," added Logan, "and sometimes I don't see how I shall be able to endure the life".

Alys pressed Logan to read one of his stories, and it was much admired. "Papa in particular," she went on, "was perfectly delighted with it. 'Perhaps after all literature is thy calling, Logan,' he said. 'But we need not think about that yet.' 'Why not?' said Logan boldly. 'In fact, Papa, I *have* been thinking about it for some time and I want very much to leave business and devote myself to a life of study.'"

And so Robert agreed to let him come home at once, and to give him the same allowance he had been having. Logan's decision was the last straw. With him studying and writing in England, as he planned, America would be empty indeed, and Robert and Hannah made up their minds to move the family to London for good. The next few months were spent settling their affairs; Logan was extremely useful, and so tactful that his father took his help as a favour. Hannah commented, "It is an unspeakable comfort to me."

Alys had one more year at Bryn Mawr, and Robert wanted her to give it up and change over to an English college, but Alys was worried about her cousin Madge Whitall, who was in great trouble. Madge's mother, the wife of Hannah's brother James, suffered from "melancholia", and now Madge was following in the same path. She was very badly affected by her mother's depression, and the doctor said that she must on no account stay at home. She was not well enough, however, to go back to Bryn Mawr. She would have a bad spell lasting four or five days, when she was drowned in guilt feelings and religious pessimism, and then pull out for a couple of weeks and return to her normal cheerful self before falling prey to the next bout. So in the autumn of 1887 Hannah begged her brother to let Madge go to England with them in the spring, and this was finally arranged. Alys took a year off college to go with her and look after her.

Another heavy trouble fell on the family that winter. Hannah's sister Mary Thomas was found to have an inoperable breast cancer. Mary herself had long been a convinced believer in

"Mind Cure", and Hannah found her "delighted at the prospect of an early death and . . . trying to cheer everybody else." But she was only fifty-three and dearly loved, not only by her husband and her eight children, but by everyone who knew her. Hannah had never been convinced by the claims of the faith healers, and wrote to Priscilla:

> The one great grief to all of us is that six months ago she *could* have been cured, when she first began to think she had the trouble, but then she trusted the Lord for healing and fully believed *it was done* and went on believing this all summer so fully that she never said anything to anyone about it. And all the while it was growing as rapidly as it was possible for it to do . . . my sister is simply the victim of the faith cure teaching.

All through the winter she faded, and in April, before finally leaving for England, Hannah went to say goodbye, for it was clear that they would not meet again. She wrote to Alys from Baltimore: "Aunt Mary sends thee 1,000 thanks for taking care of father and letting me go to her. We were very happy together and it will always be lovely to remember. We could not let ourselves cry when we said farewell this morning. It would not have done any good. If it wasn't for you children I should feel desolate enough." Mary Thomas died in July, and the last real tie with America went with her.

Before they sailed, Hannah and the children achieved a further success in their delicate handling of Robert and his money affairs. He agreed to settle their shares of the family money on them at once, instead of handing it out in the form of allowances. It was a rather vague and unbusinesslike arrangement, and was to lead to a number of difficulties in the future, but at least it would help to prevent him squandering everything.

They took leave of Walt Whitman, too. Hannah wrote to Mary about their old friend:

> Dr Bucke . . . thinks Walt Whitman very much failed, and says he scarcely leaves the house. Dr Bucke tried to get him to

make some arrangements about his papers etc if he should die, but he would not enter into the subject, merely saying "No doubt everything will be taken care of." He enjoys the oysters father has supplied him with several times a week, very much, and often says to people that "the Smiths have been his Salvation". Do, darling, remember him distinctly; write the story of thy acquaintance with him and of all thee knows about him . . . some day it will be very valuable. Tell everything about his careless ways etc . . . and the time thee was there and had to get in through the window and found him so forlorn.

Mary had discovered a house for them only four doors away from her own in Grosvenor Road, and despite Hannah's preference for living in lodgings to avoid having to do the housekeeping, they took this. In May 1888 they finally departed. "Our children are the comet," she told Mary, "and father and I are only the tail, and of course where the comet goes, there we *have* to go, *nolens volens*. Fortunately in this case it is *volens*, for both father and I enjoy going to London."

PASTURES NEW

Hannah and Family

ON HER ARRIVAL Hannah was at once enraptured by her grand-child Ray. "When I tell thee," she wrote to her friends, "that she sucks my watch and uses my spectacles as a hammer, thee will understand which of us is the mistress and which is the slave. She is in short a perfectly delicious baby, and I am a perfectly idiotic grandmother."

Logan decided that Oxford was the place for him, and on Frank's advice chose Balliol. He passed the entrance examination and soon settled in happily there, writing to Alys:

As thee sees, I am in Balliol, but thee can't know how charming it is. . . . I begin work about 9, sitting at the desk by my window, into which a gargoyle grins at me. About 11 I put on my gown (it is the thing not to wear caps any more than you can help) and go out and take a piece of Latin prose to my tutor. . . . I have been to about 5 or 6 lunch or breakfast parties in the last week, so thee sees that the opportunities for social intercourse are almost infinite. . . . I met Henry James yester-day . . . He is small and very French in appearance and has a disagreeable sneering way of talking. It is only his manner that makes people dislike him however, I think, for after I had talked to him a while he seemed very much like Prof. James. He said a number of clever things, most of which I have forgotten. In speaking of New York, however, he said that it was impossible to have a picturesque address there, and he told me that he had gone back to New York to be a good American citizen, but at the end of the year he had quietly packed up his few belongings and come away.

When Robert arrived, with Alys and Madge Whitall, the

family took a house for the summer, deep in the Welsh hills. It
was a biggish property with twenty acres of park, and shooting
available over 2,000 acres, and although damp and a bit decrepit,
it delighted Hannah's soul by purporting to have a ghost, an old
lady continually packing and repacking in the attic. Logan
enjoyed the fishing and shooting, and Robert the peace, but
Hannah and the girls found it too quiet and too wet for their
taste.

She was still fascinated by the strange social customs of the
English:

> It is a very interesting glimpse into English County life, and
> makes me understand a great many things we have met with in
> English books that nothing but actual experience would make
> plain. For instance we know now with how much interest
> people who move into a new County watch to see whether the
> County families will call on them. Evidently the vicar of the
> church that is on "our" estate thinks *this* is the most important
> element to be ascertained in settling on a home. . . . I do not
> myself think that the "County Society" around us is particularly
> brilliant, and to tell the truth, except as a study of English
> customs . . . it is all rather a bore to me.

The "County" did indeed call, and Hannah was soon in retreat.
"I wish", she wrote to her daughters while away on a short trip,
"you would pay off all our calls while I am away. DO! There are
six to pay . . . you can go in detachments. Let me be spared any
further sacrifices in this line. I have bought a novel to read called
Cut by the County with which I shall arm myself against the next
county we live in. I prefer being 'cut'."

Mary and Frank joined them with the baby, and Hannah worshipped while Mary made another unsuccessful attempt to get
Frank to give her proper philosophy lessons. She complained later
that all he did was to make her help him in his own work. "He
had finished his magnificent training, so I must scamp and hurry
over mine, to work where he already is. . . . There is no method in
the matter presented to me to be assimilated, no course arranged."

Wales, they all agreed, was too far from London for a permanent summer home; their friends would be discouraged from visiting them there, and they returned to London for the winter resolved to find something nearer next year. Hannah settled the family into 44 Grosvenor Road. The Costelloe home at number 40, with its alluring nursery, was so close that, as she said, "We can run in and out to Mary's without bonnets." She was fully prepared to be as active in England as she had been in America, undeterred by the fact that she was a foreigner:

> I do not feel myself to be any different as an English subject than as an American. I have not the vote in either place, as I am not a citizen of either and have no call to be patriotic. In fact, I do not see how *women* can ever feel like anything but aliens in whatever country they may live, for they have no part or lot in any, except the part and lot of being taxed and legislated for by men.

Nevertheless she was soon caught up in the excitement of politics. First there was a Parliamentary by-election in Holborn, where Frank spoke four or five times a day for the Radical candidate, and after that he stood as a candidate for the newly-created London County Council. Hannah wrote home: "I must say that English politics are wonderfully interesting just now. In a very little while the elections for County Councillors under the new Local Government Bill are to come off, and the burning question is whether *women* are eligible. It is not perfectly clear in the Bill, and several women are going to contest it." Frank was elected and so were two women, Lady Sandhurst and Miss Cobden, but objections were raised, the case was taken to court—where Frank was one of the defending barristers—and on appeal it was decided against the women. Despite repeated appeals by the London County Council, it was not until 1907 that women obtained the right to stand as candidates.

After Christmas the Smiths went south: Logan to Sicily with an Oxford friend; Robert, Hannah, Alys and Madge to the Riviera. Robert had got himself into another financial muddle, as Hannah told Mary: "Father is certainly astray on money matters. It is not his fault, poor fellow, and we must be as patient as we can. It is a great comfort that his decay takes the form of inertia, for if he was like Uncle Horace he would set us all wild." Horace Smith's manic-depressive illness was already becoming apparent, and was to alarm his family in the years to come.

After Ray's birth Mary, like Hannah before her, determined to have no more children for a while, and a combination of squeamishness, the principles she then held, and Frank Costelloe's Catholicism led to their relying on abstinence rather than "checks". Mary wrote to Hannah early in 1888:

[Dr Garrett Anderson]* asked me whether I was pregnant again and I said "no", and then she asked me how I knew, so I told her that we had made up our minds not to have another child at once. Thee can hardly think what a lecture she gave me —I should think a woman would be ashamed to say such things. She said if I was *her* daughter she would warn me most seriously that such a way of life was wrong and wicked and all sorts of terrible things . . . So I asked "Isn't it very bad for a woman's health to have as many children as she possibly can?" "Certainly it is," she said, "but there are plenty of other ways besides abstinence of avoiding that!" . . . I do think it is *wicked* in physicians to give such advice to their patients. It is a fortunate thing I married a man who agreed with my principles—I think it would almost have turned me to *hating* my husband if he had wanted me to use any of Dr Garrett Anderson's "other ways".

Soon, however, a child was coming again, and an unwanted one. Mary was beginning to feel very disillusioned with her marriage and wrote in her diary in the New Year:

It was wicked beyond words for us to dream of having a child if we were not prepared to give something up for it. He is not prepared to give up any of his activities or pursuits to help me lead a quiet, restful, healthy life—we had no Xmas holiday, we

* One of the first two women doctors to practise in England and sister of Mrs Fawcett, the Suffrage leader.

never have an evening, and he is always behindhand and worried with his work, and of course I am dragged along in his wake. I cannot live a separate life. But this has been misery for several months. I think I will never have another child unless the conditions can be *entirely changed*.

The rest of the family was in Mentone, where Alys and Madge (whenever she was well enough) were having a gay time with the English colony, going to teas, dinners and balls. Hannah's treats were different. Some three years previously she had met the spiritualist and mystic, Laurence Oliphant, with Lord and Lady Mount Temple. He had lived for some years in Palestine, where (she said) he actually owned the Plain of Armageddon, and had come over to England to propagate his doctrine of the Sympneuma, the missing half of each soul in the spirit world, with which a spiritual union could be attained—perhaps by earthly means. Hannah had then described his views as "pure unadulterated trash", and was now perturbed to hear further details from a Lady Caithness in Nice. She wrote to one of her English friends:

Mrs Oliphant has made our dear Ladye [Mount Temple] think that the objectionable part of their practices has been given up. But I know that this is not the case. I heard and saw letters from Mrs Oliphant herself, written since Laurence's death, telling an entirely different story. In one she said that Laurence had taught her that true love was *always* sexual love, and that the "sympneumatic life" is only to be imparted by bodily contact. I *know* that the common custom of the community at Haifa is to get into bed with one another in order to impart this life. . . . What *can* be done? Not for the world would *I* undertake a crusade against it, for it is after all only a frightfully exaggerated development of the subtle doctrine concerning the physical manifestation of the Holy Spirit which led my dear husband astray, and to rake all that past would be grievous indeed . . . Moreover there does seem to be some truth at the bottom of it all.

She still had a soft spot for heresy and her "dear fanatics".

They went on to Italy, where Hannah remarked: "Rome is full of priests in all their varied and picturesque dresses. I confess it does give me solid satisfaction to see *men* obliged to walk around in this muddy Rome with long flapping skirts twisting round their ankles at every step. It seems to introduce a little more fairness into things."

Leaving Madge and Alys in Nancy, where they were to try a new hypnotic doctor for Madge's melancholia, Hannah hurried home for the birth of the new child in March 1889. It was another girl, christened Catherine Elizabeth, and called Karin, and while Mary did not have such a difficult time as with Ray's birth, she did not recover properly, and her mother took her down to the country while they hunted for another family house for the summer. A very suitable one was triumphantly found, on a south-facing hill overlooking the little Sussex village of Fernhurst.

Friday's Hill House was big and ugly, but there was a lovely view of the Sussex Weald and the South Downs, and it was only forty-five miles from London. There was a billiard-room, two coach-houses, two cottages, a conservatory, and a tennis court, together with ten acres of grounds and nearly two hundred of woodland. There were fourteen bedrooms in all, enough for the staff and family and some nine or ten guests, though Hannah had to move into the little sewing-room christened "The Last Resort" when things got too crowded, as they frequently did. One room was made into a studio sitting-room for the young people, where they were able to smoke in secrecy, and one into a picture gallery. Logan used to keep the studio supplied with canvases, oil paints and brushes, and all visitors were required to paint a picture, which was then hung in the "gallery". They finally accumulated about sixty pictures which Hannah reported to be "amazing", though unfortunately none survive.

Hannah was soon giving her American friends news of their progress. "The Rector has already called, and if he spreads a good report of us perhaps we may have some visitors." The report must have been favourable, for a fortnight later she wrote:

Yesterday Lady Russell, a delightful old lady, the widow of

Lord John Russell, called in the morning, and invited us to her place to "afternoon tea". . . . We have also had calls from several of the County people, and now Lady Russell has called I suppose we must consider ourselves fairly endorsed and may breathe freely! Not that we are anxious for callers, quite the contrary, but it is rather an interesting experience after all, and there are certainly a great many very nice people scattered about in English country houses.

Lady Russell, widow of Lord John Russell, who had been Prime Minister earlier in the century, had been staying at her son Rollo's house at Hindhead, nearby. A little later that summer, Rollo Russell brought his young nephew Bertrand, then just seventeen, to call on the newcomers. They stayed on for supper that evening, and Bertie wrote in his *Autobiography*:

[Alys] was very beautiful. She was more emancipated than any young woman I had known, since she was at college and had crossed the Atlantic alone. . . . She was kind, and made me feel not shy. I fell in love with her at first sight. I did not see any of the family again that summer, but in subsequent years during the three months that I spent annually with my uncle Rollo, I used to walk the four miles to their house every Sunday, arriving to lunch and staying to supper.

Alys was unaware of the shy schoolboy's admiration. She was already deeply involved in philanthropic work, and on August Bank Holidays, as was then the custom, brought down twenty girls from her factory girls' club. "It was a busy day, as you may imagine," wrote Hannah, "but the girls seemed to enjoy it thoroughly. . . . It was touching to see the pale faces of those poor London girls brighten up . . . with pathetic glee when they were turned loose into the pasture field beside our barns with liberty to do as they pleased." Sometimes, however, they proved a handful, as in 1891 when Hannah reported:

The girls numbered about twenty-seven and were from a butterscotch factory. . . . They were wild and rude beyond anything you could conceive of . . . [they] danced on the rail-way platform, they sang songs all through the streets, the most awfully vulgar songs, they tried to flirt with every man they met, they kissed the railway porters, they rushed into public houses . . . they screamed and hallooed, and in short seemed more like a pack of monkeys than human beings.

Logan, who used to bring down equivalent groups of boys, seems to have had an easier time. "Logan said they had had really a delightful time," wrote Hannah, "and the boys behaved very well. Certainly a great deal is done in England for the happiness of poor people. Probably it is this that holds absolute rebellion in check, for certainly the immense gap between the 'classes' and the 'masses' would otherwise seem calculated to bring revolution about every day in the year."

Meanwhile Robert, so Hannah reported, had "fallen completely in love with English country life in general and with this place in particular. We tell him he is already turning into an English Squire and Frank says he sees signs of him developing strong Tory tendencies! He walks around and views his premises by the hour, and plans all sorts of improvements." Among other things he had a big sun-room built up in the branches of one of the trees, which he called his "Bô Tree" and hoped to use for Buddhist-style meditation. Hannah wrote: "I go up sometimes, but the winding stairs are rather steep and disagreeable for me, and my skirts catch uncomfortably." So he could meditate in peace.

Hannah had made a new aristocratic friend: Lady Henry Somerset, a cousin of Virginia Woolf and a family connection of Bertie Russell. Isabel Somerset's story was just such as would appeal most to Hannah, who retailed it with gusto to her friends in America:

Her story is a sad one in spite of all her great possessions. She was married right out of the schoolroom to the second son of the Duke of Beaufort, Lord Henry Somerset. Two days after the marriage he said to her: "We may as well come to a clear understanding of things. I am not in love with you nor you with me. . . . We have come together for convenience. I expect to go my way and you may go yours." . . . She very soon discovered that Lord Henry was a dreadfully wicked man who only wanted to use her and her money as shields to cover his monstrous sins. . . . She fought a brave battle for twelve years, and then was driven by the excess of his wickedness and violence to leave him and get a judicial separation.

The truth was that Lord Henry was a homosexual, and after providing his wife with a son, he was found to be having an affair with one of his footmen. Isabel—against the canons of the world she lived in—insisted on a public scandal and a legal separation, whereupon Lord Henry was forced to resign his seat in Parliament and his various posts and honours and flee to Italy, while Isabel found herself *persona non grata* in Society and presently took to good works. At the time she became friends with Hannah she was already widely known in Temperance circles, and she soon became President of the British Women's Temperance Association, of which Hannah was already Treasurer and was later to be Secretary. Hannah's beloved friend Frances Willard was now President of the Women's Christian Temperance Union in America, and Hannah was able to bring the two together, whereupon they became close friends.

Madge Whitall had unhappily not been cured in France, and her attacks were now getting worse than ever. The doctors finally sent her to a nursing home and advised against all visitors, so Alys felt that in the circumstances it would be best for her to go back and finish her final year at Bryn Mawr, and she sailed in September 1889. The following April, still no better, Madge returned to Philadelphia; she contracted TB and died in 1892, to Alys's abiding grief.

Mary was still ailing, and it was becoming clear that there was real trouble between her and Frank. Hannah's growing dislike of her son-in-law was now unconcealed, while Mary's complaints were becoming almost hysterical. Frank put her condition down to morbid neurosis and inherited mental instability, but even though she admitted there might be some truth in this, Mary still blamed him. In matters of religion, too, she was breaking away. "With all his certainty," she wrote, "whom has Frank ever convinced of the things he can 'prove'? No-one, not even his wife. . . . I cannot play the lie any longer of pretending to be a Catholic."

By October she was in such a state that the doctor decided she was near a breakdown and ordered her abroad, so Hannah took her to Switzerland to rest and recover. A new pair of spectacles seemed for the moment to have cleared up the trouble and Hannah was jubilant, but in April 1890 Mary was again writing in her diary:

> How I long for a Soul—but truly there is no time to get it. . . .
> The other day I could have killed myself for the longing I
> had to change it all, to be in real relations to others, with
> the Universe . . . I have wondered sometimes if all marriages
> are like this. . . . How I wish Frank had been able to show
> me a little about religion. I think it would all have been
> different.

She struggled on through the spring and early summer. Frank was chosen again as a Radical candidate for Chelsea in the next election, roundly defeating George Bernard Shaw in the candidate's ballot, and the regular round of social and political life went on. Mary entertained and was entertained without much enthusiasm. "I went to Lady Victoria's party last night," she wrote to Hannah. "She received us in the usual manner of the English hostess, which leaves on one's mind the impression that somehow you have either mistaken the day or come without an invitation." Frank was a very sociable man, and had a great many friends. He was one of the early members of the Fabian Group of social and political reformers, and Bernard Shaw, Graham Wallas and Sidney Webb were frequent guests, forming the nucleus of what he hoped would become Mary's political salon. There were less politically-minded visitors too, such as Oscar Wilde and his wife, and Count Stenbock, Ray's godfather. There were also many

Americans, friends of Walt Whitman, or of the family in Philadelphia, or others arriving with introductions.

During the summer of 1890 a young man called Bernhard
Berenson arrived in London and Mary invited him down to
Friday's Hill for the August Bank Holiday weekend. He was a
Bostonian of Lithuanian Jewish origin, twenty-five years old—a
year younger than Mary—and some two or three inches shorter
than her five foot eight. He was handsome and elegant, with dark
curly hair and wide-set grey eyes. He had been at Harvard at the
same time as Mary and Logan, but they had not met there, though
he had been pointed out to her at one of the University concerts
as the most brilliant member of his Sophomore Class. After
Harvard, encouraged by the wealthy Mrs Jack Gardner, and
financed by a group of friends, he went to study in Europe. Early
in 1888, while he was at Oxford for a while, a Harvard friend of
Mary's called Gertrude Burton, who had been much enamoured
of him, urged Mary to make his acquaintance and she had invited
him to dine. He had gone on to Italy and Germany, unsure as yet
in what direction to turn his extraordinary talents and his almost
fanatical love of beauty. His first visit to Italy had convinced him
that he must devote his life to learning all there was to learn and
enjoying all there was to enjoy about Italian art, and that Italy
was where he must live. By the summer of 1890, when he
returned to England, the Smiths had taken a long lease of Friday's
Hill House, and were settled in there for the second summer,
while Frank and Mary had been lucky enough to find a smaller
house called Friday's Hill Cottage, just across the road.

Both Hannah and Mary left descriptions of that weekend.
Hannah wrote to her friends:

We found at home as a visitor, a young genius named Bernhard
Berenson, an Americanized Russian, who is considered by those
who know him to be one of the most rising young men of the
world. He has devoted himself especially to pictures, and seems
to know *everything* about *every* picture that has ever been
painted. And the way he demolished the idols of the young
people was something perfectly delicious. He *proved* by the

most masterly criticism that most of the old pictures they admired were either bad originals or bad copies, and . . . the worst of it is that his criticisms were so pungent that one was almost compelled to be convinced utterly against one's will. . . . He does not paint himself, but is an art critic. You are sure to hear of him some day.

Mary looked back on it much later—the meals, the drives and the talks by the camp fire all through the night:

He has since confessed to me that he thought my conversation very silly but my pink satin dress very becoming. And in spite of my silly and artificial conversation I suppose he must have felt in me a spirit that reached towards the things he cared for. Fascinated I listened to his talk about Provencal poetry, about the Greek anthology, about Russian novels and the operas of Wagner. . . . Even my dear Quaker mother listened to his strange doctrines in admiring silence. . . . At last I felt I really *was* at the centre of things, not sitting on a bench in Boston listening to a lecturer, but partaking, in imagination at least, of the real feast.

. . . When this beautiful and mysterious youth appeared, for whom nothing in the world existed except a few lines of poetry which he held to be perfect and the pictures and music he held to be beautiful, I felt like a dry sponge that was put in water. Instinctively I recognized that those were the real values for me, however wicked and self-indulgent they might be.

A strong dislike for a course of action or a way of life had always been sufficient proof for her that she would be right to abandon it, and the combination of personal charm and a doctrine that openly rejected Frank's political and religious ideals in favour of purely aesthetic ones could not have burst upon her at a more opportune moment.

THE RUNAWAY

Mary and Bernhard

MARY SPENT ALL that August with Bernhard—or B.B., as his friends called him—visiting galleries and museums in and around London and talking endlessly. Frank too found him excellent company, and he dined frequently at 40 Grosvenor Road, and stayed again at Friday's Hill Cottage.

Early in September Mary and Frank went for a trip down the Loire, joining B.B. for a few days in Paris on the way back. Again Bernhard and Mary toured the galleries enthusiastically while Frank was visiting his own friends, and finally, standing on the Pont d'Austerlitz, they promised to write to each other. A day or two later Bernhard answered her first letter: "No, you did no wrong in letting me know how much you hated our parting. You are the one reality to me and if I couldn't have hung on to that, I don't know what I might have done these past four days, considering how terribly skinless I have been feeling."

Mary and Frank returned to London, but the correspondence went on almost daily. It was first and foremost a *catalogue raisonné* of the pictures B.B. saw as he travelled round the galleries of Germany, and Mary found his long descriptions enthralling, for her passion for art was a genuine and lasting one, even though it went hand in hand with a growing feeling for Bernhard himself.

Her first reaction was that his way of life must be wrong. She wrote to Gertrude Burton, who had introduced them:

I do feel that he ought to take some thought for his future. . . . He feels, I think with reason, that a few more years of the enjoyment and appreciation of beauty in Italy would give him that exquisite and rare culture which only one person in a thousand could ever attain. Because it is so beautiful, he dimly feels that it *must* be of use in the world, merely the existence of a supremely cultured person, whether he does anything practical or not. . . . The flaw is in his leaving out the moral and social elements, but how to make him see this I don't know.

She sent him various Fabian pamphlets to read. Bernhard was very scornful of Bernard Shaw's effort. "Mr Shaw's attempt to rise to moral heights is perfectly ludicrous. I shall read the other essays with great interest, but if they are all written as pellucidly I'd as soon drink the Thames in London." He was much more impressed by Sidney Webb's contribution, but noted:

Mr Webb is probably not aware how very hard [socialism] is for one of my sort, for instance, for whom culture has been a religion. It is a bad religion, I see . . . yet when this has been all your inspiration it is so terribly hard to give it up for something so directly opposed to it as Socialism, even in Mr Webb's meaning. . . . I suspect you do not realize how impossible it is to drive the two, culture and Socialism, as a team. . . . I am afraid you will end up making me feel that it is my duty to give up everything I have cherished hitherto. . . . I don't want that to happen.

And, as Mary wrote later, "Of course it didn't happen . . . indeed he very soon turned the tables and tried to pull into his orbit."

There was another direction in which she tried to influence Bernhard, and here, despite his continuing opposition, she did in the end succeed. "About this time," she recalled, "I began to urge him to *write*, as I saw clearly that only by this means could he make himself a position in the world, and a man is apt to be bitter if he reaches middle age and remains entirely obscure. My insistence degenerated at times into nagging . . . but in the end I won my point."

The letters were rarely personal—Bernhard was never good at expressing his private feelings—but now and then there were traces of growing affection. "I want so much to talk to you no matter what about. It is curious, you do not draw me out, you do not make me say any very brilliant or startling things, you do not rouse me to say very much, yet *no* other person has ever been so delightful to talk to."

At Christmas Mary persuaded Frank to take her to Italy, and Bernhard met them in Florence and went on with them to Rome. "No later experience", she wrote in old age, "can efface those first three days—just three—when Bernhard, darting about in the winter cold and sleet, showed me its treasures." She was referring to the treasures of Rome, but there were other revelations during those three days:

One drive, I remember, Bernhard and I took . . . on a beautiful sunny afternoon, when Spring almost seemed to be in the air. We were talking very eagerly to each other when suddenly I saw Bernhard blush a glow of red. "What is the matter?" I asked. "Oh it is only what some people on the pavement said to each other as we passed." He was very shy about repeating it . . . and finally told [it] to me in their Italian words, which I scarcely understood. What they said was "Stanno per bacciarsi" [they are just going to kiss each other] and their comment revealed to us a great deal of what had remained latent, yet colouring everything for us; nor can I imagine anything more enchanting than to be desperately in love and yet able to sublimate that love . . . into an intense enjoyment of art and beauty.

The sublimation, of course, did not last very long. Mary and Frank went home to London, and in February B.B. followed them for a visit of several months. At first he stayed with the Costelloes, before moving into rooms of his own, and this was probably when he and Mary became lovers. On one occasion (as he told the author in 1947) he found himself in the classic French farce situation, hiding in a wardrobe clutching his trousers, when Frank came home unexpectedly early.

He gave a series of lectures at the National Gallery, yielding unwillingly to Mary's pressure to start earning money and making his name known. He and Mary were almost inseparable, spending their days in galleries, visiting private collections, and collaborating on a guide to the Hampton Court pictures, which was brought out under the name Mary Logan. This was a pseudonym she continued to use in her writing for many years, as Frank objected to her using his name.

Though Hannah was unhappy, and Robert raged against Berenson, there was as yet no open breach with Frank. One strange development that spring had been Bernhard's conversion to Catholicism. He was attracted to the Catholic church as much by art and history as by what Mary called "an underground spring of mysticism", but he had also been much impressed by a pamphlet of Frank's on the significance of the Mass. He was received into the church in the Monastery of Monte Oliveto, near Siena, in February 1891, just before coming to England. But as Mary said later: "The vaccination, if I may so express it, did not 'take' except in so far as he felt closer, by this step, to the Italy he spent his whole life in learning and loving." Mary, too, had been momentarily touched by a renewed enthusiasm for Catholicism, but in her case it burnt out in her quarrels with Frank, leaving her with a savage and lifelong hatred for religion of any kind, and most of all for Catholicism.

After Bernhard left that summer, Mary found it impossible to return to her previous life. She determined, at whatever cost to herself or anyone else, to break with Frank and go to Florence to study art with Berenson. Frank was not only a Catholic, but a conventional man, and much concerned lest scandal should affect his career. He would not agree to a divorce, but Mary insisted on leaving him for at least a year, and to this he had to consent.

When she went, Frank felt it best to show an apparent approval of her departure, so husband and wife set out together for Paris. There Frank stayed to visit Count Stenbock, while Mary went on alone to Antwerp and The Hague, and joined Berenson and his friend Enrico Costa in Brunswick. The three of them travelled together (though Mary stayed at different hotels), looking at pictures in Berlin, Dresden and Munich, and indulging in an orgy of Wagner.

She soon shed her depression in these new surroundings, and Hannah wrote: "It is a great comfort to know that thee is happier, darling daughter. I believe it *is* good for thee to be alone for a while and really 'come to thyself', and for that reason I should have been glad if thy absolute aloneness could have continued a little longer, but I do trust thee to God."

"Frank is really behaving very well," Mary wrote to her a little later, "always with the one, and most important, proviso that to hold a woman tied to you when she doesn't want to be is an anomaly in civilization. Somehow it seems to me just as absurd as women not having the vote—I turn it over and can't look at it any other way." She was touched by Hannah's loving loyalty. "I want to be always now *perfectly sincere* with thee . . . thee is the dearest, dearest mother that ever was." But this last resolve did not prevent her, during the coming years, from omitting from her letters all reference to the constant and close presence of B.B., or from allowing her mother to assume—or at least to hope—that their relations were platonic.

Mary had happily cast off all concern for convention, and felt sure, with the optimism of a much-spoilt child, that she could pursue her own path undisturbed. In September she wrote to her mother:

I seem to be getting an interior peace which is very different from the wild tumult of bitterness and uncertainty in which I was raging when I was at home. Of course the danger is that I have (I think) no orthodox standards of any kind. Thee, who is such a rebel against orthodoxy in religion, cannot be surprised or shocked if I am a rebel against orthodoxy in conduct. Frank is quite right in saying that one heresy leads to another, in the next generation at least. What he isn't right in is thinking that religious orthodoxy has much real influence on conduct. A little impartial reading of history would show him that it has practically no influence at all. . . . The one thing that is certain (to my mind) is that it does not do for me to take anyone else's views, Frank's or thine or anyone's.

She added: "Thy idea of right has gone so far as that parents shouldn't sacrifice their children to themselves—and mine goes a step further and I think it equally a mistake to sacrifice parents to children." Hannah, of course, disapproved, and though as loving as ever, she was deeply concerned over the effect of Mary's actions on other people. She wrote carefully to Carey and her Germantown friends, kept up relations with Frank, and hoped in her heart that Mary would come back when she had had her fling.

But for Mary it was a whole new and fascinating way of life. She and Bernhard worked their way south to Verona and Venice, all through September and October 1891, living on 5 lire a day each. "We attacked church after church in a slow and systematic way," she wrote later. "Afternoon was the time for the Gallery and for excursions on foot or in a small light carriage up into the hills . . . on the hunt for altar pieces of the Verona school."

As we reached Verona I registered a vow that I would go into *every single church* in Italy exploring for pictures. I need not say that the vow wasn't kept—indeed I gave up all idea of it that autumn when, after six weeks in Venice, out visiting churches from half past eight to noon, I looked out Baedeker . . . and found that he mentioned 36 churches into which we had not penetrated. Just in one small town.

Bernhard made her work extremely hard, as he did himself, sitting sometimes for hours on end on the steps behind an altar, or standing on the altar itself, but it was all a delight to her, and she willingly undertook—and carried through—the long arduous business of training her visual memory and acquiring a critical knowledge of Italian painting. Berenson was almost the only man then alive who could have taught her what she wanted to know, and she was his first and ideal pupil.

As she did all her life, Mary took careful notes of everything they saw, a habit, she said, that "Bernhard destested, for it broke in upon his absorbed raptures," but which "he was very glad to have when finally he did bring himself to write. . . . When he was writing . . . how eagerly he would call for notes, and how he would rage if there were none, or they were not detailed enough."

When they finally reached Florence, Mary moved into an apartment near the Ponte Vecchio, just a few doors from Bernhard, and next door to Gertrude Burton, who had also left her husband and was living in Europe with her two small boys. Mary had persuaded Frank to allow the children to winter with her, and Hannah joined them for a month.

After casting her motherly eye over Mary's arrangements, Hannah wrote back to Robert: "I am very glad to be here for a little while. It will be a great protection from scandal that I have been here for part of the winter." And to Logan: "Sister is well chaperoned by having her children and Gertrude here, and she is very busy studying and is leading a quiet life." She went on optimistically: "Berenson is, of course, very prevalent, but there is nothing at all lover-like in their intercourse, and they seem to meet only for study and writing."

Hannah was still hoping that Mary would come back at the end of the year of absence, but Mary had no intention of doing any such thing. She realised that she would no longer be able to rely on Frank for financial assistance, and while she had her own modest allowance, it was not enough for the travelling she and Bernhard wanted to do. B.B. was as yet making practically nothing, so she determined to earn herself, by writing articles on art. At first she could only get her work accepted by the editors of Temperance and Feminist papers, who knew and admired her mother, and who paid very badly.

Logan, who was now busily practising to become a writer, was happy (as always) to offer advice on style and presentation:

I should only say that thy interesting letters would be the better for printing if thee took a little more care of thy sentence forms. A series of short sentences laid down one after the other gets rather monotonous and jerky. One should try to get a periodic style, I think; long sentences, with qualifications in them, tangling and untangling themselves (as Stevenson puts it) like knots of string; interspersed now and then with one or more quite short ones, and all bound up [in] paragraphs with some uniformity of meaning, form and texture of style that both rests and interests the eye and silent ear with which one reads.

Mary was duly grateful. "Tell Logan", she wrote to Hannah, "that after reading *The Women's Herald* I realized to the full the justice of his criticisms as to my style of slamming down one sentence on top of another. It sounds about as thumpy as a regiment of soldiers crossing a bridge."

She was still trying to make Berenson write himself, but he was unwilling and inhibited, and indeed his original ideas were still unformed and not ready for expression. He was happy that Mary should use what she was learning from him, and gradually her articles became more lively and telling. They began to be taken by more authoritative periodicals such as the Paris *Gazette des Beaux Arts*, the *Spectator* and the *Atlantic Monthly*.

Mary brought the children home in May. When she made it clear that she was returning to Florence and not coming back to him, there were terrible scenes with Frank, scenes which, as always, had an immediate and dramatic effect on her physical health. Frank was determined that she should never be allowed to take the children abroad again, as he was convinced—probably due to some unwise threat on her part—that she would steal Ray and that Hannah would help her. Finally he forced her to sign a separation agreement which limited her access to the children to about four weeks a year, and made her promise not to disturb his career and reputation.

While all this was being discussed, Mary made some notes of the terms she was anxious to obtain, in order of preference:

1) Divorce with Ray, 2) Separation with right to Ray and to have her utterly to myself, 3) Separation and rights to child half the time, 4) Separation and right to have her when I am in England, also right to oversee her general education, decide upon her governesses, holiday visits etc. Guarantee that she is not to be made a Catholic (an arrangement not very likely to work harmoniously, even if I could exact the guarantee), 5) Divorce and complete separation from the children.

Not only does this betray a singular ignorance of the Catholic standpoint, but there is no mention of Karin in the document. Neither Mary nor Hannah was as fond of her as of Ray. They were all, even Alys, in the habit of talking and writing as though there was only one child, referring to the loss of "Ray" and the approaching reunion with "Ray", without any reference to Karin's existence. Whatever the reason for this—whether it was that Ray was the firstborn daughter (always a potent factor in that family), or because her temperament was less excitable and uneven, or because Karin's birth had not been wanted or, as Mary herself believed, because Karin looked increasingly like her father, while Ray was large and fair and handsome, like a true Whitall—it remained the case throughout their lives.

Mary's list of conditions indicated that she was prepared to give Karin to her father entirely, if only Ray could be given to her and Hannah, and it appears as if for her part Mary would even have accepted the loss of Ray if that had been the only way of securing a divorce. However Frank had the law, his religion and social convention on his side. He was increasingly mistrustful of Mary's and Hannah's influence, and was determined to bring up his children as Catholics. Her virtual defeat over the separation and the children was a terrible and unexpected blow to Mary, and for years she suffered from recurrent guilt, misery and illness when she thought about them.

Throughout the autumn of 1892 she was ill with inflammation of the womb, and came back to London to have an operation and to be nursed by her mother. On her return to Florence she wrote gloomily: "I have been simply tortured about the children, partly no doubt from being nervous. I have even thought of giving up everything for them—but it would be ultimate misery for they are sure to grow up different from what I should like, and then they would have me broken on their hands to take care of." Hannah's answer was a simple one:

I trust it will all work out for thy best welfare. But I cannot help feeling there would be far more likelihood of this if thee were not forsaking thy manifest duties to secure it. No reasoning can ever shake me in my deep conviction that a mother's first and most sacred duty is to her children; and I cannot feel that anything will really prosper that involves the neglect of them.

Mary protested: "It is a struggle between a person and a mother in me, and I am dreadfully torn all the time when I am not actually occupied in work. But it is not fair to say I desert them and whenever thee says it I must protest. I would give anything but what I solemnly feel no person has a right to demand of another—and that is my liberty of action." And Hannah apparently acquiesced: "I am sorry darling, that my frankness in expressing my feelings about thy duty to thy children has hurt thy feelings so much. . . . I have no desire to nag thee, and having told thee how I feel . . . I must now leave it."

Leaving it, however, was the last thing that Hannah could do, and the letters she wrote to Mary, literally every day they were apart, were full of explicit and implicit reproaches and horrific tales of how the children were faring in their mother's absence. She used every kind of argument and applied every possible kind of moral pressure to try to get her to come back. At the same time she conducted a long war of attrition against Frank and his mother, a cross, pious old lady with displeasing table manners, whom nobody seemed to like very much. Hannah also shamelessly bribed the children with treats in her efforts to keep in touch with them and retain some kind of influence over their upbringing and religious training. She believed absolutely, and had taught Mary to believe, that in justice children belonged entirely to their mothers, and that Frank's behaviour was unconscionable and tyrannical.

Both Frank and Mary suffered under Hannah's onslaughts in their different ways. Frank, though he conscientiously wanted to be fair, was a very busy man who had never been very successful in organizing his own private affairs, let alone those of his family, and he became more and more maddeningly elusive as this seemed to be his only defence against Hannah. In Mary's case the Chinese water torture of continuous appeal and reproach had the result of making her defensive and resentful, and more and more bitter against Frank.

Early in 1893 Hannah was involved in a deplorable family scene:

> During the conversation [Frank] told Logan and Alys how indignant he was about my going in . . . and taking the carpets out of his house without saying anything to him. . . . When Logan said they were *thy* carpets, he said that according to English law all the furniture was now his. . . . Logan was splendid and fought for me bravely. . . . Now thee *must not* write to Frank about this. It will only make things worse for me . . . let me *entreat* thee to consider well before thee does anything that aggravates Frank. While we can keep on fairly friendly terms we can have the children, but the moment he is made angry we shall lose them altogether.

Later that year Frank claimed that "scandalous" rumours were circulating in London about Mary's relations with Berenson, and the nature of her illness the previous Christmas, rumours which Mary most forcefully denied. She felt that Hannah's appeasement was the wrong way to treat Frank and was sure she could use the threat of scandal, should she turn up in London, to force his hand. Hannah was very much alarmed at this prospect:

> I am sure if thee does not stir Frank up thee can go on living thy life as thee thinks right, and no-one will interfere. And it certainly is far more generous to B not to involve him in a public scandal. . . . Frank (naturally) feels very bitterly towards Berenson, and he said to me once that if matters came to an open issue he could and would ruin B. . . . Remember darling, thee *must not* on any account say a word to Frank of *anything* I write to thee. Neither must thee to Berenson, but of course thee would not do that.

Mary agreed to be "kinder", and a new arrangement was made, but a week later Hannah was writing again: "Oh my darling daughter, thee is making it all so much more difficult by thy 'kind' letters to Frank. He has shown me one or two, and I cannot help feeling how likely they are to anger him. Could thee not soften them a little by beginning 'Dear Frank', which after all is only a conventional term." But Mary could not bring herself to yield. "As to your remarks about me having no right to interfere in your household," she wrote to Frank in October 1893, "I must remind you that both as the children's mother and as their legal guardian, I have every right to interfere. . . . Very much your best plan would be to be perfectly frank with me in any plans you may make for them." This was too much for Frank—though it will be noted that he retained the affectionate Quaker "Thee" he had adopted on his marriage, while Mary had dropped it:

I have sometimes thought [he wrote to Hannah] that thee is tempted to write these things to M. in the hope of working on her feelings to make her come back. No-one would rejoice so much as I if she could return in any practicable and proper way. But under present conditions, to try to force her back as a check on me and against my will is, thee must surely see, a suicidal policy.

He warned Mary: "If thy mother has again complained to thee . . . she has only come one step nearer to a result which neither thee nor she would enjoy. . . . These recurrent threats, although they are highly unpleasant to me, do not do anything to advance the objects which I suppose thee desires—rather the contrary."

Things calmed down in the end, though the situation remained agonizing for all of them until Frank's early death in 1899 (which Bertie Russell called "a stroke of great good luck"). Hannah went on pleading with Mary, still unable to understand how a woman could possibly prefer any man to her children. "Give up Berenson," she wrote in 1894, "(for a few years at least) and come home and be as friendly with Frank as thee can. . . . Surely, surely, darling precious daughter, thee will be able for all our sakes and thy own, to make the little sacrifice, or even great, if it *is* great."

In the intervals of this guerilla war, Mary enjoyed life enormously, despite her nervous ill-health. She was careful to keep a strictly separate household of her own, and was not ostracized, as Hannah had feared she might be. Indeed English and American friends visiting Italy made a point of calling on her and inviting her from the first. Lady Carlisle, Bertie Russell's alarming aunt, asked her to dine with her family when they visited Florence in 1893, and William James and his wife, who came several times, met and dined with her frequently. Mary noted critically that the Professor had "a curious mind, almost incapable of *thought* in the sense of following an idea out to any length. An anecdote or amusing trait he catches in a second; but any line of reasoning seems to bore him and his mind hops away."

Florence was an ideal place for the unconventional Anglo-Saxon at this time. Lord Henry Somerset, the errant husband of Hannah's friend Isabel, had taken refuge there (though he moved in different circles and Mary never met him) and the large expatriate community abounded in "Sapphists", eccentrics and those whose marital arrangements were irregular. This gave rise to a lot of agreeable gossip and a kaleidoscope of feuds, and it also provided a number of intelligent and amusing people among whom Bernhard and Mary found many friends.

One of the first of these was Violet Paget, a brilliant if erratic talker and writer on art and travel under the name of Vernon Lee, who lived with her family and a passionate female friend at Maiano, near Fiesole. Another early friend of Mary's was Maud Cruttwell, also endeavouring to work in the field of art appreciation; a kind if not very exciting or profound creature, she, like Vernon Lee, tended to dress in shortish tweed skirts and a man's collar and tie, with her hair in a stiffly curled fringe. In January 1895 Mary moved up to Fiesole, sharing the expenses of the Villa Rosa for a time with Maud, while Bernhard settled in just two doors off, at the Villa Kraus.

Maud was an excellent housekeeper, and Mary retained a lasting if somewhat mocking affection for her. "Miss Cruttwell", she wrote in her diary in 1902, "said that she could not bear the thought of a man sleeping in her apartment even if she weren't there. It reminds me of how pleased she was to ride behind my donkey when she thought it was a female ass, and how disgusted she was when she found out it was a 'maschio'."

While Mary was sharing the villa with Maud, they were visited by two remarkable friends from England; Katherine Bradley and Edith Cooper, aunt and niece, were passionately attached to each other, and were known jointly to their friends as the poet "Michael Field" or "The Mikes" for short. These two ladies wrote no fewer than twenty-eight verse dramas, all dripping with truly Jacobean gore, and steeped in sex and sin. Their first work, Callirhoe, had been praised by Browning, but thereafter the critics had been all too silent. They were a touchy and somewhat difficult pair, though judging by the number and quality of their friends they must have had great charm. Their visit to Fiesole was, however, a considerable strain.

> They think they are a Great Poet [Mary wrote to Hannah], unappreciated at present but certain to be famous and adored in the next generation—and they think their souls are united and that it is good for them to be together. As a matter of fact the utter mistake of both these theories is "obvious to the meanest intelligence" . . . Michael (Katherine) makes constant demands for sympathy, and it has been hard to preserve even a decent appearance of it. To anyone less resolutely obtuse, my feelings would have been plain. . . . Please do not let me forget that I will never live in the house with them again. Remind me if I grow weak . . . but after all, there's something rather attractive about them.

Mary was as drawn to eccentrics as Hannah had been to fanatics.

Among the closest of Bernhard's early friends were Carl Loeser and Carlo Placci. Loeser was a wealthy American, now settled in Florence, who had a high opinion of his talents as a connoisseur. He had known Bernhard since they were at Harvard together, and had been generous to him in his early travels, but Bernhard was becoming more and more impatient with what he considered to be his fantasies, his pretensions and his propensity for malicious gossip; a quarrel finally arose between them which was not patched up for years. Placci was a highly sociable Italian, and an assiduous courtier of European royalty and nobility. He was unstable in his views, and swung from atheism and extreme socialism to equally extreme Catholicism, right-wing politics, and violent anti-Dreyfus propaganda, which last resulted in a period of estrangement between him and B.B. and Mary. However, peace was always made after their quarrels, and this volatile, pyrotechnic talker and musician remained one of their dearest friends until the Second World War finally separated them.

With all these, and many others, Mary and Bernhard played out, through the years, the game of quarrel and reconciliation which seemed to be a necessary concomitant of all their friendships. Mary charted their progress at the end of each year in her diary, listing their friends under different headings: "1) Really personally affectionately liked, 2) Friendly, 3) Viewed with indifference, and 4) R.I.P."

A YOUNG MAN'S FANCY

Alys and Bertie

UNLIKE THE STORMY Mary, Alys was an ideal daughter: virtuous, hard-working, beautiful and happy. If Hannah secretly preferred her elder daughter, she was nevertheless genuinely very fond of Alys: "Never did a mother have a dearer, more comforting daughter than I have in thee. My one chief earthly consolation in everything is that 'I have Alys, anyhow'." She was invaluable at home, running the household harmoniously, playing word games with Robert and looking after him while Hannah was away at her many meetings, and a diplomat in dealing with Frank, who came to like her very much, and called her "Al". She enthusiastically took up the kind of philanthropic work Hannah most approved of, running a working girls' club in London, starting all kinds of village activites in Fernhurst, and becoming the "Y" (Youth Branch) Organizer for Lady Henry's temperance society, the BWTA. This involved a lot of travelling round the country, running her own youth meetings and minuting Lady Henry's, and they became very friendly.

In spite of all this virtue, her manners were very easy and uninhibited by comparison with the strict conventionality required of well-born English girls. Her extreme earnestness, however, and her very literal mind, made her appear a little forced and insincere in conversation. She was far more reserved, though less devious, than Mary, and in spite of her hero-worshipping love for her mother, and her life-long urge to be "good", she always kept her inner feelings, blameless as they were, very much to herself.

Bertie Russell was twenty-one in 1893, and the same summer became Seventh Wrangler in the Mathematical Tripos at Cambridge, with one more year to go before taking his Moral Science Tripos. He had had a most oppressive and peculiar childhood; his parents died when he was a baby, and he was brought up by his grandmother Lady Russell. She was a remarkable woman, known, when her husband was Prime Minister, as "The Deadly Nightshade", on account of the malign nocturnal influence she was reputed to wield over him. She genuinely loved Bertie, but subjected him to a mixture of austere Nonconformist piety and emotional blackmail which drove him to retire into solitude and reserve. In 1893 he still lived in a strangely out-dated world, with his grandmother and his maiden aunt, Lady Agatha, at Pembroke Lodge, a house on the edge of Richmond Park which had been granted for life to Lord John and his wife by Queen Victoria. After such a childhood, and educated at home, he not unnaturally became extremely shy and uncertain of himself. He jettisoned his religious beliefs in his teens, but remained for many years very stiff and puritanical.

Although Alys had been friendly and kind, his shyness, and a strong fear of ridicule, kept him very much in the background after their first meeting in 1889. In June 1893, Alys and a cousin of hers came to Cambridge for a visit, and he had a better opportunity for private conversation. A month later, on July 21st, which he later discovered to be her birthday, he wrote in his journal: "I dreamed last night that I was engaged to A., when I discovered that my people had deceived me, that my mother was not dead but in a madhouse. I therefore had, of course, to give up the thought of ever marrying. This dream haunts me." Nobody had told him, at this stage, of the amount of mental instability there had been in his family, but he must have been subconsciously aware of the threat, which was to become a very real one a year later. He went on:

I think of A all day long. Like Meschdanoff in Turgenjeff, I am haunted by a doubt of my real feelings. Still more horrible, I half fear the amusement of my relatives. . . . I incline to think that my passion is imaginary when I reflect that I "love love" just now, and envy those who have a mutual love. But I think it has been genuine, not only now but ever since I first met her, when I reflect on the minute recollection I have of every detail of my meetings with her.

During the Long Vacation she came again, and they went on the river. Bertie wrote:

The greatest day in my life hitherto. A. and a cousin came to stay the night and she stayed afterwards by herself. We went tête-à-tête in a canoe and discussed love and marriage. How absurd to an older person it would seem to have to argue on a question of social ethics before acquiring the minutest right to speak one's own feelings. I gave her my little essay on the impropriety of not marrying if in any way above the average: this led to a discussion. I explained how in my view love, sympathy, friendship (whichever you will) was the greatest thing attainable, was indeed the only thing well worth having; she maintained: Independence. . . . We agreed to a large extent that marriage gave the best opportunity for such spiritual love and that friendship between man and woman is impossible. But I found, what I had always imagined in women, an aversion to sexual intercourse and a shrinking from it only to be overcome by the desire for children. . . . Whether she remained blind to my feelings throughout I know not. . . . I regretted her departure; however we shall meet again, she said, as though it were pleasant . . . and she consented to occasional correspondence by which much may be done. Never before was she so "vertraulich". I intended to show her some of the more intelligible passages in McTaggart's paper about love in its philosophical aspect: was it an omen that on returning home it had mysteriously disappeared?

Alys was fully as priggish as Bertie. With his little essay on Eugenics, and his kind offer of simple philosophical instruction, his style of courtship might not have appealed to everyone, but to Alys it seemed natural and right. They started writing to each other, as they had agreed, though at first the letters were very stilted. He did, moreover, send her McTaggart's paper, and added his first touch of humour: "I have come to the conclusion that all that is important is straightforward and all that is hard . . . is unimportant: but as I did not understand the hard parts you may perhaps wonder how I came to that conclusion. You will still have an opportunity of displaying your boasted stupidity when I come, by discussing it."

He had been invited to Friday's Hill in mid-September, and described what happened in his journal:

All is accomplished: my wildest hopes had not imagined such success. . . . The first morning she and I went up the Bô-tree: I said I made few demands on life and these were not to be granted: she said all wishes could be obtained by perseverance: I felt certain she knew what I meant so felt encouraged but could hardly believe my good fortune. So I talked about friends in general and said I always cared more about them than they about me. *She*: You don't trust them. *I*: I don't—After a pause, and with the greatest hesitation, after a concentrated struggle in myself, I said: I am sure you don't care for me as I care for you. *She*: No, but I have entire sympathy with you and what more can you want. . . . *I*: I have tried but it isn't like any other; I have fought hard but I cannot take it calmly. Then there was a long pause. At last she said in a rather unsteady voice: I think if I were conscientious I should put an end to this friendship for your sake, but I care about it too much myself. . . . After a pause and with some hesitation (as no word of marriage had yet been said) I told her of my dream. . . . After some talk about it she said: I wish you would put away the thought of marriage: friendship is so much nicer, I don't want to marry, at least for a long, long time. . . . *I*: I will try and be calm, and I could be more easily if I saw more of you. *She*: We ought to see each other if we are ever to think of it (marriage I suppose)— Then we were silent when for the first time I felt an intense happiness with all but no admixture of pain.

Next morning they went for a walk in the woods and discussed it all once more, and decided "to get to know each other intimately: as we of course both feel that without great intimacy it is folly to become engaged."

They decided to be frank with their respective families, telling them that "it is a mutual alliance not for lovemaking but only for friendship". Throughout the autumn they wrote to each other twice a week, and very soon Bertie was telling of the good effect love had on his work. "I cannot imagine now being (as I used to be)," he wrote, "so sick of work and the whole world I lived in that I was forced for days to take refuge in a novel and live the life of the people I was reading about."

And so they began the long and absorbing task of discovering each other's tastes and beliefs and opinions, and getting to know each other. The next time they met, they rode round South London on a tram, discussing sexual relations—which Alys deplored.

I don't believe [she wrote] that it is a very wholesome relation between men and women who love each other for spiritual and intellectual reasons. I am afraid it might introduce an element that would lower the others, always excepting, of course, when they mean to have children. . . . Most thoughtful women agree with me, and so, I am told, do a few men, tho' not many, I imagine.

Bertie, as virginal as she, and nearly as prudish, replied: "I have at times thought as you do about marriage; so lately as last May term I remember a discussion in which I expressed the opinion that love was degraded by sexual intercourse; but nobody seemed to agree with me and I came to think the idea due to a morbid reaction."

They knew already that they shared the same Radical political beliefs, but when it came to religion there was a clash. Alys was an unbigoted Quaker, like her mother, and Bertie wrote:

I am afraid it is almost necessary that we should have a good deal of discussion on theological questions: I am really sorry because I shall unavoidably appear in rather a brutal light as I am so utterly out of sympathy with Christianity. . . . I am convinced that as soon as we begin to reflect seriously on religion we shall find Pantheism a far finer, a far more inspiring faith.

In October, much to Bertie's disappointment, Alys decided to accompany Lady Henry Somerset to a Temperance Convention in Chicago, where the World Fair was being held. She thought a lot about Bertie while she was away, and about the difficulty of combining an independent life, and the kind of work she thought valuable, with marriage—which Hannah had consistently taught her to mistrust. She was back in England by the end of the month, still undecided and still arguing. However her defences were beginning to crumble, and meeting Bertie again hastened the process. In mid-December she wrote:

> It is a temptation to say affectionate things, and even to hold your hand, especially as such things seem so conducive to perfect sympathy, but I am afraid they are a mistake. . . . I am afraid I am a bore tonight, but I cannot help it. I have had a hundred different minds about you this week, each one different, which makes it difficult to write. You will need infinite patience, and then you will see that I am not worth it.

To this Bertie replied: "I assure you it is not for want of trying to find faults in you that I have not found them. . . . Once (about six weeks ago) I spent a day hunting for these faults, with no effect . . . but I think I can criticize your intellect just as well as anybody else's: I suppose it is because it is not intellect I care about in people."

On January 4th he came up to see her from Pembroke Lodge and described the visit in his *Autobiography*:

> It was on this occasion that I first kissed Alys. . . . Although she still said that she had not made up her mind whether to marry me or not, we spent the whole day, with the exception of meal-times, in kissing, with hardly a word spoken from morning to night, except for an interlude during which I read "Epipsychidion" aloud.

Alys wrote a day or so later: "I feel as if there were no need for words after the absolute satisfactoriness of our last meeting. . . .

Lion* thinks thee would make an excellent husband. So does Mariechen, who considers thee cleverer than any of the young men we know, and very distinguished looking." She was confiding in her contemporaries, even if she had still not completely capitulated. She had also begun to use the intimate Quaker "Thee", which he too adopted towards her.

They went on diligently working through all their possible differences and she wrote: "I thought the difference in age nothing, as thee looks so much older and I so much younger than our real ages." (She was nearly five years older than he was.) "I have determined never to think of it again. We know that to ourselves it does not make the slightest difference and the only possible pity would be if I were to take advantage of thy youth, which I shall try not to do." Bertie answered: "I think the difference of age is a very small matter . . . and I fail to see any method thee can invent for 'taking advantage' of my youth even if thee were to set about to try to find one."

The next point revealed a more perilous situation. "I have suddenly realized the fact," wrote Alys, "that I am really a sociable creature. . . . I am afraid that is not thy disposition. . . . I am afraid thee would not like thy home to be a sort of hotel, which is my ideal." Bertie replied:

I am not of a sociable disposition, that is to say from my earliest childhood I have had so much solitude that it has become a sort of necessity and I find myself oppressed by the thoughts I have no time to think unless I have a good deal of solitary leisure. . . . I have an awkward habit of getting unable to work if I have to see too many strangers. . . . However the question will no doubt arrange itself when it arises.

And of course the question did arise, and Alys had to devote herself for many years to preserving for Bertie the solitude he required.

By the end of January they were back on the subject of religion. Bertie wrote:

* Lion Fitzpatrick, a friend of Alys, who later married Bobby Philimore.

[It] would only become very serious, I think, if we had any children to bring up: I could hardly reconcile it to my conscience to have any children of mine brought up Christians. Has thee thought any more about religion lately? I cannot argue well with thee, for when I am with thee thy religion seems so right that I lose all wish to change it: and yet at other times I am so strongly anti-religious that I am afraid it might in future become serious.

"I have indeed thought a great deal about religion lately," answered Alys. "I do not *wish* to believe in God—on the contrary, I am so much influenced by thee that I rather wish to believe or not believe as thee does—but I simply cannot help believing in God. I have no other orthodox Xtian beliefs, but that one seems to me more a fact and part of myself than anything." And a little while later she wrote rather sadly:

If I lose my belief in God, I shall have to give up all my Temperance work, or at least the sort I am doing now. I only realized it today when . . . Lady Henry said she feared it was impossible for agnostics to work with us. It came over me with a sort of horror, because I had hoped I had really found my work and place in life, and could now go steadily on . . . but I suppose it is only one of the disagreeable facts that has to be faced, and I shall not let it interfere with my trying to think honestly.

By February she had admitted that she loved him. "Thee has all the qualities I would wish thee to have; in my eyes thee is perfect, but hitherto I have not dared to acknowledge it even to myself, because it was contrary to all my previous theories. But I don't care now, and I will let those previous theories take the course of many others thee has upset." When Alys surrendered, she did so almost too wholeheartedly.

Hannah was not at all overawed by Bertie's background; she approved of his politics and morals, but she still retained her suspicions of all men in their capacity of husbands, and she wanted to postpone as long as possible her loss of Alys. Alys agreed that they should postpone marriage for at least a year, but Bertie became more and more impatient, and the thought of another year's wait was intolerable to him. He found love a great spur to his work as well as a great happiness, but separation and uncertainty made him almost desperate.

Lady Russell found their occasional meetings and correspondence, which were all she had yet been told about, deeply shocking, and regarded Alys as a harpy, pursuing Bertie for snobbish reasons. Bertie went to stay with cousins in Rome for Easter, and arranged to stop over in Paris on the way home to meet Alys, who would be there with Hannah and Logan. When she heard of this, Lady Russell sent for Alys, who wrote in her diary:

Reached Pembridge Lodge at 4 o'clock, and saw Lady Russell alone for half an hour, then Lady Agatha came in. . . . I left at 5, as the conversation was painful and very fruitless. They think I am behaving in a very dishonourable and indelicate manner in seeing so much of Bertie and writing twice a week. And they do not understand how I can "pursue" him to Paris. I saw it was hopeless to argue with Lady R. so I only repeated that I could not see the thing as she did. . . . I felt very sorry for them both but fortunately my conscience is good and what they said didn't influence me in the least.

To Bertie they had said that "she was no lady, a baby-snatcher, a low-class adventuress, a person incapable of all finer feelings, a woman whose vulgarity would perpetually put me to shame". He reproached his grandmother, and reported to Alys:

[I said that] I couldn't help feeling that she had been "unkind" to thee. This word seemed to sting her like an adder, far more than I had anticipated, and so it did when I spoke about difficulty in our relations. To this she said in a voice half choked with tears (as her voice was throughout) that such difficulty was only on my side (which seemed to me natural enough, since she has hitherto been the aggressor), and to the other she replied in an agonized tone (which was perfectly real) that though she had many times to speak plainly to people in a similar situation before, nobody had *ever* told her she was unkind. The idea of blame from a younger person is so foreign to her mind that my words seemed like a combination of sacrilege and cruelty. . . . She . . . said she thought she was doing thee a kindness in speaking frankly to thee about everything . . . that she felt so relieved in her conscience (or rather in her temper, which faulty analysis mistook for conscience) by her talk with thee, but that now she regretted it: that she would write to thy mother to visit her, though I don't know what good she could hope from such a visit.

Hannah was uneasy and told Mary that the Dowager Duchess of Bedford, Lady Henry's sister, approved of the match and advised them not to worry about Lady Russell, as she always opposed marriages in her family. But she warned: "Nothing must be announced; *especially from our side* until Bertie has had it out with the old lady." He did "have it out", and despite all Lady Russell's efforts to get him to agree to a six months delay (supported in this instance by Hannah) he refused utterly, and by the middle of April their engagement was agreed, though it was not to be made public before his final Tripos at the end of May.

Before then, however, the news began to leak out. As Hannah explained to Mary: "[Alys] and Bertie have been acting like such idiots in going about together that people have begun to talk, and Lady Henry told us on Tuesday that for Alys's sake the engagement must be announced at once." Hannah was always very nervous about the possibility of scandal in connection with either of her daughters, but Bertie's outlook was aristocratically offhand. "I think thee and thy mother have always had a very exaggerated fear of scandals from having grown up in Philadelphia where they are so rare; here in Europe one is hardly respectable without a few family scandals, and they never make any difference to anybody."

The announcement was agreed, and Alys now had to face all the high-born relatives. She reported that Bertie's aunt, Lady Stanley, "objected to his marrying an American girl and out of his class, but spoke sensibly and kindly. The P[embroke] L[odge] people wished to defer the announcement a few days longer, but B. insisted it should come out at once."

She went out there a few days later for "the solemn betrothal kiss from Lady R. and Ly Agatha" and had a long talk with Lady Russell. "She wishes me to prove to the world that I am a domestic character and have no 'theories', but only natural instincts like other 'nice' girls. All the world knew, she said, that the marriage was not made by their family, but encouraged exclusively by mine . . . but she tried to be kind."

They had a brief spell of happiness. Bertie had taken his examinations and, as expected, had got a First Class with Distinctions. Their letters became more cheerful; Bertie wondered whether his frankness had ever shocked her, and Alys replied: "I have analysed it out that the only word I was shocked at in thy letter was 'copulate', and that was because I had never heard it used of anything but earthworms before."

But Lady Russell had not given up hope of breaking the engagement, and her new weapon was to cause both Alys and Bertie a great deal of unhappiness. She claimed that there was insanity in his family. His father, he was told, had been epileptic; he had an uncle in a mental hospital, and Aunt Agatha's engagement to a curate, many years ago, had been broken off on account of her insane delusions. This, she claimed, combined with the fact that there was the same tendency in Alys's family, made such a marriage highly unwise.

At first Alys was not much distressed.

I do not wonder thy uncle is worried about the "race", [she wrote] for it seems they all think I have an uncle who is, or has been shut up in an asylum. I think I was able to reassure them on this point, for tho' Uncle Horace is subject to nervous depression, he has never been treated for mental disease, and his three children are all healthy.

But the dreadful warnings went on until Bertie felt that he was being driven insane himself, and doctor after doctor became involved. One of them wrote to Alys: "Were I arranging from a psychological point of view, a marriage union, I should not fix upon one between the families in question." And there were gloomy consultations. On 22 June she wrote in her diary:

> B. came up and said Dr Anderson [Lady Russell's doctor] had gone off to see Dr Tuke and Blandford, promising to come and tell us the result at two o'clock if possible. It was awful waiting, the most miserable morning of our lives. We tried to read Browning but could do nothing. B. said he felt sure the doctors' opinion would be favourable, but I said we must discuss what we should do if they were not. We talked it over on the river steamboat and I said my own mind was made up that I should still wish to marry, even if we could not have children. B. had felt the same, but had not wished to say so, thinking the sacrifice would be too great for me, as I seem so particularly fitted to have children.

They had another long session the next day with all the doctors, after which they walked up and down Richmond Green, discussing it. "B. felt", she wrote, "that if the risk of his marrying into a family so slightly tainted as ours was so very great, that there would still be risk in his marrying a perfectly healthy person. As I agreed with him in this, he went back and told Dr A. of our plan of marrying without children."

This Dr Anderson (unlike Elizabeth Garrett Anderson) was horrified, and wrote to Alys: "The more I reflect upon all the circumstances, the more I am inclined to consider such a proposed union as unhallowed and unnatural. . . . I cannot rest without making known to you my deliberately weighed professional opinion that such a course would have a disastrous effect upon his nervous system." Alys was very angry at his sending her such a letter, and told Bertie: "I was perfectly furious when it came last night, not so much at him as at thy grandmother for inciting him to write such a letter. . . . I still consider it perfectly *unpardonable*." Bertie soothed her down and went off to yet another doctor, this time a less conventional and more independent one, and reported the results to Dr Anderson: "A physician . . . who . . . has a wide professional experience of the effects of preventive checks . . . told me that in the course of a long and extended experience of them, he had found harm only when the parties believed themselves to be living in sin."

With this they won through the medical trial, but Lady Russell now claimed that all this worry had brought upon her "a disease like cancer", and persuaded the doctors to appeal to Bertie to promise a separation of at least three months to put her mind at rest. Much distressed, for he was genuinely fond of her, he reluctantly agreed, but only on condition that they should marry immediately the three months were over. Alys wrote to him:

> We had foolishly given up expecting new blows, and this one was such an unexpected shock. But now we do not need to feel superstitious—thy Grandmother is neither Fate nor Destiny, but only an old lady who leaves no stone unturned to get her own way. . . . I will *never consent* if it is going to make thee too depressed. After all we are free agents, and if I were reading about us in a novel, I should say "Why don't these foolish young people brace up and take matters in their own hands".

But Bertie felt that his possible depression did not outweigh his real duty to his grandmother and agreed to go. A convenient offer from Lord Dufferin, ambassador in Paris, to take Bertie as an attaché for three months was accepted, though it was not a world into which Bertie had any wish to penetrate, and without seeing Alys—as that would mean starting the three months all over again—he left for France in September.

He wrote two letters a day to Alys throughout the period, and they told in minute detail all his thoughts and feelings. For the most part he was bored, depressed and homesick; shocked by French morals, and insufficiently stimulated by the work and company at the Embassy. He recovered gradually from the terrible drama of the summer, and began once more to analyse his relationship with Alys.

Thee stood for me [he wrote] as the woman of the future, not the transitional struggling woman—for everything transitional is crude and strained and unhappy—but the woman born with the victory already won, and almost unconscious of other possibilities—which thanks to thy mother thee really is to a great extent. Hardly any other woman has been independent always without having to struggle. And that I suppose is one reason (the other, and more important being that thee is fat!) why thee is so much less angular and pugnacious than most advanced women.

Alys, for her part, was calm and happy at first. She admitted to becoming less antagonistic to the idea of sex, and Bertie wrote: "I am sure thy former views came from the notion that there was never any desire on the woman's part, which is utterly untrue. I have never been able to see any harm in moderate intercourse where it is perfectly mutual and *quite* subordinate."

Alys was still worried about his superior intellect, and he replied: "I'm too egotistic to mind thy not having more than the very fair share of brains thee has—provided thee is sympathetic it will always be enough—and thee has managed to get most of thy opinions those that clever people have, which is the greatest point." "If thee had more brains", he went on frankly, "thee would not care so much about mine and then I would not be so much stimulated. . . . However I feel that if thee were strongly to take up anything I thought illogical or foolish I might be very disagreeable—it is as well to realize the danger so as to guard against it." And sometimes he was less tolerant.

Thee *must* think for thyself instead of taking scraps from different people—that is what makes thy opinions so disjointed, because thee takes different opinions from different people, thinking two subjects independent—but no two subjects are really independent. . . . Thee wastes thy mind, not from modesty but from a combination of laziness and pride.

Bertie never expected to find a woman with a brain he could

really respect, and in this, his first love affair, as in his later ventures, he maintained that what he really valued in a woman was appreciation and sensitivity. The sensitivity which he himself offered in return was not outstanding, and the intellect which he brought to bear on his personal relations did little to soften his outspoken and often hurtful comments.

He came over to England for a week at the end of October, to read a paper at Cambridge, but did not see Alys, in obedience to their agreement. When he went back to Paris on 4 November, for the last few weeks of his attachment, he travelled across with Mary, who had stayed on in England later than usual that year.

Although Alys had come to dislike Frank—largely for the unhappiness he caused her mother—she found Mary even more uncongenial.

I am very annoyed with M [she wrote to Bertie] as well as Frank. . . . I wouldn't mind her telling lies to Mother if she didn't make such professions of sincerity and talk so much against liars and hypocrites. And also she makes use of Mother so unscrupulously, shifts off all her duties on her, and accepts every kind of sacrifice without making any sacrifices in return, and all the time deceiving her. She knows that Mother might give the children up if she didn't tell her lies. I wish to goodness Mother would give them up. It makes me miserable to see her suffer so about them.

Two days later Mary settled into the same hotel as Bertie, hoping "to get to know him". As the days passed Bertie described their growing friendship in somewhat tactless detail. His defence of Mary's lies struck an ominous note, to start with:

I think thee is always a little hard and priggish when thee talks about Mariechen. . . . It seems to me rather hard upon her to object to her telling lies to thy mother: *thee* never needs to, because thee and thy mother are extraordinarily alike, and can therefore understand each other—but Mariechen is more like thy father, and it is naturally incomprehensible to thy mother that that should be the case with a woman, especially an American woman, still more a woman who is her own daughter. . . . As to her falling in love with different people, that is a matter of temperament, and can't be helped. It is objected to, conventionally, but I never could understand why constancy should be a virtue, because it is simply *impossible* to love people because one ought to.

At first he was fairly critical: "She seems genuinely interested in metaphysics and is always getting me to talk about it, which I enjoy very much. . . . But . . . every now and then one hits a hard rock of stony selfishness beneath the silken exterior, which gives one a sort of shock." But gradually the letters became more enthusiastic: "She is a *perfectly* charming companion, and has made these last 10 days really enjoyable, which I should hardly have supposed it possible for anyone to do under the circumstances;" "she is really, as she says herself, simply in pursuit of enjoyment—only she pursues it in a very graceful manner," and finally, "she is so nice and emotional that she fits my present mood to perfection."

Alys did her best to endure all this stoically. "It *is* nice for thee to have Mariechen there to breakfast every morning . . . and I hope she will be rewarded by finding thee very stimulating. She's of a peculiar nature that can only be stimulated by young men, and I don't mean to say that in a mean way." "I am *so* glad thee has got M. to make the time pass for thee, Dearest. Thee may fall in love with her all thee likes, but I *shall* be mad if she converts thee to Nietzsche." "Why should I mind thy kissing [M.]? It is a pleasant and interesting experience if the person is pleasant . . . and one might as well do it when it seems *à propos.*"

At home, however, the cheerful face was less in evidence, and her diary for 9 November reads: "For some reason or other I have been perfectly miserable the last few days. I am so afraid I shall not be able to make B. happy, I am so dull. Cried." And on the 12th: "Felt depressed and teary." And finally on 15 November: "Cried most of the morning, but felt better after some sleep. Mariechen left Bertie yesterday."

Bertie had not fallen in love with Mary, but he had clearly been both dazzled and impressed by her, even if letting down her hair and exchanging fairly fraternal kisses was as far as they went. What had so upset and alarmed Alys was that he had absorbed Mary's far from complimentary opinions of her, and his letters were not only depressingly full of his enjoyment of Mary, but more and more critical of Alys.

Under Mary's influence Bertie had come to sympathize whole-heartedly with her behaviour to Frank. He had always felt, more-over, that Alys was altogether too "practical" and philanthropic, and had feared that she might try to force him in that direction, too. Mary's advice was that he get Alys to give up all her own activities and devote herself entirely to helping him in his own far more important work.

This advice he passed on at once, and Alys wrote back:

I found thy letter when I got back . . . and it made me so miser-able that I tore it right up. . . . Thy letters have all been utterly unsympathetic since Mariechen has been there, but I tried not to mind because I knew it only meant that thee was happy and busy. But this one seems more critical and superior than any, and was just too much for me. . . . I never mind *thy* criticisms, Dearest, but I do mind echoes of Mariechen. Thee knows how utterly unsympathetic she has always been to anything I have really cared about, and since her last week at home I have had such a loathing of her morals and conduct that I can hardly think of her without shuddering.

 . . . It has made me really unhappy that thee should write so very much about my giving up practical work and how much happier it would make thee, when I feel that I can't do it and still be myself. That was always one great drawback in my mind last year, that our taste in work was so different, and all thee has written brings back all my old fears and doubts about our ulti-mate congeniality. And then it is so provoking to have thee reinforce thy arguments by Mariechen's when thee can't know that she used to be just as much down on anyone who did any-thing but practical work. . . . Of course thee doesn't know her very well and I have purposely refrained from writing anything about her to thee this week so that thee might form thy own impression. What I do mind is thy taking her say-so about me.

Bertie was overcome by repentance, and admitted that he had "abandoned [himself] too recklessly to M." and had been brutal in his way of putting things. His apologies were copious and graceful, and the minute they met, when the three months were at last at an end, he was entirely forgiven.

Their troubles were still not quite over, for Lady Russell was fighting a desperate rearguard action. Hannah and Alys went to call on her to discuss arrangements for the wedding which, with Bertie's complete agreement, was to be held in Quaker Meeting, as quietly as possible, just before Christmas. Alys noted in her diary: "Mother and I called at P.L. They objected to all our arrangements and Lady R. said nasty things to Mother, who said nothing." She complained to Bertie who was somewhat unsympathetic:

> It was brutal of my people to annoy thy mother—they think her inhuman, I believe, and incapable of really suffering from anything they say. . . . I never expect thee to stand other people's worrying thy mother—but I dare say what [Lady R.] said wasn't half as bad as thy mother represented it, for thee knows how she loses her head when the family, and thee in particular, are attacked, and how incapable she grows of reporting accurately.

There is an indication here of his later irritation with Alys for her "excessive" devotion to Hannah, and perhaps a trace of resentment that anyone other than himself should criticize his "people".

Lady Russell was in fact capable of being very venomous indeed. One of the final thorns she proffered concerned the wording of the wedding invitations, which she maintained should omit Bertie's title of "the Honourable", whereas all the rest of his aristocratic relatives, including his brother Frank, Lord Russell, declared it must go in. As Americans, the Smiths had to take the best advice they could get on so ticklish a point, but when they decided to include it, and told Lady Russell, she replied:

Of course where different people give different advice, you were obliged to reject that of the persons whom you might think least competent to give it, or least concerned in the matter, which *last* you could hardly think of us. You need not have feared, as Americans, that you would be thought to pay too little deference to titles—the invariable charge is the other way.

The last shot in the locker came from Lady Agatha, who wrote: "Rollo reminds us that December 14th [the day first fixed for the wedding] was the day of the death of Prince Albert and of Princess Alice—and considering our situation with regard to the Queen, we felt we could none of us like the wedding being on that day."

So they were married a day earlier, 13 December 1894, in the Quaker Meeting at Westminster. Lady Russell and Lady Agatha did not attend, but Bertie's brother and his aunt Lady Stanley were there, and Hannah wrote cheerfully to Mary that there had been "lovely little sermonettes . . . two prayers and short intervals of silence which Lady Stanley . . . employed in dropping her stick and shawl and her various belongings which someone had to rush forward and pick up".

Immediately after the wedding they set off to Holland and Germany for their honeymoon.

Part III

CONSEQUENCES

STORM WARNING

Alys and Bertie

IT ALL LOOKED most auspicious. Bertie later said of the honeymoon that although they were both completely inexperienced, they found their predicament not embarrassing but comical, and that Alys had taken quite naturally to the sexual relations she had envisaged with such distaste. She wrote to her mother three days after the wedding, saying: "No immediate prospect of skating, I fear, but we have enough to amuse ourselves without that!" and Hannah replied: "And now do write me a few private particulars. How do thy nightgowns work; does thee like them as well as pyjamas? Does Bertie like the pyjamas . . . who gets up first . . . I want all the particulars." She destroyed the answer, as Alys requested, but it enabled her to relieve old Lady Russell's mind during one of the painful sessions the two ladies had together. "I may tell thee in the strictest confidence," Hannah wrote to her daughter, "that her great fear seemed to be that you did not live together as man and wife, but I told her that I was sure you did, and this seemed a *great* relief to her."

Bertie later complained that Alys's nightgowns were all made of flannel and most unalluring, but this was due to her fear of rheumatism. As Hannah told Mary: "She gets it at once if she leaves off her flannel nightgowns. . . . When she was [in Florence] she had to wear woollen stockings on her hands and arms as well as her feet, and leave no part of her body uncovered with flannel but her face, or she got rheumatism at once." In their various ways, indeed, the whole family retained a strong residue of Quaker "plainness" in their attitude to clothes. Alys did her best to be elegant and even fashionable, but it never occurred to her that underclothes should also be chosen for aesthetic reasons.

In 1896 she learned to ride a bicycle, for which purpose she wore what she called "Rational Dress", which she described in an interview for a paper called *The Wheelwoman*: "I always wear loose Turkish trousers, Zouave jacket and broad sash round my waist. It may not be beautiful, but I can answer for its great comfort, and honestly I do not think skirts are either suitable or safe for cycling." This costume caused something of a furore in Fernhurst, as she noted in her journal:

> I called on Lady Gatacre at Verdley Place, but as she was out I left a message inviting her to tea the following day. She had seen me bicycling in knickerbockers about five weeks previously, and now wrote as follows: "Dear Mrs Russell, I had your message yesterday. Since I met you bicycling in the Lodsworth road, it has been impossible for me to consider you as a friend. I should not have expressed my opinion if it had not been for your invitation, which I therefore decline."

Alys used to go on cycling trips in Italy with Bertie, taking a spare wraparound skirt to put on as they entered a town. There the reaction was much more favourable, as she recorded in 1899, also in *The Wheelwoman*: "With or without a skirt, I always attracted a great deal of attention, but of a kindly sort. . . . Crowds of children followed me when I walked about, but only out of pure curiosity . . . 'Certe colonne di gambe' [real columns of legs] one man was overheard saying in an approving tone."

She was lucky to be born when she was, for her legs were indeed columnar, as were Hannah's and Mary's—great Cretan pillars, sloping straight down from thigh to heel. Karin, too, inherited the Whitall legs, unlike Ray, whose limbs, though massive, were normally shaped. While the older generation, in their sweeping skirts, were unmoved by the inheritance, Karin, always the unlucky one, lived in an era of rising hemlines, and her "columns" were a real trial.

Alys and Bertie continued their honeymoon in Berlin, where they wanted to study Socialism. Thence they travelled down to Italy, to stay with Mary in Fiesole. Mary told Hannah: "Bertie and Alys seem really very happy. I notice that she has been very much influenced by his way of thinking, but that is natural as he is really so clever. They are eating their breakfast in the dining room now, and I hear peals of laughter from moment to moment."

Mary observed the couple with an eye that was both amused and critical. Before their marriage she had already noticed Alys's total conversion to all Bertie's doctrinaire theories.

Bertie's idea [she had written to B.B.] is to have the State provide "procreation tickets" of a certain colour, and have heavy fines for those who dare to have children with those whose ticket doesn't correspond—thus eliminating disease. The congenial ones could marry all the same, even if their tickets weren't right, but must use checks. . . . They are both against marriage in the present sense, altogether. Alys has a little penny pamphlet containing pictures and prices of half a dozen varieties of check, all safe and harmless, from one shilling to 2/6. . . . Shall I send thee one? . . . Among all his friends, Alys says, these questions are hotly discussed.

Mary had clearly changed her mind about "checks" since her visit to Dr Garrett Anderson.

In Florence the Russells' daily activities were more cultural than doctrinaire, and Mary noted in her diary: "Bertie read aloud the Book of Job, and we read parts of *Prometheus Unbound*. Poor Alys gets *so* bored and sleepy with all these talks and readings and keeps continually looking at her watch and tries to cheer herself up by thinking of other things." As she wrote to a friend, "We call her 'Conventionality in Progress' . . . but I trust under Bertie's guidance she may grow more of a person. I see some signs already."

The honeymoon pair went on for an idyllic trip down the Adriatic, and finally returned to Friday's Hill, where Bertie worked on his dissertation for a Trinity College fellowship, which he duly obtained. The following year they paid a visit to America, to meet Alys's family and friends, and stayed with Carey Thomas at Bryn Mawr. Bertie lectured on Mathematics and Socialism, and Alys on Temperance and Suffrage, while in private she had discussions with the girls about paid motherhood and free love—she had to apologize to Carey for this afterwards, as the Trustees of the College got to hear of it and were outraged. They went on to Boston, and when they wrote to Professor James and his wife, suggesting a visit, they were much amused to receive a reply from the puritanically honest Mrs James which read: "We shall be very glad to see you", with the "very" crossed through though still clearly visible.

They called in on Mary again in 1896. Bertie went bicycling with B.B. and there was, as usual, endless conversation.

We were confessing our ambitions last night [Mary noted]. Bertie owned to the modest desire to write "a dialectic logic of all the sciences; and an ethic that should apply to politics". Alys followed with the hope that she might bring the Woman's Movement and Socialism into closer rapport. Bernhard seemed to be bent on writing a psychological aesthetic of the Fine Arts. My wishes soared no higher than writing a Classic Guide to the pictures in the Louvre.

On their return to England Bertie and Alys moved into "The Millhanger", a little cottage a mile or so away from Friday's Hill, where they built on a couple of workrooms for Bertie. The next few years were, he said himself, among the happiest and the most intellectually fruitful of his life. He abandoned politics for the time being in favour of mathematics and philosophy, and started to write his first major work, *The Principles of Mathematics*. Alys provided just the background he needed, giving him love and admiration, protecting him from strangers, coping with practical problems (Bertie was hopelessly and deliberately unpractical and never even learned to do up a parcel), while maintaining an equable and sunny temper. She had not given up her practical work and once removed from Mary's influence Bertie seemed to have entirely come round to it. "There was a time," he wrote to Alys in 1896, "when thy work seemed to me rather uninteresting, but now I feel quite the opposite. It seems to me rather splendid to wake up middle-class country girls and get them in touch with more advanced and thoughtful people." The loss of her faith, which Bertie had succeeded in demolishing a month or so after their marriage, did not after all appear to prevent her from working for the BWTA, and she spent a lot of her time travelling round the country, sometimes with her mother, sometimes with Lady Henry Somerset, organizing and speaking for Temperance and Suffrage, while Bertie stayed at home and worked on his book.

Throughout these years their letters were very loving, if without the desperate urgency of the engagement days. "I am getting very anxious to see thee," wrote Bertie to Alys in 1897. "We met a man and his wife walking over the pass today and I felt quite a pang of envy." "I only realize when I am away from thee how very much thee is to me and how I can't think of anything except in reference to thee."

And occasionally there was laughter, too. "Cleopatra was really fine this afternoon," wrote Alys. "Her death was marvellously tragic, but I did not weep because I knew that it happened so long ago." Alys was famed for bursting into tears on the slightest provocation, and Bertie could not resist mocking her. "I am . . . much amused", he replied, "that long-ago sorrows don't affect thee. Thee believes, apparently, in the reality of past time when it is only a little past, but not when it is much past. Try this metaphysic on Moore, as I don't believe it has occurred to him." And a little later: "I read my paper last night to an audience of about 10 people. 'That Owl', Masterman, was there, and two Scotchmen. As for the rest they left most of the discussion to Moore, and he and I soon lapsed into a duologue, which emptied the room of all but one Scotchman. No-one could understand what we were saying, and he was the only man who thought he could. Moore told me afterwards, by way of a friendly goodnight, that I too hadn't perceived what we were arguing about."

Bertie had come to know the philosopher G. E. Moore, author of *Principia Ethica*, and later the prophet of Bloomsbury, when they were undergraduates at Cambridge. They were both elected to the exclusive intellectual discussion group known both as "The Society" and as "The Apostles", and Bertie liked and admired Moore, though often disagreeing with his views.

Each year the Russells spent the spring term at Cambridge, where Bertie was able to renew old friendships and make intellectually-exciting new ones. Coming out of his solitary shell, he increasingly entered into and enjoyed the congenial, shop-talking Cambridge life. Alys did her best, but naturally she could not participate in this. All she could do was exercise her undoubted talents for hospitality and housekeeping, and display her somewhat artificial social manners, which were not always as effective as she hoped in putting Bertie's erudite friends at their ease. Some years later, referring to a dinner with the alarming Dr Jowett of Balliol, she described her technique. "I prepared a number of funny stories beforehand, and launched them at suitable intervals on suitable occasions with great success. I practised the same technique with Mr Baddeley, the Head of Bedales School, when I and my niece lunched with him, and made a real sensation among the children when he laughed at my jokes."

Everything seemed peaceful and trouble-free and Bertie was clearly happy, but the fickle element in his nature was already beginning to stir in its Puritan strait-jacket. Whatever Alys may have noticed, however, her pride and unbreakable reserve would never have let her admit it to anyone, even to herself. He was still aware, for instance, of Mary's attractions, and teased Alys about this in 1897. "[Mary and I] had a jolly tête-à-tête dinner last night, and revived the pleasing feelings of Paris, without their very serious drawbacks." And again: "Last night I elicited from M. a most thrilling adventure of the heart concerning which I will tell thee all when thee comes—she didn't want it written. . . . She was more charming than ever, and I enjoyed having her to myself, as well as the opportunity to kiss her 'on suitable occasions'."

All this must have given Alys a pang: it certainly startled Mary, who wrote to B.B.: "Bertie was *very* affectionate and I didn't quite know what to do. But I think I managed all right by taking a perfectly natural tone of friendliness. I do not want to put it into his head that I notice anything, because then he would get the idea that I thought something more intimate *was* possible, however undesirable, and I do not believe he really thought it."

And then there was an American girl called Sally Fairchild, who came as a visitor to Friday's Hill in 1899. "An aristocratic Bostonian," Bertie called her later, and he observed: "In the face she was not strikingly beautiful, but her movements were the most graceful that I have ever seen." He may well have been struck at the time by the contrast with Alys, whose face was lovely, but who was awkward and clumsy in her movements. Alys showed no signs of jealousy, but the rest of the family could see only too clearly what was happening. Mary wrote to Bernhard: "Poor Mother is dreadfully worried about Bertie's evident flirtation with Miss Fairchild. They go for long walks every evening, and Bertie has deserted his hitherto invariable habits of study and cards, from which nothing used to be able to tear him. And of course they have nothing in common except flirtation." And a week later:

She and Bertie stayed out walking till midnight last night. Mother was awfully worried, as they were out till 2 the night before. But Alys seems quite delighted. I suppose her idea is that Bertie tends to be too much of a hermit and that anything that brings him out of his shell is a blessing. But I am afraid if she knew as much about him as I do, she wouldn't be contented that a well-known flirt should be his distraction.

This time nothing disastrous happened, and Bertie returned to his books. However, Mary's sharp sisterly eye was on the watch for further signs of trouble. The next time Bertie and Alys came to stay with her in Florence, she wrote in her diary:

I had an amusing talk with Alys and Bertie last night. Alys says she hates men and despises conversation and thinks smoking "a filthy habit". But she adores Bertie and so has fashioned her life to be occupied chiefly in these three things. But it is quite true, and it accounts for the queer icy streaks one comes across in her every now and then. . . . I wonder if, à la longue, even love can bridge such fundamental differences as there are between her and Bertie. Bertie says he has resigned himself to being *always bored* after he is thirty. "At home, even?" Alys asked. "Especially at home," Bertie answered remorselessly.

EARLY WORKS

Logan

LOGAN LEFT BALLIOL in 1891, with a Second Class degree: a tall, fair, heavily-built young man, already beginning to go bald, with a "nervous" constitution, a tendency to sleeplessness, and an unexpected love of boats and sailing. He had made many friends at Balliol, notably Philip Morrell, who later married Lady Ottoline Cavendish Bentinck. The handsome son of an Oxford solicitor, Philip was probably the person Logan cared for most deeply in his whole life, though he was later to turn against him, and still more bitterly against Ottoline, when she became involved with his brother-in-law Bertie Russell.

He also made friends with a number of more or less politically-minded young aristocrats such as Willie Peel, the son of the Speaker of the House of Commons and grandson of the Tory Prime Minister, Sir Robert Peel, with whom he shared digs in Headington. These aristocratic friends were not without their special attractions. "I think I was best known in Oxford," he admits in *Unforgotten Years*, "as belonging to the not very estimable type of social reformer who combines extreme democratic views with no very pronounced dislike of the society of lords."

Oxford made an indelible impression on him in many ways. "If I have to any degree attained to a clean heart and a new spirit," he wrote, "I owe it to these years of careful tuition and personal guidance at Balliol." It gave him the third great influence on his literary style (the others being Walt Whitman and Henry James): that of Walter Pater, whose famous injunction—"to burn with a hard gem-like flame"—was the catchphrase of his cultural generation, and whose prose many of them tried to imitate. Oxford also gave Logan the all-male atmosphere then so typical of English institutions, so congenial to his temperament and so refreshingly different from his matriarchal family life. But at the end, one suspects, he developed a lurking fear that Oxford had cut him off from his roots and taught him to hunger for a style and excellence which, along with social self-confidence, he was committed to strive for, but might never achieve.

His religious faith had entirely vanished—on his own account, it disappeared up a cherry tree when he was eleven—but, for both moral and fastidious reasons, he retained a strong tendency towards puritan asceticism, co-existing uneasily with a taste for cynical and sometimes malicious gossip. He still shared the family passion for philanthropy, and to some extent preserved it all his life.

During the summer of 1891 Logan stayed at Friday's Hill, where his parents happily kept open house for their own and their children's friends. Here, what Hannah called the "clash-ma-clavers" was unending and uninhibited; guests as diverse as Mrs Bramwell Booth of the Salvation Army, George Santayana the philosopher, Mrs Hodgson Burnett (author of *Little Lord Fauntleroy*), Bernard Shaw and the Sidney Webbs were all equally welcome.

Logan decided that he would spend the next few winters in Paris, where he could find peace and a propitious climate for his literary exercises. He took a small flat in the "artists' quarter" of Montparnasse, and alternated spells of hard literary work with social explorations of a new and fascinating kind. He made friends with many of the English and American art students who flooded into the city in the nineties, and whose devotion to their chosen pursuit was, for the most part, equalled by their lack of talent. He also made friends with many of the more serious writers and painters, including Roger Fry, whom he came to know through the Quaker connection.

Many more friends came to him through his acquaintance with the three Kinsella sisters, Joe, Kate and Louise. They were Irish-American girls from Boston who had a flat in Paris, and he wrote home: "One sister paints and has a studio, one sings, and the other looks beautiful and collects old books and tapestries." Louise, the beautiful one, was forever sitting to her artist friends. Hannah hoped that Logan might be in love with her, but after staying with him in 1894 she reported: "Logan declares he is *not* in love with Miss Louise Kinsella, nor thinking of it; and we see no signs as if he were." But they remained friends for many years.

Through the Kinsellas Logan came to know Whistler. He wrote to Hannah: "He is a little French-looking man, and talks very fast in a nasal American voice, and is certainly the wittiest and best talker I ever heard. . . . Whistler is rather poor just now, and wants to paint Miss Louise Kinsella; that is why, I think, he is so nice to me, because I am trying to arrange it." The portrait did materialize, and Logan himself was enrolled to pose in the clothes of Whistler's fashionable sitters when they could not spare the time themselves.

Will Rothenstein was another of the Kinsella circle; barely twenty at this time, but clearly a brilliant painter, he was invited for the whole summer of 1893 to Friday's Hill. He was much impressed by the free and unconventional atmosphere, and Hannah wrote to her American friends: "One young Englishman named Rothenstein seems really to have a remarkable talent, and the great Whistler even predicts for him a great career. I tell you this as it *may* be a prophecy." During the visit he painted one portrait of Alys in yellow silk, and another in a memorable dress decorated with green beetles' wings. Roger Fry, who also painted her, much admired the two portraits, but (as was often the case with Rothenstein) they were not liked by the subject, nor by Hannah, who thought they made her daughter look like a "Piccadilly lady".

All the Smith family were now hard at work, with the exception of Robert, who pottered round Friday's Hill, playing word games and chess with his brother Horace. He was idle and depressed, and wrote to Mary:

Bear in mind, dear Poll, that thee has the fearful curse of our inheritance of NERVES—and that while never actually insane, thy greatgrandfather—grandfather—greatuncle Richard and two of his children, Nelly Howland and Dillwyn—thy two

uncles—thy father—his cousins Stewardson and Richard M.
Smith—nearly the whole family have suffered beyond description. The lesson is to keep oneself free from all excitement and
overwork—sleep as much as possible—and be very distrustful
of our own intellectual and moral conclusions.

Horace Smith and his wife Margaret now spent much of their
time in England; their daughter had married an Englishman, and
when they were not visiting her in Birmingham they stayed with
Robert and Hannah. Horace's state of mind varied from extreme
excitability to equally extreme depression—an exaggerated version of Robert's own temperament. In March 1893, for instance,
when his wife took him to Paris, Logan described how "Uncle
Horace, without telling Aunt Maggie, got up a concert and invited all the hotel and everyone he knew in Paris. I went as I
thought I ought: but I was very sorry for poor Aunt Maggie,
for she never knows what he may be doing." By September the
pendulum had swung right over, and Hannah told Mary:

Poor Uncle H. is in the depths again. It is evidently melancholia.
I pity Aunt Margaret from the bottom of my heart. She says
she sees nothing before her but to spend the rest of her life
wandering the world with him. It is dreadful. And he is so
sweet and gentle and patient when he is in one of these spells
that you cannot find it in your heart to be angry with him.

Logan's first literary work, a book of short stories about Oxford
called *The Youth of Parnassus*, was accepted by Macmillan and
published in 1895. When it came out he wrote to Mary: "I am
pleased on the whole; 'pretty' and 'charming' would be the most
I should say . . . but it is not more than a piece of school work,
an effort towards technical efficiency." It got a few kindly reviews,
and one less kind one which said: "These stories tell us nothing,
and tell it very indifferently. When Mr Smith has gained a larger
knowledge of life and acquired a literary style of his own, he
might try again, but until he has done both these things we assure
him . . . he does but waste his own time and ours." He sent this

b

a) Frank Costelloe,
c. 1885
b) Mary Costelloe,
1886
c) Wedding breakfast
of Frank Costelloe and
Mary Smith in Balliol
Hall, 3 September
1885. Dr Jowett is
seated at the head of
the cross table on the
left.

a

b

c
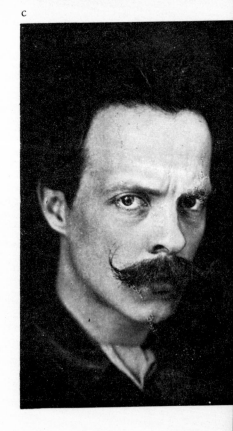

a) Friday's Hill House, 1894
b) Bernhard Berenson at
Harvard, 1887
c) Hermann Obrist, c. 1894

c

a) The Pearsall Smith family at Friday's Hill House, 1894. Back row: Alys, Logan. Seated: Robert, Karin Costelloe, Hannah, Ray Costelloe, Mary Costelloe
b) Alys Pearsall Smith, 1894
c) Bertrand Russell and Alys Pearsall Smith, 1894

a

b

c

a) Whitall women: Mary, Hannah
and Alys, 1898
b) Hannah and Robert at Friday's
Hill House, 1894

c) Horace Smith, 1889

a) Bertie and Alys Russell, 1907
(Bertie's election photograph)
c) Ray Costelloe, c. 1908

b) Alys Russell campaigning for
Women's Suffrage, 1910
d) Karin Costelloe, c. 1908

a

b

c

a) Bernhard Berenson,
1909
b) Mary Berenson,
c. 1914
c) I Tatti

a

b

a) Ray Costelloe, the
Rev. Anna Shaw and
Ellie Rendel in Buffalo,
1909
b) Hannah at Court
Place, 1909

a
b

a) The Strachey family, c. 1893:
James, Lytton, Oliver, Ralph, Dick,
Sir Richard Strachey, Lady Strachey,
Elinor (Rendel), Dorothy (Bussy),
Philippa, Pernel, Marjorie
b) Oliver Strachey, 1911
c) Mud House in 1936: Mary Berenson,
Roger, Ray Strachey

c

b

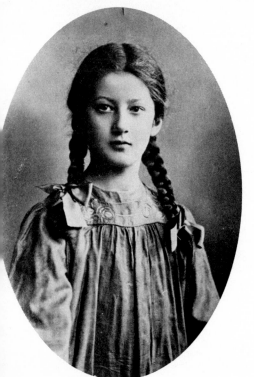

a) Adrian Stephen, c. 1928
b) Virginia Woolf at the
Mud House, 1938
c) Julia Strachey, c. 1911

a

b

c

a) Ray Strachey with her children,
Christopher and Barbara, Mud
House, 1928
b) Karin Stephen and her children
Ann (left) and Judith, 1926

c) Ray Strachey canvassing in
Chiswick and Brentford during the
General Election of 1923

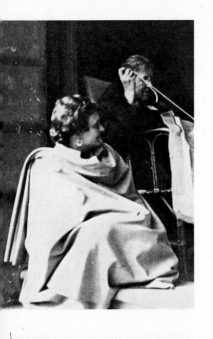

b
d

) Nicky Mariano and Mary
erenson at I Tatti, 1929
) Logan Pearsall Smith, c. 1931
) Ray Strachey, 1940
) Karin Stephen, 1927

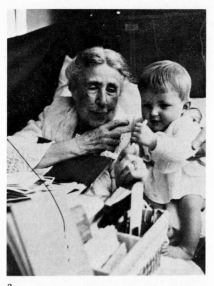
a

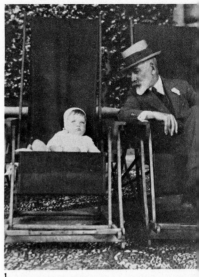
b

c

d

a) Mary Berenson in old age with
Roger, 1935
b) Bernard Berenson with Roger
at I Tatti, 1935
c) Bertrand Russell in the 1940s.

d) Alys Russell in Wellington
Square, 1948

to Mary, commenting: "I more or less expected something of the kind, but I thought I should mind it more—this seems so off the point somehow." Many years later he still had a soft spot for his only excursion into fiction. "On re-reading it the other day," he wrote in *Unforgotten Years*, "I felt that it was not entirely devoid of merit."

He sent a copy to Henry James, and described the outcome in his Journal:

> Henry James was kind enough to ask me to come and see him and talk about my book. I still have the feeling that he is a "Master", one who knows, feels, in an accomplished way. I remember the sense of initiation, of participation in great things as if it were a great moment, when in the dim light, with the whispering fire, he gets my book, puts on his big spectacles and turns the pages. . . . I feel a little echo of the emotion with which years ago in America, I should have looked forward to such a scene. But his advice—no—no.

He never said what that advice had been.

He next tried to write a novel "à la Turgenieff", and a play about Sin ("in its British sense") and Society. Alys got hold of part of this opus, and sent it to Shaw for an opinion; "I shall soon hear of its futility," Logan commented. Neither of these early efforts survive, and for the most part he was content to practise the craft of writing prose without a specific end in view.

Many of his friends had left Paris by 1895, and he spent the next few winters mainly in Italy, returning for the family reunions in the summer months. He stayed a good deal in Venice, and also in Florence with Mary; he got on extremely well with her, and tolerably with B.B. He enjoyed the spectrum of social life he found there, and the copious opportunities for gossip about the "Virgins of the Hills", as the more unconventional ladies of the colony were called. When it came to work, however, he moved to Venice. "I have really come abroad," he told Mary, "to think out my next piece of work and for that I need complete solitude."

He found Venice enchanting. He wrote to his closest friend, Philip Morrell, who visited him there in 1896, and to whom he used the affectionate Quaker address:

What has become of thee, my dear Philip, since thee went off over the lagoons into the great world of noise and fierce people? . . . For a long time after thee left I was quite alone and melancholy, but the days passed, and then came a precious time of work and thought and ideas. . . . Oh Philip, solitude is the thing, solitude and a few books and memories; the waves and agitations of the soul grow quiet, and it can calmly reflect the images of the things it loves.

Back at Friday's Hill for the summer, he described his daily life to Philip:

I have been pursuing the usual cheerful course of my working days, . . . coming down late, to the annoyance of my father (which I rather enjoy) reading the paper a little to see if any pleasant disasters have happened to the great successful philis-tines, and then coming up here with a sort of itching in my fingers to get to work. I hum over prose to myself, hunt for words, cross out my chosen adjectives, go to the window and look out, stick cloves into oranges and put them in the sun; get to work again, read a page of Lamb or the etymological diction-ary, while flies buzz about and I hear the great clock strike.

In 1897 there was a breach with Philip, for no recorded reason, but after more than a year they were reconciled when Logan wrote a letter of warm sympathy after the suicide of Philip's brother. The correspondence flowed on again, dealing with Walpole and Burton, prose and gardens, displaying urbane affection and equally urbane irony.

I am trying to read Paul's epistles, in order to finish the Bible. What stuff! Of all letter writers he is the dullest, he even manages to bore you when he writes about fornication, a sub-

ject on which it is so hard to be dull. I rub my eyes and wonder
what the centuries have seen in that Paul, and to think that they
might have been reading Plato!

In 1897, when he was thirty-two, Logan rented a house of his
own, called High Buildings, in Fernhurst, the village at the foot
of Friday's Hill, where he spent much of his time during the next
nine years. There he indulged in long hours of reading and
gardening, sometimes happy, although his happiness was tinged
with melancholy, and sometimes in despair at the difficulties of
his self-set task. "Summer days," he wrote in his journal, "with
all the doors open, the soft wind blowing through the house, with
the bees scavenging in the lavender stalks, swallows dipping in the
water. . . . I pick and enjoy these days one by one like ripe peaches
from the garden walls, . . . but I was often depressed in these two
months . . . depressed, as I was happy, for no reason." He confessed
to Philip:

> I am in despair about writing—I can't do it. I know exactly
> what prose should be, a rich, subdued texture, a brocade with
> threads of gold and wonderful flowers, yet all grave, severe,
> with a faint perfume of seventeenth-century roses. . . . It ought
> to be noble, fine, like the voice of a beautiful Vergil-loving
> youth reading the lessons at twilight in an Oxford chapel. . . .
> To write, and to write well, isn't so hard, but oh to write just
> in the key of good prose—no, no that isn't for Logan.

Oddly enough, he was also ambitious for popular acclaim. He
wrote in his journal in 1895: "This morning when I woke I felt
suddenly that I wanted success—not the real kind of success, the
esteem of a few good judges, but popular, gross success."

Bertie had started by liking and even admiring Logan, but as
time went on he began to believe that Logan had been warped
by the evil influence of his mother, though his wit continued to
delight him. But in early marriage Bertie was a stern moralist.
He found Logan's conversation frivolous and malicious, and told
Alys that he did not have a high opinion of his abilities. "He has

a passion to be first rate and says other people's good work makes him miserable. I haven't got the passion myself, and was surprised to find that he had it. It is unfortunate for him, as he will obviously not get it satisfied."

Logan, while saying that he approved intellectually of Bertie and Alys's lovemaking, found it "rather mildly disgusting". He always claimed that he did not want a life of adventure, and that his blood "did not stir to passion". "My idea of a happy ending to a love story," he wrote, "is to begin at the engagement, where the hack writer ends, and show how they escape from the storms and wild beasts back into the safe harbour of celibacy." It was a harbour he himself was never to leave.

Meanwhile he was trying to live on his allowance of £300 a year, borrowing as often as he could from Mary or Bertie. Even that comparatively modest income was threatened when the American slump of 1893 affected Laurel Hill Cemetery and Whitall-Tatum Glass, whence the family money still came. The income decreased sharply and Whitall-Tatum abruptly decided to hand over the capital it had been holding for the seceding branch of the family, and leave them to invest it elsewhere.

They all finally bought annuities, and on Mary's advice Logan tried to make some extra money by buying and selling Italian antiques and furniture. The decorative arts had attracted him since childhood, and he had acquired excellent taste and considerable expertise in furniture, tapestries and *objets d'art*. It was the ideal time to make money in these fields in Italy: prices were absurdly low, the formalities involved in shipping purchases of this kind out of the country were minimal, and could be enormously eased by hand-greasing.

He started by undertaking commissions for friends, but Mary urged him to make a proper business of it, and finally he started an elegant little antique shop in Pimlico, with his friends, Philip Morrell and Percy Feilding. It was called "Miss Toplady"—a joke referring to the fact that the proprietors were too exquisite to talk money, and always referred clients to "the lady who lives at the top of the house" for such details. This lady was Logan's cousin, Grace Thomas Worthington, whose marriage had just broken up. She was exceedingly poor, and brought her three children over to England to shelter under the welcoming wing of Aunt Hannah. All the family were very fond of her, and the children made ideal playmates for Ray and Karin. An allowance was scraped together, a cottage rented for her in Fernhurst, and a job found for her at Toplady's. Bertie paid for her elder son Val to go to a public school and then to Oxford, and Karin and her daughter Mary, known as "Pug", became inseparable.

Toplady's was never a great financial success, because Logan found it degrading to charge for his treasures. There were too many "special clients" and too many cherished things he could not bring himself to sell, but it provided a living for Grace for some years.

Hannah, meanwhile, was still delighting in the varied interests and entertainments of the English scene, though a wider experience of life was adding a sardonic touch to her moral fervour. She had become good friends with Oscar Wilde's wife, Constance, and was horrified—if not surprised—at the revelations at his trial. She wrote to Mary in 1895:

Everybody thinks that Oscar Wilde is going to get off after all! It is outrageous for no human being doubts his guilt. *I* believe the judge and jury are all guilty of the same thing, and dare not convict him. We are writing out resolutions for our [BWTA] Annual Council and I handed one to Lady Henry which read as follows—"Resolved that it is the sense of this Council that all men should be castrated." It is the only effectual remedy I know.

Mary was more tolerant, and wrote in her diary:

Oscar Wilde is imprisoned for two years with hard labour; it makes me quite miserable, for although I came to the conclusion he was somehow a loathsome beast when he was here last spring, yet surely he was so much more use than harm, even granting the charges are true. And when you think how common the vice is, it is sickening to think that the punishment

has fallen on the most brilliant of them all. To have known him
so well! It is horrible to think what his feelings must be. Poor
Oscar! I have a secret hope it may turn out well for him in the
end.

Hannah's religious activities were as wide-reaching as ever.
Her books of Bible exposition and homely wisdom, presented in
good, simple, forceful English, had been reprinted again and again
in England and America, and translated into many languages,
including Cantonese. They brought her an ever-flowing stream
of visitors, drawn by doubts or unhappiness to sit at her feet and
take comfort from her unshakeable common sense. One caller
complained that she had never been able to understand the
doctrine of the Trinity. "But it is perfectly simple," said Hannah,
"all you have to do is to think of a Threepenny Bit."

She had also written a little book on bringing up children,
called *Educate our Mothers* in England and *Child Culture* in
America, in which she tried to pass on her notions of raising
children by means of loving praise instead of discipline, based on
her own experience as a mother and grandmother. Ray and Karin
were a perpetual delight to her, and she tried to spoil them even
more than she had spoiled her own children, to make up for their
mother's absence.

Ray described how she did this in the book she wrote about
her, *A Quaker Grandmother*:

Her creed about grandmothers was very complete. . . . Grandmothers are old, their life is past. . . . They therefore are free
to devote themselves to the children. . . . But they must be
very careful not to interfere. They must step aside and let the
younger generation have its way. "It stands to reason", she
would say, "that young people *must* know better than we
do.". . . They should see to it that their grandchildren should
have plenty of fun. . . . She really enjoyed our pleasures more
than we did, and cared more than we did when they failed.
As, however, we were almost continuously happy, I think she
was, too.

The duty of providing "treats" and "fun" for the children was carried out so thoroughly that Ray said they could only remember one occasion when she disappointed them:

We had set our hearts on having a pet elephant, and went, as was our custom, to ask Gram for one. . . . In her desire not to disappoint us, she actually went to Whiteley's (who advertised to provide anything on earth) to ask them if she could hire one for us. She would have done it, and brought us the creature, had she not discovered that it had to be fed daily on a ton or so of hay. The difficulty and expense of procuring hay in such quantities was finally too much for her, and she brought down only toy elephants, with which we, heartless wretches, were far from satisfied.

IN FULL CAREER

Mary and Bernhard

OUT IN FLORENCE, B.B. and Mary were hard at work. Primarily this involved seeing, digesting, comparing and remembering, and they would often spend two hours in front of a picture, studying one small detail. They were also building up a unique collection of photographs of paintings, a professional aid which was only just becoming available. This was always Mary's province, and she began to systematize and index the collection, which she claimed amounted to 12–15,000 items by 1896, and 20,000 by 1899.

They had also begun what was to become a regular annual series of viewing trips. At first, when virtually all the money they had was Mary's small allowance, they did not go far afield, but even so they covered a lot of ground. In 1892, for instance, they went to Modena and Bergamo in May, and to Ravenna, Ancona, Macerate, Fabbriano, Citta di Castello, Perugia, Foligno, Viterbo and Orvieto in October and November. Later, when money was more plentiful, they went further: Provence, Spain, Hungary, usually travelling at least twice a year; and in later years they went to Sweden, Greece, Egypt, Palestine and the southern shores of the Mediterranean, looking and enjoying in the same careful way.

Conditions were far from luxurious on those early trips. There was virtually no tourist trade, and in any case the places they needed to visit were often small, with only one primitive inn. Every summer Mary suffered what was to be a lifelong martyrdom to fleas. She did not advertise to her family that all these journeys were taken in the company of Bernhard, but she did report regularly on the flea problem. In 1891 she was writing to Alys from Verona:

I am literally devoured, *devoured* with fleas! A flea actually hopped into my soup tonight—and was there drowned, to my great satisfaction. My noontide rests are converted into flea-hunts, sometimes crowned with success, but generally resulting in exasperation. My clothes are ruined with anti-insect powder, and I lie at night on it, as on the sands of the sea. I assure thee there is not a single inch of my body without at least one raging bite, and they are multiplying minute by minute.

Next year at Ancona she was beseeching Hannah for help. "Do make enquiries about fleas. . . . I undress every few hours and always catch one or two, in spite of innumerable camphor bags sewn all over my clothes. What *is* one to do? Thee always finds a remedy for everything. I am sure thee can for this." She tried anything anyone recommended, even dog soap, and when her children grew old enough to appreciate her letters, fleas became a running theme. Finally Hannah passed on a tip from Aunt Margaret Smith which was the most effective of all:

Aunt M. says . . . she has found it a great relief to sleep on a very fuzzy blanket, as they get entangled in the fuzz and cannot hop. She says if thee will stick the fuzzy corners inside thy nightgown all the fleas will collect in them . . . but it must be a fuzzy blanket, not a smooth one.

Both Mary and Bernhard were often ill at this time: she suffered from gynaecological troubles, bronchitis, catarrh, sleep-lessness and headaches, while Bernhard, always quivering at the edge of nervous exhaustion, endured catastrophic bouts of in-digestion. But nothing could deter them for more than an hour or two, and for Mary, if not for Bernhard, there was always good food of some sort to be enjoyed.

At home the work was less exhausting, but no less continuous. Mary was still trying to make Bernhard write, and when at first she did not succeed, she wrote herself. She was learning Greek, German and the piano, and also took singing lessons for a time.

For the first time yesterday [she wrote to Alys] my "real voice" came out. It is a very low, rather powerful—and I may add indescribably hideous—contralto. It is just the voice I *didn't* want to have. I wanted a light clear voice to sing nice little tinkling things—and lo and behold I have an "organ" suited only to the bellowing of passionate, moving songs. I should not have begun had I known.

She and Bernhard would read aloud almost every night—poetry, history, the Bible, or books on whatever theme they were pursuing at the moment. She loved every minute of the life.

In the long run Mary made a fair amount of money from her articles, and became tolerably well-known in the field, as Mary Logan. Bernhard was always highly nervous at the prospect of anyone stealing his ideas, and quarrelled on this account, at one time or another, with almost all his friends and professional colleagues, such as Vernon Lee, Carl Loeser and Roger Fry, but with Mary he was prepared to be generous. She wrote to Hannah in 1893:

Where another person would have kept his professional secrets and best ideas to himself, or at any rate would have used me to do *his* work, he has placed at my disposal all he knows, and has urged me to work for myself and in my own name far more than I have done. He has been busy a year helping me to collect materials for my Botticelli, which is, I hope, going to be a thorough and very thoughtful piece of work.

They had already worked together in 1891, on the guide to the pictures at Hampton Court which appeared under her name, and on an essay on the Venetian painters of the Renaissance. In the summer of 1893 she submitted this for publication, and wrote to her father:

Thee remembers the essay on Venetian Painting which I gave thee to read a year and a half ago? Well, I offered it to Putnam then along with some badly arranged Hampton Court material. He said he liked it, and if it could be combined with something less cumbrous and of more general interest than the H.C. stuff, he would print it. As I was not in possession of sufficient knowledge to do anything else with it, I gave it to Berenson and advised him to make lists of all the genuine works of the Venetian painters. This he did, and I submitted it to Mr Putnam last summer and he accepted it at once. My idea, of course, was to have both names, because I thought, and still think, that the best way to answer scandal is to tell the exact truth as openly as possible, namely that we have been doing serious and scholarly work together. Mr Putnam wanted both names, but mother opposed it so decidedly that I yielded the point and asked Mr Putnam to leave out my name. This I thought was only fair, as the smaller part of the work is mine, and then I am using his notes for my Hampton Court book, which is to appear in my name. So that is the way it has been arranged and Mr Putnam has sent all the proofs to me. It is going to be a useful little book for those who care for the subject. But human nature is queer! One thinks one isn't ambitious, and is only anxious to have peace to do quiet scholarly work, no matter who gets the credit, yet I find myself much more interested in the publication of the Hampton Court affair than in the *Venetian Painters of the Renaissance*, although I hope that may have a small success—which is the most to be hoped for a book of that character.

The following April she wrote to Hannah: "A number of papers have reviewed [*Venetian Painters*] very favourably, but I am glad my name is not attached to it in any way, not only for personal reasons, but because it is too small a book to bear two names. Everyone complains of this shortness." By 1896, however, it had already run into three editions, and it is now revered as the first of Berenson's "Four Gospels" on the Italian painters.

Mary made no claim to being responsible for the expertise involved. She was always clear that it was B.B. who was the leader, and she who followed behind, and in later years she happily refered to the *Venetian Painters* as "B.B.'s book", as he did himself. In fact, he trusted and relied on her judgment as well as her style. As the years passed he would commission her every year to check all the new pictures at the London dealers for him, and provide attributions and judgments which, even when they could not be checked against photographs, he was perfectly happy to accept. Already in 1896 he wrote:

Gutekunst knows of a Velasquez which may do for Mrs J. [Mrs Jack Gardner]. I am very anxious that you should see it, as I do not like to deal in such big game without autopsy. Please be aware of your responsibilities, but I should not ask you to do this, if I did not believe you as competent as any living person to have an opinion.

B.B. was always touchy about his literary style, though he sometimes submitted to criticism and emendations from various friends, such as Vernon Lee and Bob Trevelyan, as well as Mary. English was not even his birthright tongue, though he was a brilliant linguist and claimed to have known twenty-six languages, and he was aware that his own use of it was sometimes less than perfect. His autobiographical *Sketch for a Self Portrait* is full of reasons for his revulsion against writing—his "penshyness" as he called it. He hated to steal time from true appreciation of beauty; he admitted to a lack of discipline in arranging his arguments; and above all he claimed that his nature was that of a talker, and one who talked best, he said, to an audience of the adolescent-minded, such as society women, who could encourage and respond without opposing the flow of his ideas, or evoking competition.

In 1894 Mary met a half-Swiss, half-Scottish sculptor, called Obrist, at dinner with Professor James; he was a strange young man: pop-eyed, with a sweeping moustache and a mistrustful frown, obstinate, opinionated and a little deaf. She and B.B. became very friendly with him and admired his art nouveau sculpture and his embroidery designs. All three of them went off in April, with some other friends, on a brief tour of Italian towns, and Mary's dangerous bent for flirtation led her to lengths she later greatly regretted.

At the time she tried to conceal everything from Bernhard, who set off for America in August in a loving but suspicious mood. "Back of all you said and were nearly aware of," he wrote to her from Boston in September, "there transpired a feeling towards O. of an unpractical kind—to say the least. But I must trust you to take care of yourself." And a few days later: "I wonder whether you or any other woman could ever satisfy all I crave for. Yes, I think you could—if I had you; but there's the rub, I fear in some ways I have been too much like a father to you, I have helped to form you, to start you, and you feel the natural inclination to leave me and to try for yourself."

That year (1894), Mary stayed on in England with the children until November. On her way back to Florence she broke her journey in Paris where she enchanted Bertie Russell (and borrowed £100 from him). She did not attend Alys's wedding because Frank insisted that he must not be forced to meet her, but soon after Christmas she brought Obrist for a brief visit to Friday's Hill. The affair was coming to an end, and Logan wrote to Alys: "Poor Mariechen got bored, towards the end [of his visit] I think; she had to entertain him and talk to him all day long, and from any part of the house you could hear her voice pouring into his melancholy ear, everything she knew and a great deal she didn't."

Throughout 1895 she and Bernhard struggled towards a reconciliation, and in November she noted in her diary: "In the evening Bernhard and I read over the correspondence between Obrist and myself. . . . I must confess, it was much duller than I thought it would be. It bored us to death." But bored or not, Bernhard was "very, very angry, and hated me bitterly for many moments together".

There seems to be nothing left to start afresh with—nothing . . . to be a person who is fickle in soul, to have loved once, as I really loved Bernhard, and then to waver, to be unable to hold fast the good thing. . . . When I left [Frank] I thought my love for Bernhard was *for ever* . . . and then I couldn't hold firm, but yielded to the delight of feelings that sprung up (for it *is* wonderful to be "in love"). . . . And yet if it had been Bernhard, should I have blamed him? Sometimes I think not, for

Love, in whatever form it comes is a God . . . Why should we put faithfulness before it?

She was to have plenty of opportunity to discover whether she was more or less jealous than Bernhard, but meanwhile they made up their quarrel and Bernhard forgave her, writing: "All I ask of you is to be scrupulously honest and sincere with me. It is my first and last request—and condition." To Obrist, B.B. behaved in an outstandingly generous and civilized way. A year later he wrote to Mary: "Do not think I am irritated with O. I am very fond of him. But he is not the friend of my dreams. . . . I want us both to help O. to the utmost—thee also to join in if thee can pump all sentiment out of the concern."

Obrist, however, was convinced that B.B. was stealing his ideas—a complaint which inhabitants of the world of art criticism have never been slow to make of each other. In June 1895 Mary wrote to him: "I beg of thee, dear artist, to lay aside thy really ungrounded suspicion that B.B. could take any ideas of thine and use them without thy consent and giving thee no credit. . . . I have never known him do such a thing consciously . . . and furthermore the book is already written." The book was the *Florentine Painters of the Renaissance*, and whatever may be the truth about Mary's part in the *Venetian Painters*, it was this second book—somewhat different in style and approach—which was to present to the world Berenson's theory of Tactile Values, for which he became famous.

Throughout 1895, as they quarrelled and made up, Bernhard and Mary worked together on the book, and Mary's admiration grew. She wrote in her diary in June:

All this time at Fiesole grappling with the Book, and enjoying it very much. Every day we saw deeper into the "why" of real art enjoyment. Practically the whole will come out in Bernhard's books, but I do wish I had kept a record of our discussions from day to day. However I was lazy and did not—and so I have missed the detailed memory of one of the happiest and most *growing* months of our lives.

When she went back to Friday's Hill that summer Mary discussed B.B.'s ideas: "Bertie and I are at it hammer and tongs," she wrote to Bernhard, "over thy theory of 'pleasure' which he begs to dispute in toto, basing himself upon the more recent psychologists." She gave a long description of his arguments and finished: "I wish thee were here to thrash it out thyself with Bertie. . . . I am doing my best since thee isn't here." B.B. was nervous of Mary's well-known lack of discretion, and wrote back: "I am sorry to hear that you have shown my MSS even to Russell. Not that I fear his misusing it in any way, but on principle, and partly because it implies that you are talking about it and giving it away in spite of yourself." "I think it inadvisable to make any changes in the MSS," he went on a few days later, "I see clearly what Russell is driving at, but this far I do not see that it matters at all. . . . However, do elicit all you can out of [him] and I shall be grateful."

Berenson had really begun to write at last. Even before the *Florentine Painters* came out, his book on Lorenzo Lotto was published and the *Central Italian Painters* followed a year later, as well as a number of articles. Mary wrote glowing reviews of the Lotto book—as Mary Logan—and wrote in her diary in the summer of 1895: "I have been simply overwhelmed by Bernhard's genius."

The years of B.B.'s real emergence as an art expert saw not only differences with Obrist, who snarled protectively over his ideas, but violent quarrels with Vernon Lee, whom Berenson accused of plagiarism, and with Carl Loeser. In 1895 they also quarrelled with "The Mikes", to Mary's regret. "Bernhard", she wrote in her diary, "cannot endure any friendship that imposes concealment and pretence, and although he has often enough said pretty frankly what he thought of their work, yet they always fall back into posing before us as *poets*, which we don't for an instant think they are—but only agreeable human beings."

There was no doubt that Bernhard was a quarrelsome man. One of their friends told them that he had developed a reputation for being "a man who cannot bear other men, as he is furiously jealous of their reputation", Mary noted in her diary. "We are both supposed to be very unstable and changeable in our opinions . . . I see the justice of the remark." Mary was always trying to prevent or resolve Bernhard's quarrels. In 1897 she wrote to him: "It would be a mistake to quarrel with Miss Paget [Vernon Lee]. It's always a mistake to quarrel; the thing to do is just to drop people quietly. And then the person accusing another of stealing his ideas is always in a ridiculous position. . . . I am *sure* thy best pose is a dignified approval of their work." She herself found the situation funny, and noted her amusement at the sight of "these maiden ladies, dressed in stiff shirts with wrinkles where most women have a certain fulness, crossing their legs and putting their hands in their pockets and taking this petty little squabble with all the seriousness of a European war at least". But Bernhard was always too tautly insecure and nerve-wracked to follow her confident and sensible advice.

There were incessant quarrels between B.B. and Mary, too. She wrote in 1896:

> Bernard seems so nervous and cross that unless he had told me out and out that it was not so, I should not have been able to help thinking that he disliked me intensely. Everything I do and say gets on his nerves, whenever he looks at me it is to tell me that I am fat, or red, or hairy or slouchy or untidy, and these remarks he makes—and others on my Americanisms and general stupidity—in bitter tones with a frown and not the slightest appearance of finding anything nice in me. It may be a way of expressing affection, to be greatly concerned with another person's faults and defects, but it is not the happiest way.

Luckily Mary herself, though she had many other faults, did not cherish rancour, and except when her health was affected she was unquenchably gay, stimulating and good-tempered.

These were crucial and worrying days for B.B. He was just beginning to become known and to make money. In 1895, a year after the publication of *Venetian Painters*, there was an exhibition of Venetian painting in London which—as was so often the case in those early days—gave a large number of wildly mistaken attributions. In his disgust, B.B. had a pamphlet privately printed, giving the correct attributions as he then saw them, an action which caused a scandal in London art circles, and stirred up a bitterness and dislike which was never wholly dispersed.

But his growing reputation brought success as well as controversy. He sent a copy of *Venetian Painters* to Isabella Gardner, who had been his patroness at Harvard. Isabella was a remarkable woman; wife of a wealthy member of an old Bostonian family, she was a dominant character, ostentatiously extravagant but shrewd, and, as Bernhard used to say, "as tyrannical and wilful as a female Caligula". She was much impressed by her protégé's growing reputation, and used him to buy the collection of Italian paintings she was assembling at Fenway Court, her Boston house. For years he chose nearly all her pictures for her, including the Velasquez Mary had reported on in 1896, and his taste and expertise made hers one of the most remarkable private collections.

The commissions from her and the other wealthy collectors who occasionally made use of his services began to bring in large sums of money. Mary was frankly delighted. "I rejoiced at the thought of the money," she wrote, "but Bernhard did not feel any *real* pleasure in it." Indeed he was paying the price for success which he was to deplore all his life. In entering the savage arena of art dealing, as distinct from art appreciation and scholarship, he was faced with an endless battle to preserve his integrity, a battle which, whether successful or not, left him with an abiding sense of guilt.

Late in 1898 Isabella Gardner's husband died, and her trustees had less sympathy with her grandiose ideas of expenditure. Suspicions also arose as to B.B.'s financial probity and put him into a panic. He asked Mary in desperation if he could count on her under threat of disgrace, and she replied that of course he could. The dispute raged for months; he was accused of inflating prices, of making illicit bribes, of taking double commissions and of changing dealers without Mrs Gardner's authority. His worry brought on an almost suicidal depression, and made him more than ever dependent on Mary. From Friday's Hill she wrote him letter after letter of encouragement and shrewd tactical advice. He was to explain that it was impossible to move in the art world without the use of bribes—as was indeed the case—and that if they did not trust him he would provide accounts, but that Mrs Gardner must allow a margin for necessary but anonymous payments. Bernhard was deeply grateful; this time he followed her advice, and in due course the purchases started again.

At the end of 1897 they were forced out of their Fiesole villas by the noise of B.B.'s landlord rehearsing his brass band in the courtyard, and now that they were more prosperous they decided to move into pleasanter accommodation further down the hill. Mary took the charming Villa Frullino, in San Domenico, and B.B. again lodged nearby in Via Camerata. They were now able to furnish in a much more distinguished style, buying Aubusson carpets and good china and "resplendent" green tapestry chairs.

Mary, however, was in disgrace again. In the spring of 1897 she became friendly with a young Englishman called Wilfred Blaydes who, anxious to avoid becoming a barrister, had come to Florence to take up a vaguely literary career. This time Mary did not try to conceal her sins from Bernhard, and when she was back in England with her family in July, she wrote to him:

> My only excuse, or rather explanation, for my *inexcusable* behaviour to thee was that I had allowed myself to fall under the influence of an emotion genuine and sincere from its own point of view, which for the moment shut my eyes to every other point of view. . . . From the point of view outside the feelings, I did things which cause me to turn hot and cold all over, but from the inside point of view, well, they were quite different. . . . I have given thee a formal *business* promise that I shall never again (if it continues to matter to thee) take another excursus into my own inside point of view apart from thine.

Bernhard's reaction was, understandably, a little cool. He said that it would be better to be apart for a while. "You can practise a great deal, see your children, read and even think a little. Thinking will do you no harm. Indeed, much depends on how clearheaded I find you when we meet again. I love you very much, and I wish it made me happy as it used to." He went to St Moritz for the summer, and wrote long letters telling of the fascinating society ladies—La this and La that—whom he met there, in letters that did not conclude with the customary complement of four crosses. Mary wrote back: "I had such a dreadful night —nothing but dreams of the Grazioli—and such torturing ones." The crosses were absent all summer; they were a symbol of something sacred, Bernhard said, which she had abused, and it was not until October that he relented enough to vouchsafe two.

Mary got back to Italy to find that Blaydes was still impassioned; she wrote in her diary: "A telegram came from W.B., asking me to meet him in the Duomo at 3. . . . I had already written to him the reasons why we must not see each other any more . . . so left him after half an hour and came up here to weep. Dear Bernhard comforted me very much—and he could not help saying it was an original situation for *him*. But he was equal to it."

Blaydes recovered and found himself a bride without too much delay, and B.B. dined with him in London in his usual civilized fashion. Mary felt that it was not right for them to conceal their affair from the bride, and urged Wilfred to tell her. Bernhard was furious; he told Mary that he did not wish to be known as a complaisant lover and that "a person who, left to herself would be making a grisly fiasco of her existence should be humbler and not so cocksure of what others ought to do". Blaydes meanwhile borrowed money from both of them, and went on trying to borrow more for years. Bernhard remained unfailingly helpful, and finally told Mary that though Blaydes was not quite his kind of person, he had acquired a feeling of responsibility for his bread and butter and a certain fondness for the man.

Though Bernhard hated the dubious world of the dealers,

Mary enjoyed it with tremendous gusto and was soon entering the fray on her own account, buying and selling, and pitting her wits against the professionals. She was the one who handled their finances at this time, as Bernhard hated to get involved with money matters. She made nearly £800—a large sum in those days—on a Guardi she picked up in Venice, and had great fun mounting an anonymous sale in 1900.

Uncle Logan and I had great sport with the dealer [she wrote to her family]. We . . . took him round to see a "really quite remarkable little collection of pictures for sale" . . . i.e. *my* odds and ends. There they were, ranged round in a funny little room belonging to my picture restorer, who received us with perfect gravity and talked about "the proprietor" as if he were a hundred miles away. The London dealer was quite amazed to find such a remarkable collection: "never seen anything like it", "endless gratitude to me" and so on. . . . It is very amusing, but still I prefer selling straight out, without this mystery, only in these three cases for quite special reasons, I don't want it known that the pictures are mine.

The picture restorer, Cavenaghi, was so impressed by her that he offered to teach her his trade secrets—a considerable compliment.

Bernhard, too, had begun to buy pictures, but mainly for his own enjoyment and possession, and he generally sold them only when he could bear to part with them and wanted others. There was always the risk of forgery. In 1899 Mary noted in her diary: "We called on the Antiquario . . . and found nine excellent Sienese forgeries, which gave us doubts about—most of Bernhard's pictures!! The Antiquario confessed they *were* forgeries and offered him a hundred francs if he would show us the man who did them." There was a "terrific" hunt for the forger, who turned out to be a whole family of cheerful rogues in Siena, called Ioni. Mary and B.B. went to visit their workshops; they concealed nothing and gladly explained their technique, and Mary was utterly fascinated. Bernhard was less enthusiastic.

One of the greatest bargains of all was the marvellous Sassetta

altarpiece of St Francis, bought for their own house in 1900. Mary
described to her children how they acquired it:

Uncle Logan wanted us to look at some things he had found
for Toplady's, but he couldn't quite remember the shop, so we
drove about in the dusk, seeking for it. At last we came on it
just as they were closing the shutters, a tiny little out-of-the-
way, hole-and-corner place. We went in to see his things, and
lo, on the wall a marvellous altar piece by one of the rarest
painters in Italy, an early Sienese named Sassetta, of whom, as
it happens, nobody knows anything except . . . Mr Berenson
(who was with us). . . . I consulted Mr Berenson with a look
and saw that he had recognized the picture too, and . . . I found
the chance to say under my breath "What do you advise me
to offer for it?" "Up to 5000 francs (£200)," he said. In a
casual way I presently asked the dealer if he wanted to sell the
picture and at what price. He began to praise it up, but I said,
"O well, it's too big for a house, and so you will not easily
find a buyer." "Alas yes," he admitted, "it was true, and for
that reason he only asked a small price." "What price?" I
asked. "Three thousand francs," he said. "Well," I said in a
careless sort of way, "if you would let me have it for two
thousand francs I should take it." Upon this a man appeared,
the real proprietor of the picture, who had been hiding behind
a piece of furniture, and he said, "I accept your offer," and great
smiles of joy illuminated everybody's face, for they thought I
was buying an unknown silly picture, and I knew I was buying
a masterpiece. So I drove away . . . quite elated and excited,
though I shall no doubt feel less so when I have to pay the £80
on Monday.

In accordance with B.B.'s wishes the painting still hangs at I
Tatti, and is said to be worth well over a million dollars.

Perhaps the adventure she found most exciting of all was
smuggling a great picture of the Madonna out of Italy. This story
she relayed to her children (ten and eleven years old at the time)
and to her mother, as a kind of serial. "The great excitement of

the day," she started the tale on a postcard to the family in November 1899, "was a telegram from an agent I sent down to Umbria to look up a splendid picture I heard was secretly for sale." Two days later the story proceeds:

> The great excitement of yesterday was when I stopped at the bank in the morning and found a telegram from the picture agent saying that as he had taken a false name, he couldn't draw the 12,000 [francs] I had sent him. In the mean time, some other dealers had got wind of the picture and had telegraphed a higher offer to the monks who owned it. Last night the biggest picture dealer of Florence came up. . . . He will have to be taken into partnership, I think, and join me in putting down the price again.

A week later, again on a postcard, she described how the picture was got away: "The night they stole out of the town was fiercely stormy, wind and rain and bitter cold. The picture was wrapped in 3 blankets and an oilskin and put on a common cart. Three men held it, and they drove 50 miles over a wild mountain pass to get it out of the Papal States." This drew a warning protest from Hannah: "Is it safe for thee to send particulars of thy proposed purchase of that picture through the mail on *postcards*? It seems to me very risky, for anyone might read them, and give information in quarters thee would not wish." But the risk was half the fun for Mary, and she felt no qualms of conscience at smuggling the picture out of the country, since she regarded it as a rescue operation. "I shan't be happy till it is safely out of Italy. . . . If the Italian Government took decent care of the picture I should hesitate to snatch it away, but they let this one, for example, go to ruin, and the agent says we have got it *just* in time to save it peeling off entirely."

In the new year she described to them (this time under cover) the way in which the picture was got out of the country:

> Did I tell you my invention for getting it out? We had a huge trunk made with a false bottom in which the picture was

safely packed away. To explain the size and shape of the trunk
I had a lot of *dolls* made, and Signor Gagliardi went as a com-
mercial traveller in the doll trade. They were, though, large,
cheap and worthless dolls, or I should have sent one to you. He
went on Tuesday, and sent a telegram yesterday morning from
Basle to say it was all right.

When she circulated this letter round the family, Hannah added
in the margin: "A profound secret".

SAFELY GATHERED

Robert and Frank

AS THE YEARS passed, Robert seemed to drift away from the others, and his continual grouches and feuds made life with him a distinct burden on the rest of the family. He consoled himself by acquiring a "polished female friend", but was unable to keep this a secret from Hannah or the children. "I do *hope* thee kept a copy of that letter to 'P.'," Hannah wrote to Mary in 1895; she had made a surprising discovery while arrangements for the annuities were proceeding. "It is very evident that he has purchased that annuity of £100 for her! How intolerable it is. I feel as if I could hardly bear the sight of him." P. lived in Lambeth, across the Thames from Grosvenor Road, and when he was in London, Robert could be seen walking across Vauxhall Bridge every morning to visit her, while Hannah and Alys would lurk behind the curtains and point him out to each other in fine female fury.

Bertie was inexpressibly shocked. Not at Robert's behaviour, but at Hannah, for her impropriety in so undermining a father's authority and dignity by discussing his private life with his daughters. Bertie was coming to dislike Hannah more and more, a dislike that was greatly compounded by the love and admiration freely expressed by the rest of the family—particularly Alys. He considered her cruel and dishonest, and did not scruple to say so, causing Alys, who could not understand his attitude, considerable distress. The family's reaction to P. disgusted and infuriated him. When they were at Friday's Hill Hannah would collect the fragments of P.'s letters from the wastepaper basket where Robert had innocently thrown them, piece them together and read them aloud for the amusement of her children. In Hannah's eyes, Robert's actions were "unspeakable" and "intolerable", and it was a pious duty to make sure that her daughters should appreciate the true nature of man in general and husbands in particular. But Bertie's aristocratic and patriarchal instincts took over, and he never forgot or forgave her.

Hannah, for her part, did not forgive Robert. She had long lost all respect for him, and while her sense of her "manifest duty" kept her by his side, caring diligently for his welfare—as she had expected Mary to care for Frank's—and keeping him amused, she regarded him as a bad husband and an unsatisfactory human being.

Robert was always happiest in the country, with his Bô-tree, his garden, his horses and his chickens, and when the family began to get poorer he threatened that they might have to give up the London house. This drove Hannah almost to despair, and she wrote round to all the family urging them to support her. "I fear father is going to object to our keeping on 44 [Grosvenor Road]," she told Mary, "and my only hold on him will be if Logan wants it. While the children are at Number 40 I simply *must* have 44, but I do not want to use that argument or thee and I will be saddled with the rent." Logan rallied to her support and told Mary: "I wrote to reassure her and tell her that we can soon cow the old gentleman if he tries any tricks." Hannah was finally forced to use Ray and Karin's welfare to influence Robert. "These poor little motherless children are my manifest duty, the more so that they have such a selfish inconsiderate father. What their lives would be without me I shudder to contemplate, and I feel it is my duty to stick by them through everything, and am unspeakably thankful that I am so comfortably placed in this delightful house." They stayed.

Robert took increasing refuge in illness, which brought him good care and nursing, but little sympathy: "Poor father has *cancer* in the stomach now! The truth is that he has been eating enormously all winter and had got a very severe attack of indigestion, and is dreadfully frightened about himself. . . . One's sympathies are dried up when people make such a fuss of themselves." And she reminded Robert: "I remember Mother Smith telling me that thee always had *something* the matter with thee, but generally not more than one thing at a time, and if one part was attacked, the other parts would have a respite."

In 1897 he went off to the south of France, and stayed there for three months, despite Hannah's almost daily letters urging him to come home where he could be nursed properly. Finally he got a bad attack of influenza, and sent for Logan, who rushed to his bedside and wrote to Mary:

He really has been very ill—the doctor says that last week he was in a most critical state, but now he is slowly getting better. If, however, he is likely to die, as is still possible, I will let thee know, for I cannot help feeling that the poor old thing ought to have some of us with him when it all stops—there is something pathetic about him, like a sick animal that is grateful for the least kindness. All his old platitudes and grievances and boasts— they are life to him, and he clings to them, as we cling to the things that make our lives; and it is both sad and comic to sit by him and hear him mumbling over them in the darkened room. . . . If one has any feeling for life one can't help but be touched by illness and old age. There really is a nice old person in father . . . he has really been lying here miserable for weeks, wanting company but not sending for either thee or me because of expense, but also because he thought we should be so bored.

Robert recovered, and Logan managed to get him home by mid-April. Horace and Maggie were staying with them, and Horace was having one of his "Happies", as the family called his euphoric spells, and was being difficult. "Uncle Horace is deter-mined to go to the West Indies", Hannah wrote to her daughters, "and Aunt M. does not see how she can bear it, and yet she can't let him go alone, for when the reaction comes, he can't even buy himself a railroad ticket." And a little later: "Uncle Horace is still on the rampage. He came into the study yesterday and executed a war dance while he shouted out that he had got a new fad. . . . I see no hope of anything but a continuation of these alternations of excitement and depression for perhaps ten more years." Robert, on the other hand, was "down". "Father has had another attack in which he was certain that he was going to die, and even went so far as to wash his feet preparatory to being laid out," Hannah told Alys. "What a burden these two old useless men are! Remember when I arrive at that condition *I insist on a companion to take care of me*. Thee must just step in and get me one, no matter what I say."

Robert died in April 1898, and Bertie's dislike of his mother-in-law erupted once again at her attitude to the occasion and the "impiety" of her refusal to honour Robert's request to give the gardener £5. Logan, he recorded, burst into tears at this point, and joined him—though only temporarily—in his disapproval.

Hannah was always brusque about death; she regarded it as a great boon to the deceased, who were now happily reunited with their Heavenly Father, and usually a boon to the survivors, too. She would congratulate her friends when their aged parents or other elderly relatives were "safely gathered"—a response they sometimes found disconcerting. She was no less downright about her own death, rejoicing if at any time she thought it was likely, forbidding her family to think of mourning her, and making them promise to put her into the care of professionals if she began to become troublesome. But despite his own praise of honesty and practice of bluntness, Bertie could not see the merits of either where Hannah was concerned.

Indeed Hannah's composure seemed a little on the stern side even to Mary, who wrote to Bernhard after receiving a letter from her mother: "Father's death appeared to leave her very calm. She even enclosed in the same envelope a long account of a woman who has come to preach Free Love in London, *and a joke* about a person taking up music in later life." Logan and Mary were both moved by their father's death, and Mary wrote to Hannah:

Poor Father! He did not win much love in his life, and what he won he couldn't keep—I suppose no-one will feel existence poorer for his death, and yet one has a great deal of human emotion over such an event. We shall soon remember only what was engaging about him—and the *habit* of him will be hard to break. I can't help feeling as if he were taking a great interest in the disposal of his body—trotting around himself to give the last touches.

With Robert gone, the family's attention centred once more on their financial situation which was not very favourable. The money from Laurel Hill Cemetery, which constituted the larger part of the family income, had—for the moment—dropped to virtually nothing. Hannah had very little of her own, and all the family money had been tied up in complicated trusts to keep it out of Robert's over-generous hands. Furthermore, in addition to Logan's expenses at High Buildings, they had two large houses to keep up, neither of which Hannah could think of giving up as she felt they were her only guarantee of keeping in touch with the grandchildren. Bertie came to the rescue with reason and generosity to the fore, so long as he did not have to meet Hannah, and he agreed to pay part of the rent of Friday's Hill until their finances took a turn for the better.

Hannah, Mary noted, was "blossoming forth in a surprising way since father's death". Though she was still as fiercely anti-drink as ever, and "whenever she passes a public house she says 'That's Thy housekeeping, Lord, not mine!'" she was prevailed upon by Mary and Logan to allow wine to be served at Friday's Hill—a remarkable concession indeed. She was still deeply interested in politics, and ready to contribute to any cause she felt might improve the unhappy social conditions of the day. She had always been ready to react indignantly to oppression anywhere in the world, but her reactions to the Armenian massacres and the Graeco-Turkish conflict in Crete* were unusually fierce, even for her. She wrote to her American friends:

* In 1894–6 there was a nationalist revolt against Turkish rule among the two million Christian Armenians living in the Ottoman Empire. These risings were brutally suppressed, both in the provinces and in Constantinople, where thousands were killed in a three-day massacre in August 1896. The atrocities outraged the conscience of Western Europe (particularly British Liberals) but although diplomatic protests halted the killing, the Great Powers would not intervene to support Armenian independence. In Crete, a nationalist revolt against Turkish rule in 1897 was followed by the intervention of Greek troops. The Greeks were quickly defeated by the Turks, but the Great Powers united in bringing pressure on the Sultan to grant autonomy to Crete, and Prince George of Greece became Governor under Turkish suzerainty.

I confess my Quaker testimony on war has become very unstable of late. There seems no way in which this matter *can* be
settled but by a war that will exterminate Turkey. . . . I assure
you I have actually wished I was a man and young enough to go
to Greece to help them fight, and I almost wondered at some of
the meetings, where I had been stirred to the very depths, that
I did not come out with a helmet on my head.

In fact she was ready to be indignant about almost anything, as
she wrote to Alys. "I am just off to attend a meeting 'to protest'.
What I am to protest about, I have no idea, but I feel in a tremendously protesting mood."

And there were always the children, who were as absorbing as
ever. She took them skating, and sat on the edge of Battersea
ponds holding their coats until she got chilblains on her feet. In
warmer weather she took them rowing on the lake, and they
forced her to creep on her hands and knees to the rowing bench.
She even let them persuade her—aged sixty-six, black gown,
white cap, arthritis and all—to accompany them down the water
chute at the Earls Court Exhibition. She was fully rewarded, she
told her friends, when Ray told her "even your wrinkles have a
smiling turn at their ends".

When Mary descended on them there was drama and excitement and fascination, but she soon got bored. Unlike Hannah, she
found the idea of the children more attractive than their actual
presence and she would write to B.B., "Children, dear as they are,
are appallingly sordidizing, unless you can have them under *just*
the right conditions", and "of course it isn't a life I could lead all
the time". It became a family joke that in true "Gummidge"
fashion she was bound to come down with some disease or other
—"my" bronchitis, "my" digestive trouble or "my" splitting
headache—as soon as she got home to them.

Mary retained her early preference for Ray, often wondering
what the reasons for this might be: "[Karin] is a little angel—yet
none of us love her as we do Ray. I suppose the reason is physio-
logical—she resembles her father and his relatives, while Ray
belongs almost exclusively to our side, more and more as she gets

older." She took them riding one summer and Karin fell and got concussion (much to Frank's rage); Mary wrote: "I could not help feeling thankful beyond words that it wasn't Ray. There is an unspeakable difference in my feelings for them. I wonder if mothers generally have these strong preferences. Karin is awfully sweet and I hate her to suffer and I love her. But Ray—it is another world."

Karin, of course, was well aware of it. One night she was very upset and, as Mary wrote to B.B.:

After much trouble I got it out of them what it was—from poor little sobbing Karin who "didn't quite know how to explain what she meant"—but it finally came out that she thinks we all love Ray the most and pet her and leave herself out in the cold. This alas! is true—Ray belongs to us in character and temperament, and poor Karin is painfully like her father—and I fear there is no avoiding the consequences. But I felt it is pitiful that she should begin to recognize it, and so touching, this instinctive *claim* a child makes on love, that I took her up in my arms and comforted her as well as I could . . . but I felt it to be the first drop of rain in what is pretty sure to be a big pour one day. For these fatal differences of nature cannot, it seems, be changed.

There were still troubled times with Frank, too, trying to fight some "intolerable" course of action on his part, but he was not at all well, having increasing trouble with his ears. In the summer of 1899, he had to have an operation on his ear and jaw, and became so ill that he was seriously disturbed about his inability to earn. Hannah told Mary:

The difficulty he has in opening his mouth came on *before* the operation. . . . If it should be permanent his career is over, for he can hardly talk, and could not make a public speech to save his life. He can only manage to eat by cutting everything up very small and putting it in his mouth in tiny quantities. Poor fellow, one cannot help pitying him very much.

Frank could no longer afford to keep Friday's Hill Cottage, and asked Alys whether the family could take over the rent, which he would pay only when he used it. After discussing this with Bertie and Logan, Alys suggested to Mary that this might be a way of forcing Frank to make more generous and reliable arrangements for her to see the children, but she did not want Hannah to know, and ended her letter "DON'T THEE SAY A WORD TO MOTHER".

Frank refused to bind himself to any *quid pro quo*, but Mary, paying no attention to Alys's plea, had told Hannah everything, and Hannah agreed to pay the rent unconditionally, finding the money as best she could. Alys was furious with Mary. "Thee is really a fiend. I really am awfully provoked with thee for writing to Mother, when I especially asked thee not to. . . . Now Mother has an uneasy feeling that I am deceiving her and she has only got a new thing to worry over."

Frank's condition deteriorated rapidly, and in October Hannah wrote to Mary:

> The doctors were afraid the same trouble *might* come in the other ear. If it does I should consider his case hopeless. But I am afraid to wish for the poor fellow's death, as we have no idea what dispositions he may have made of the children. . . . I am going to get the last law about the custody of children and will send it to thee.

Realizing that he had cancer, and that death was imminent, Frank made a new Will, specifically excluding Mary or any of her family from the guardianship of his daughters and appointing instead five Catholic friends, two of whom were priests. He stipulated that the children should not live with their relations but in lodgings, under the care of their young German governess; that they should continue to go to the school he had chosen, and should be trained to earn their own livings before the guardianship ended. He added:

> I give all these directions in no hostile spirit toward my wife . . .
> but for the protection of my children . . . against the influences

to which they would infallibly be exposed if they lived with her no matter under what promises and guarantees. The nature of these dangers and the reasonableness of my precautions will I believe be admitted even by her.

One of the guardian priests, who did not approve of the Will, told Hannah about it in advance, and advised her to take precautions, so she found a sympathetic solicitor and without telling Frank they had the children made Wards in Chancery. All this was worked out between Hannah and Mary while Frank was failing. "I think it is wise," Hannah advised her, "for thee to lie low and not obtrude thyself on his notice until we see how this illness is going to turn out." And for once Mary did lie low.

Alys wrote to B.B.—by now the most prosperous member of the family—in December:

Mary will have told you that we are all absolutely united in the determination to break the Will, and that we are following the advice of a very sensible solicitor. It may be only my natural optimism, but I feel sure that it will come all right, even if we have to fight for it. . . . We can only wait and see. Just now we are expecting a telegram every minute to hear of the end.

Mary returned to sit by Frank's bedside. "I have just been summoned in," she wrote to B.B. "He is fully conscious and we have had a reconciliation scene. He kissed my hand. I am now in hopes that he may be able to make a new Will. I have sent for the doctor and Father Brown. They will join me in urging it." But he made no move, and she wrote three days later:

When I see him it is awful—that weary wreck of all his life and his ambitions come to nothing, and the horrible pathos of leaving no-one to mourn his going. When I do not see him I feel such anger and indignation and hatred on account of his Will that I could almost echo Bertie's wish to restore him to life and torture him for years. Thee can't conceive how painful it is to be swinging from one feeling to the other. But on the whole a sort of sickened pity predominates.

Frank died of cancer of the ear on 22 December 1899, aged only forty-four. Hannah and Mary rushed the children from number 40 to number 44 Grosvenor Road within the hour, in the knowledge that once there they could only be removed by a Court order. Dr Flanagan, the most prejudiced of the guardians, was furious. "[He] was so angry with my taking the children," wrote Mary to B.B., "that he was terrible to see. It was a shocking spectacle, his impotent rage. It frightened me very much, not for fear of consequences, but just as a spectacle."

Mary wrote to Aunt Lill:

It is an awfully sad thing to go thus, leaving behind you confusion and bitterness, and almost no regret. . . . Alas while testimonies to his cleverness and usefulness abound, there seems almost no-one to mourn him as a friend, and none who can regret him in any closer relation. The English law decrees that he can control the children's religion, even after he is dead. . . . Therefore in taking them into our care we have to give pledges not to disturb the teaching they have already received. But so far they seem very little affected by their religious training, and I hope, when they come to maturity, they will easily be able to throw off the senseless superstitions with which Roman Catholicism has filled their darling little heads. I will write and tell thee as soon as some definite arrangement is come to. The chief Trustee is entirely on our side, so we cannot have any serious difficulties.

Mary was a little optimistic for they did have a lot of trouble with Dr Flanagan and one of the other guardians. They had to bring the matter to Court to get legal control for Hannah, and to deposit securities providing an income of £200 a year for each child. Hannah was finally granted custody, though it was still necessary to get the Court's permission every time the children went abroad, and she had to undertake solemnly to bring them up as Catholics. She was most scrupulous about this, though the situation was not one in which a lively faith in their father's church could be expected to flourish for long—as indeed he had feared.

All this did nothing to endear Frank's memory to Hannah, as she openly admitted six months later. "The sign is down at No. 40," she wrote to Mary, "and new curtains are at the windows: and I love to look at the house and think that there are no more miseries enclosed behind its doors for us! It seems an incredible blessing! I dreamed last night that Frank came back, and it was unspeakably awful. But he must be full of worms by now, thank goodness!"

She was not to be left in peace for long. In May 1900 Mary and Bernhard rented a villa called I Tatti, on the hillside between Settignano and Fiesole, and, with Logan's assistance, set about altering and furnishing it to their taste. They proposed to marry as soon as possible after the conventional year's delay, and the only problem was how to break the news to Hannah. Logan did the deed and, as expected, Hannah took a highly pessimistic view of such an idiotic procedure.

> I had no idea [she wrote to Mary] Logan was telling me of a *fact*, and I confess I am very much surprised, and very much afraid it is going to make serious complications as regards the children. But I have nothing to say about it, as thee must, at thy age, settle thy own life. I endured Frank for a great many years, although I disliked him, and I can endure Berenson in the same way. . . . I always see myself as a patient ox pulling a cart, that has got to be full of some sort of load. . . . Frank has been lifted out now, so there is room for Berenson; and very likely he will be an easier load to pull.

Logan told Mary: "I think the main objection is now to the institution of marriage itself; and she cannot understand the folly of a widow marrying again." And later: "She doesn't seem to have any personal objections to B.B. any more, but is only afraid of the change the evil rites may produce in his character."

In the end Mary was even able to persuade Hannah that a Catholic wedding—since both she and Bernhard were nominally Catholics—would "take the wind out of the sails" of the Catholic guardians. "I should laugh", she wrote to her mother, "to see thy Quaker bonnet presiding over a group of the (practically all unbelieving) Catholics assembled to give 'correctness' to the ceremony."

Logan by now regarded himself as an expert on furniture and decoration, and set to work on the new villa with enthusiasm. All their ideas were extremely grandiose—and expensive—and Hannah struck a warning note.

Thee needn't think [Mary retorted] [that] Logan and I persuade, browbeat or hypnotize B.B. into spending money. It is quite often the other way, except that all the money passes through my hands, as he doesn't want to be bothered. But he is even worse than Logan in some ways, and I'm not a famous brake where money is concerned. However I cannot feel worried about it, for we are sure to make a great deal.

Hannah's other worry was that B.B. might still be a Russian by nationality, and that Mary would be subject to some sort of barbarous anti-feminist property laws. Here, too, Mary was able to reassure her. "Thee will be relieved to hear that there is no possible doubt whatever of B.B.'s being an American citizen. . . . There is no need for a 'Separation of Goods' for by Massachusetts law they are as separate as in England."

B.B. had been working on his book on Florentine drawings which had involved formidable and prolonged concentration, and Mary reported: "Poor B.B.! he is so miserable and ill, he looks quite worn and with a strange look almost of fright. It goes to my heart, and I am awfully glad I shall soon be able to take better care of him. . . . He says he would really give up the business of living if it were not for my good health and spirits."

Mary now hoped to bring him and the children closer together. "I want thee once to see a little of the children," she wrote to him from England in July, "for thee will, I am almost sure, find them inoffensive, and it may be that thee will actually like them." But B.B.'s response was not enormously encouraging:

> To be really frank with you—it is now or never—I feel them as a sore spot. To me they have never been anything but a source of worry and distress . . . never for an instant been a source of pleasure. So in my inner inwards there is no inclination towards them. You understand I do not go so far as to have any grudge against them. My lazy preference would be that I never once heard of them again . . . and now be assured that I shall be no less considerate of them henceforth than I have been hitherto.

But it was agreed that Hannah should bring them out to Florence for the ceremony.

Meanwhile all the work in the new house proceeded at an agonizingly slow pace; Mary was making her first acquaintance with the Mediterranean workman's somewhat idiosyncratic ideas of punctuality and accuracy. She was not, however, too busy to start another flirtation. Scarcely six weeks before the wedding she met a romantic Englishman called Captain Mounteney Jephson, who had been exploring in Africa with Stanley. She sat at his feet with the enthralled attention of a Desdemona, and the conversation soon turned to his unhappy love affairs and broken engagement. Fortunately, Hannah and the children arrived at this point to break up the tête-à-tête, and Mary noted in her diary: "More talks with Jephson, but though seeing him every day, I am really too absorbed in the children and the move."

The civil wedding was held in the Palazzo Vecchio on 27 December 1900, and the religious ceremony in the tiny chapel belonging to the villa, two days later. "To the children", wrote Hannah to Alys, "it was all a huge joke. They declare that their mother is too middle-aged and fat to have a wreath of orange flowers, so they are going to make her a wreath of good big oranges!" Logan, who was suffering from toothache, could not resist leaning over to Hannah in the middle of the service and whispering: "Don't this remind thee of Haddonfield Meeting?"

PROFIT AND LOSS

The Family

LOGAN WAS AS frequent a guest at I Tatti as he had been at Frullino and Fiesole before Mary's marriage. He took refuge there in January 1902, rather than attend Philip Morrell's wedding to Ottoline Cavendish-Bentinck. Although his politeness to—if not always about—Lady Ottoline was impeccable, the marriage clearly caused him distress. He wrote in his journal a year later: "How life renews itself! On my journey last year I said 'C'est fini'; this year I go with new hopes and sweet thoughts through the English landscape." But he was always subject to swings of temperament. An entry in his journal in 1905 reads:

"An overwhelming sense of failure in all I attempt, a dreary consciousness of absolute futility, combined with a sense of the brevity and misery of human life generally."* I copied that out that I may recognize these moods when they come, learn their meaninglessness and limits, and await their sure dispersion. So I can record that after a day in which I seemed a dreary ghost of myself, with no care for books, garden or friends, I woke the next morning with little relivening touches of joy, able to work a little, to enjoy the hum of the bees and my books.

Philip and Ottoline travelled in Italy for their honeymoon, and Mary caught a glimpse of them. Viewing the strange and beautiful bride with a mocking eye, she wrote to her mother:

Who should get into our carriage . . . at Orvieto but Philip and Lady Ottoline. . . . We looked out and saw a tall drooping figure in a fur coat and low neck hung all over with jewels and crowned by an immense poke bonnet, on which nodded and

* A. C. Benson, *Upton Letters*, p. 292.

trembled an immense array of ribbons and funereal feathers and ends of lace. They got into our carriage and Lady Ottoline, with a *thirsty* air, began a long "culture" conversation with B.B., to our intense amusement. . . . Once settled in the train [she] removed the poke bonnet and tied a lace shawl over her head, fastening it on with strange jewels. Altogether it was a "sight" but she looked very sweet and nice.

Logan gradually came to be very fond of Ottoline, and used to say that he went to see the Morrells on her account, not on Philip's, and Hannah, too, came to like them both. "Philip and Lady Ottoline came to lunch yesterday," she wrote in August. "She had a hat that was the wonder of all beholders. . . . Talk with her is like gliding over gentle sea waves, with a pleasing up and down motion, but never even sighting land."

Logan was still agonizing over his writing, nor was it yet crowned by any very notable success. He had lost much of his admiration for Pater, and was drawing inspiration instead from Baudelaire's *Prose Poems*. He was also developing his native gift for irony. "I dreamt last night," he wrote in his journal, "that the Lord appeared to me, and the Lord spake and said: 'The only way to treat modern life is the ironic—you cannot make it romantic.'"

By degrees he worked out a format of his own: small, sharp, often sour-sweet nutshell comments on life, which he called "Trivia". When he had collected and polished some forty-five of these, he put them together with a foreword stating that they had been edited "from the papers of one Mr Anthony Woodhouse". He had the little book printed at his own expense in 1902, but only 30 of the 300 copies were sold: almost the only letter of appreciation received was from the poet Robert Bridges, then a stranger, and it led to a lifelong friendship. His mother was not among the admirers of *Trivia*. "Logan gave me his little book to read last night," she wrote to Mary. "It is certainly very quaint and interesting. But it is what I would suppose would be called very 'precious', as it begins nowhere and ends nowhere and leads to nothing."

Logan was depressed by his failure, and turned to a more

learned but less original project: the life of Sir Henry Wotton, a sixteenth-century poet and diplomat, to be published by the Oxford University Press. This involved many pleasant hours researching in the archives in Oxford, London and Italy, but when finally published it made no great stir.

Hannah greatly enjoyed the years following Frank's death. She had at last got complete control of the children's upbringing, and the first thing she did, in spite of Frank's last wishes, was to send them to Kensington High School, a good modern day school instead of the rather second-rate convent school they had been attending. Ray and Karin, as they grew older, emerged as very different personalities. Karin was hasty, tactless, emotional and rowdy. She had built up for herself—probably as a defence against the family favouritism—a kind of cult of Irishness, Catholicism and the memory of her dead father. She was quite outstandingly intelligent, but her insensitivity, immaturity and addiction to schoolboy slang did not yet allow this to become apparent. She was attractive to look at—apart from her fat legs—and already at fifteen her effervescent affections were directed towards the boys of her acquaintance, whereas Ray found boys "perfect asses". Even as a small girl, Karin had suffered like her father from ear trouble, and the medical examination for the new school revealed that she was a little deaf. The specialist to whom she was taken, however, found nothing in particular wrong, and merely recommended that her adenoids be removed.

Ray was large, handsome, obstinate, competent and reserved. She hated the family favouritism, both on her own account and on Karin's. "I wish Gram would not pet me so much," she wrote in her diary on 1902, when she was fifteen. "I can't do anything without it being published and admired and talked about till I am more than heartily sick of it. . . . She seems to think I am a perfect being. . . . She doesn't seem to care half as much about Karin—I wonder if Karin minds. She certainly would not if she knew how horrid it is not to have any privacy." The efforts of her elders to prise out her thoughts and feelings were unending, but she had not won the nickname "The Oyster" for nothing. "Karin has

certainly inherited thy delightful outspokenness," wrote Hannah
to her daughter, "and I am doing all I can to cultivate it. Ray on
the other hand, has inherited Uncle Logan's reserve, and considers
it very undignified and very un-English to show her feelings in
any way. . . . Self-control, Ray calls it."

Ray's rejection of this inquisitiveness was passionate:

> It is only the personal things they are after [she wrote in 1904].
> That horrible way in which people ask you questions and
> expect you to pour out the secrets of your heart—and then if
> you do in any measure, they patronize you and torture you
> ever after. . . . To you it is interest, aim, occupation and pre-
> occupation—to them it is only a rather dull and insignificant
> way of finding out what kind of a wild beast you are.

She was passionate, too, about the family efforts to make her
grow up to be graceful, elegant and cultured. Not that the elders
were all that elegant, but Mary was tactlessly insistent with her
children, forcing them to take detested dancing and fencing
lessons, and closely supervising their clothes, confident that they
would thank her when they grew up. Hannah, with the remains
of her Quaker inheritance, had some sympathy with Ray's revolt
on this point, but even she found it excessive. "Ray sniffs at the
idea of thy trying to make her look graceful," she wrote to Mary,
"and I confess it seems to me a hopeless task just at present. We
cannot torture her with bones, and there is no other way. But she
has consented to give up those awful knickers for the summer and
wear her short gymnasium dress."

Ray had taken to life at High School with real enthusiasm. If not
outstanding at her lessons, she was unusually good at games, and
soon became captain, not only of cricket and swimming, but also
of the highly important hockey. Karin was not far behind, and
Hannah's life came to be ruled by new and strange factors. "I am
quite amused", she wrote to friends in America, "to find that
every morning when I get out of bed, one of my first thoughts
is . . . 'Is it good hockey weather?'"

Ray showed signs, too, of the family bent for organizing and committee work. Her sports successes led to her becoming Head of the School, and she took the burden of responsibility most seriously. "Ray is in all the glory of being on a 'Committee'," wrote Hannah. "It is too funny to think of her beginning on her career as a Committee woman. I must give her some of my . . . principles that have enabled me to pass through a long lifetime of committees without, I believe, a single quarrel. . . . They are two: 1) Be perfectly willing to give your best advice, 2) Be perfectly content not to have it followed."

She had made friends with a girl at the school called Ellie Rendel, whose mother was a much older sister of Lytton Strachey; she spent a lot of her holiday time staying with the Rendels, who bickered venomously and continuously, and found them fascinating—they were so different from her own over-affectionate and inquisitive relatives.

Hannah herself was beginning to feel that it was time for her to retire from active work. She was seventy in 1902, and was becoming increasingly crippled by arthritis. But she had no intention of becoming a cabbage. In 1903 she published her "Religious Autobiography", *The Unselfishness of God*, which explained her religious philosophy and how she reached it, and was eminently readable, with delightful descriptions of her childhood in Philadelphia. She also began to work on the revealing and entertaining papers on religious fanaticism which she left for Ray to publish after she, and the other characters involved, should be dead.* She started going to the theatre, and even went to see *La belle Otero*,† though she and Aunt Margaret found T. W. Robertson's *Caste* "a little too full of what I call horse play. . . . We are dainty old ladies, for all we are so gay."

She wrote to Alys, somewhat ambitiously perhaps:

Tell Bertie the widow Boole‡ is going to have a class to teach her husband's philosophy of mathematics, and I am going to attend it. I certainly think my brains are equal to the brains of

* Published as *Group Movements of the Past*, ed. Ray Strachey (1934).
† La Belle Otero was a celebrated Spanish gypsy dancer of the period.
‡ The widow of George Boole, the Mathematical Logician.

the other women who are going, and I feel quite eager to get some new ideas. Perhaps—who knows—I shall understand Bertie in some small degree afterwards.

Getting about, however, became more and more difficult for her and in 1903 she went to Manchester with Alys for one last BWTA National Executive meeting, after which she resigned her Secretaryship. On her return she wrote to Mary: "My sprees are over at last. My next . . . will be Heaven, and that will be a spree worth having! And no legs will interfere there." And later, "I sit and chuckle over the deliverance from care and from the necessity of doing anything which my lameness gives me. . . . I am determined to get all the fun out of it I can, and I find plenty."

Travelling even so short a distance as from London to Fernhurst was becoming difficult for her, and in 1903 they took the adventurous step of hiring a motor car. Hannah reported: "I found it most satisfactory. We travelled at the rate of about fifteen miles an hour, slowing down to twelve whenever we came in sight of a policeman. . . . At first the rapid motion took away our breaths, but we soon got used to it."

Her normal method of progress was now a bath chair, pushed by her maid, or by Logan when he was there. She had difficulty getting into bed, and Alys reported to Logan: "Mother had some new little steps for climbing into bed last evening, but they were a failure, and as she lay panting and exhausted on her bed, I thought she said 'Hell, take away the steps' though she maintains she only said 'Well'."

By September 1903 she was writing to Alys: "I had to let Rose put on my stockings . . . as I could no more reach my feet than I could reach the bottom of the bottomless pit. . . . I believe I have said a final goodbye to my silly feet, except as I can reach them to wash them with a long-handled brush." Her cheerfulness was unimpaired, and her attitude to death as practical as ever: She told Alys one day: "Remember if I die, the fireworks are on the top shelf."

Though she had painful attacks of bladder trouble and shingles, as well as continuing arthritis, and was finally unable to lie down at all and had to sleep sitting in a wheelchair, it was her family's health, not her own, that she worried about unceasingly. She and Mary exchanged recipes with enthusiasm—stomach binders against indigestion, new flea ointments and lotions, diets, hot air cures, rheumatism cures. On one occasion Mary wrote to Hannah: "I have heard of a cure for rheumatism and stiffness . . . you sit for an hour in hot black mud and are then stung all over by jelly-fishes . . . doesn't thee feel like trying it?"

But Mary was now turning more and more towards slimming cures, and new ways of shedding some of her ever-growing fat. She tried massage, diathermy, and any possible aid. "Please send me at once", she wrote to Hannah, "a box of that anti-fat soap. I may as well try it. . . . If it works it will certainly be more con-venient than all this dieting and exercise." She had to force herself to take exercise, and though she often started a diet, her devotion to good food was so overpowering that she could never keep it up for more than a few days.

During these years she had entirely thrown off the constant ail-ments from which she had suffered before Frank's death, and apart from a miscarriage in 1902, which she concealed from her worry-prone mother, she was hard at work and as healthy as she was happy. "I am happier than I have ever been," she wrote in her diary in April 1901. "Our house is beautiful and we get on *au mieux*." In August she wrote to Bernhard: "I think the future will be calm and happy." She added frankly, however: "I think it is absolutely necessary to serve [people] up with a sauce of affection —the great trouble is to make the sauce. We are neither of us good cooks, in that respect. I am apt to make too much sauce for a very few people; thee to spread the sauce too thin all round, for thy famous 'good will' doesn't warm thy heart much."

Her own goodwill was still directed towards Captain Jephson, who had lost his job as a King's Messenger through ill health, and was soon borrowing money he was annoyingly slow to repay. He was writing to Mary, but she was careful to assure B.B. that he need not be concerned as there was nothing in the letters that "even a jealous husband could object to". Although by 1903

Mary had become thoroughly bored with Jephson, as she had been in turn by Obrist and Blaydes, the friction with B.B. did not entirely vanish. The jealousy and mistrust which he undoubtedly felt, despite Mary's explanations, was not just of Jephson, but of Mary's divided heart, and of her loyalty to her family; this embittered all their relations in spite of their genuine love for and need of each other.

"I am so tired of addressing thee to London," wrote Bernhard, "and so tired of thy absence. Remember I am by nature a person who gets fonder of people when they are with him, and less fond when they are away." Mary complained: "Thee could make me even more devoted to thee if thee would give me the feeling sometimes that thee doesn't despise most of my ways and thoughts. . . . I struggle, and this is the whole truth, under a sense of being a burden to thee, of being too coolly 'seen through'. . . . It is rather icy at times."

He grudged every day Mary spent away from him with her family, and was always suspicious that she was telling him lies for their benefit or trying to "manage" him in some underhand fashion. In 1903, the year that Hannah became so lame, Mary postponed her return to Florence in the autumn by a week, to help her mother move back to London. Bernhard raged:

> You were to be away three weeks; now you propose being away another week. After 12 years you should know me; and know that I abhor all notion of being managed. . . . I wonder what leads you to suppose that I am so attached to your apron strings that the thought of being separated for 4 weeks is something I cannot look in the face. I frankly tell you, altho' I am very devoted to you I can contemplate absence from you with an equanimity that is entirely upset when you fail to "work up to contract time" or arouse the suspicion that you are trying to manage me.

Mary protested that there was no plot or "management" involved. " I *could not predict* before I came . . . how much stiffer and older Mother had got, and how Alys's illness made her what she never was before, dependent on me." On this occasion, at least, it was all perfectly true, but Bernhard's suspicions were not allayed.

In spite of this, B.B. kept his promise, and remained unfailingly generous to Mary's family. In addition to providing houses and allowances for his own family—whom, except for his sister Senda, he found almost as uncongenial as Mary's—he was always ready to come to Hannah's financial assistance whenever her irregular income was delayed, though Hannah hated to ask him.

Meanwhile he was beginning to look elsewhere himself. He had taken to spending his summers, while Mary was in England, at the bracing and fashionable resort of St Moritz, and there he developed a number of attachments. His growing affection for the dazzling Gladys Deacon, who later became Duchess of Marlborough, did not distress Mary, who found her as fascinating as he did:

> So beautiful, so brilliant [she wrote in her diary] with her "soft elixir ways"; her hard clear youthful logic . . . her lively imagination; her moods; her daring. . . . What will become of her? . . . She told me the Duchess of Marlborough was nearly broken hearted because the Duke made such love to her. Was it true? All in all I never knew a person who told so many lies as that beautiful and radiant creature.

Some of the other ladies he admired, however, were less to her taste, nor was the international aristocratic set, whose company Bernhard found so conducive to the exercise of good conversation. "Women," he wrote later, "especially certain society women, are more receptive, more appreciative and consequently more stimulating." Mary dutifully followed his lead, and entertained and was entertained by these friends, but she relieved her feelings to her mother during a visit to Cadenabbia:

> It is a great deception, as French people say, getting to know all these swells. I used to come here as a simple tourist and make dreams to myself about the wonderful great people who bore

these historic names and lived in these beautiful pleasure-palaces along the shores of the lake. Now, alas! I know how they actually put in their time—they stand on their terraces with spy-glasses and try to make out the passengers in every boat that puts onto the water. The rest of the time they gossip—not witty spirituelle gossip . . . but dull terre-à-terre remarks.

And on another visit she wrote:

Various princesses and marchionesses called and chattered from 2–6. The evening was a perfect burlesque, for they began to talk politics. Sometimes as many as 8 were shouting and scream-ing at the same time. B.B. and I sat shaking with laughter. No-one listened to more than the first words of the others; and quite often, for want of listeners, the chief shouters would break off right in the middle of a vehement address. . . . I truly can't tell thee what it is here, I sometimes feel as it couldn't be real it is such a parody of human intercourse.

Mary was always quickly bored by uncongenial people, and among B.B.'s fashionable friends she felt unappreciated and at a disadvantage, to say nothing of the element of jealousy involved. Unlike him, her thinking was so rooted in her own language that she never became really at home in any other, and furthermore her Quaker inheritance and growing embonpoint made her efforts to compete in matters of fashion unavailing. B.B. tried for many years, by moral pressure and bitter criticism, to force her to dress fashionably, but while she paid sufficient heed to his views to buy ever more elaborate corsets, and even to try to instil a clothes sense into her daughters—a highly unrewarding task—she never became truly interested herself. Her majestic figure and handsome profile, however, always created a noble, if not exactly elegant effect.

Most of their friends were still far from being fashionable, how-ever. They were English or American intellectuals or artists, for the most part, often impecunious and eccentric, and they were welcomed with unstinting warmth. The setting Bernhard and

Mary had created was already exquisite and luxurious, but it was far from snobbishly exclusive. Among their close friends, for instance, was Hutchins Hapgood, the American writer, whom they loved dearly and called "Fafner"; he was seeking, said Mary, "for God and the Absolute among thieves, anarchists, prostitutes and pederasts." And he found illumination in drink, though he could not persuade Mary to join him in his sessions.

"Trevy"—Robert Trevelyan, brother of the historian George—was another close friend; a wild, uncouth, delightful man who wrote classical poetry seated on rocks or under trees, dressed like a tramp, and was liable to plunge nude into any kind of water he came across, whether it was a secluded stream or an ornamental pond in someone's garden. At dinner one night, when B.B. deplored Matthew Arnold's use of the word "perform", he became suddenly incensed and threw his plate at Bernhard's head.

Their neighbours, Henry and Janet Ross, who owned the nearby medieval castle, Poggio Gherardo, became dear friends, although of an older generation. "Aunt Janet" was a fierce and formidable old lady. The story went that she had once horse-whipped Ouida for putting her into her novel *Friendship*, where she was portrayed as the hard selfish Lady Jane Challoner, who stole the hero from the heroine, Etoile. The story was probably apocryphal, but not unimaginable. Mary, being well used to formidable females, really liked her without being in awe of her, and Aunt Janet, in turn, became devoted to Mary.

Among the new friends they made at this time was one sent out to them with glowing recommendations from Bertie and Alys—Gilbert Murray. Murray became Professor of Greek at Oxford, and was already well known for his lyrical translations of Euripides. He was a singularly sweet-natured man, and the Berensons took to him at once. "We are enchanted with Gilbert Murray," wrote Mary to her mother. "Only B.B., who always takes his pleasures sadly, is raging at not having known him *ever* so long ago." Murray's taste in English literature, however, threat-ened to mar their instant sympathy. "Last night . . . a fearful gulf opened, a dark chasm between our spirits. It turned out that

Gilbert admired Dickens." This was nothing to the shock he had
for them a few days later.

I asked him [Mary continued] which in his secret heart he
preferred—Shakespeare or Milton. He replied that he did not
even consider Milton one of the greatest of English poets.
"Who are they?" we asked, and he replied: "Chaucer, Shakespeare, Shelley and—Tennyson ! ! !" A hush of horror fell upon
us, as if someone had thrown a smoking bomb into the midst
of the company, and we were all so frightened yet fascinated as
to be unable to move. Literally we gasped for breath . . . I went
to fetch a volume of his poems. This I handed to Murray and
asked him to read us some of the "real poetry". Mother, he
read "Come into the garden, Maud"!

During 1902 Bernhard finally finished his monumental work on
Florentine drawings. The effort had nearly killed him; he was
always delicate, suffering from crippling bouts of indigestion and
from what was vaguely called "nervous exhaustion". But the book
was, Mary proclaimed, a masterpiece. "This book of B.B.'s", she
wrote to Hannah in May, "is really a 'great work': I am myself
surprised at it. Nothing like it has ever been done about art, for it
is not only concerned with drawings but wanders off continually
into the most interesting and suggestive general speculations. He
has really achieved a thing to be proud of."

When the book was finished, the reaction was severe. Bernhard
was so weak that on one excursion to Siena he fainted on the
station platform, and Mary and the doctors urged that he should
rest. Not being allowed to work made him more nervous than
ever, and brought quarrels with Mary which in turn made the
nervousness worse. Mary seemed to be unable to avoid provoking
his frightening rages. In January 1903 she wrote in her diary:
"Came home to an awful quarrel with B.B.—our first for a long
time—over household affairs. We were both in the wrong . . . we
were both worn out with fury. The worst of quarrelling is that
we *can't* escape from each other after all these years, and we know
it." And Bernhard found himself unable to avoid venting on

Mary the fury aroused in him by other people. "B.B. received a letter from his publishers," she noted in March, "and was enraged indeed. He even tore his hair, and he wanted to write a letter that would simply end things then and there." When his anger was spent, he was full of remorse. "I found him in bed the other day, quite overcome," she added. "'I'm sick of being cross with you, Mary,' he said, 'but there is no-one else I *can* be cross with, and I've such a lot of crossness in me.' Fortunately I don't mind it, for I know it is tired nerves, and I always laugh at him."

He was engaged, too, in a long-lasting feud with Roger Fry, whom he accused of the usual art expert's crime of stealing ideas. Mary and Hannah tried, for many years, to heal this breach with a man who had frequently stayed at Friday's Hill, and whom all the family had come to be very fond of, but distaste for what he called "Roger's shallow way of rushing into print", and further and more violent differences prevented Bernhard from agreeing. One of the main battlefields was the newly-founded *Burlington Magazine*. Roger was anxious to involve B.B. both in the policy and in the financing of the new paper, but the editor, Robert Dell, favoured one of B.B.'s bitter rivals, and Roger's efforts to keep the peace were construed as disloyalty. This unfortunate episode left Bernhard with one of his almost irreversible rancours against both Fry and the English art world.

By the autumn of 1903, however, he was sufficiently recovered to set sail for America with Mary on a long business visit. They needed to find other wealthy buyers of Italian pictures, as Isabella Gardner's collection was now almost complete, and her purchases were becoming less frequent. They were anxious to convince potential patrons that this was their last chance to acquire Italian masterpieces at reasonable prices, and that Berenson's advice on the subject was indispensable.

The idea had been largely Mary's, and they spent some five months in America, moving almost exclusively among the people she called "squillionaires". They had both been full of doubts and fears about the likelihood that these "business barons", although providing possible sources of income, might be intolerably crude and uncultured. Here, as everywhere, they did indeed encounter a

great many crass mis-attributions by optimistic dealers and
gullible collectors, and Bernhard, to avoid ruffling the feelings of
the wealthy on the one hand, and telling lies on the other, was
often forced to respond with such non-committal ejaculations as
"Murder" and "Jiminy Whiskers". There was also much appallingly bad taste, of a kind described by Mary as "Sardanapalian",
and which, B.B. said, suggested an incredibly extravagant
brothel, but in spite of this they found themselves increasingly
won over by the sheer abundant energy, eccentricity and friendliness of their hosts.

Mrs Gardner herself was among the most extraordinary of the
people they met. Mary wrote home:

> Mrs Gardner came to lunch wearing lots of jewels, at least a
> million dollars worth. She said one of her friends had been
> robbed by her butler of all her jewels and this had frightened
> her so she had made up her mind to wear them all. She was a
> blaze of diamonds and rubies and pearls, and I think she had on
> sets of sapphires and emeralds under her dress, which looked
> very lumpy in spots.

In spite of the jewels, she had a number of miserly habits. "Mrs
G.'s pet hobby seems to be a hatred of spending money on light.
She saves up all her old candle ends, has only one light in her
drawing room and none anywhere else, not even in the halls."
She was also very jealous, and apparently entirely unscrupulous.
"We find", wrote Mary in January, "that [Mrs G.] is *determined*
to have no-one else in Boston but herself buy Italian pictures
through B.B. [and] she has done her utmost here to keep us from
meeting the collectors and to prejudice people against B.B. or to
warn them from approaching him 'in his delicate state of health'.
There is no lie she shrinks from."

Chicago, luckily, was beyond her influence, and a more fruitful
field.

> We went to a grand dinner [wrote Mary]. There were about 30
> people seated at table. . . . One of the men calculated for my

benefit that the "interests" represented at that table were about nine hundred million dollars. . . . B.B., quiet little uncle Bernhard, was really so witty and so very, very amusing that I assure you I felt a sort of pang at the thought of confining him again to the pokey, dingy society of Settignano! I in the meantime, was talking chiefly to the son of Abraham Lincoln, who as head of the Pullman car system "represents" nearly a hundred million.

As Mary admitted: "I daresay our heads are a little turned by flattery, for the reception B.B. gets here is very 'gratifying'." "It seems like a game played in a very diverting dream. Only, if we do, as I think we must, make money as the outcome of it all, I shall be glad, for we have an ideal of life that, alas, requires us to have enough money for ourselves and the people we love not to worry about it."

While they were in Boston they visited B.B.'s family, but Mary found them depressingly "life-diminishing". "The Berensons began to get on my nerves," she wrote in her journal of the trip, "and B.B. saw it, and was as nice as possible. He said he a little dreaded it for himself as well, as he can't do more than so much for them." In spite of this and of Mrs Gardner's machinations, Bernhard greatly appreciated their Boston visit. "I think he is really enjoying coming back to the home town where he grew up," Mary wrote home, "and being lionized by people bearing the names that all proper Bostonians are brought up to adore: Cabot, Coolidge, Kidder, Peabody, Parkman etc. They are mostly very nice people, too—interesting, particularly the men."

Mary was not so happy at returning to her own home town. "It was a great disillusion going back to Germantown. I suppose my fancy had warped my memory and made it all seem bigger and more splendid than reality. . . . It is socially very 'mortifying' to think of taking B.B. there, for I have trained him to believe that my *provenance* was really something very superior."

B.B. refused to lecture, so Mary took over, and wherever they went she spoke with great success. In Chicago she gave a talk on "How to tell a forgery", and, according to Mary, B.B. said that her delivery was "the best he had heard, simple, confidential but dignified, humourous and winning. (I have to tell you, no-one else will.)" She was offered a Chair at Chicago University with a salary of $3,000 a year.

Bernhard, too was offered a post. "There is talk of their offering the position of Director [of the New York Metropolitan Museum]," Mary indiscreetly confided to Hannah. "The salary is £3,000 a year; but not only will the talk probably come to nothing, but the position would to my way of thinking, be intolerable. B.B. is so in the flush of fast-coming impressions that he doesn't know *what* he thinks."

The suggestion came to nothing, and by March they were on their way home. "It has been an exploring visit, which is always fun", wrote Mary, "and we have found so much to like. Then we have amused ourselves so much together, talking it over—it has been a real lark from beginning to end." They brought back no major commissions to build other collections such as B.B. had assembled for Isabella Gardner, but the exercise unquestionably made Berenson better known and more highly respected in the circles where big money was spent on pictures, and their affairs continued to prosper.

BARREN TEARS

Alys and Bertie

WHEN BERTIE RUSSELL courted and married Alys he was still
wholly obedient to the strict puritan ethic in which he had been
brought up, even though he had abandoned the religious sanctions
which underlay it. He was austere, frugal and moralistic, and disapproved sternly of even the comparatively mild self-indulgence
of the Pearsall Smith household, while the sybaritic comfort
of I Tatti genuinely repelled him. "Returned yesterday from
Florence," he wrote in 1903. "The atmosphere of art and luxury
was rather trying to me, and at first I couldn't understand why I
had liked B.B., but gradually got to like him again." Even this
liking, however, was not of an uncritical kind. "If only", he
commented, "he would not permit himself the physical liberties
which Jews indulge in of touching one and putting their hands on
one's shoulder and so on."

He himself lived in what was then considered, for one of his
class, great simplicity. By 1908, Hannah wrote to her friends in
America, "Alys herself has come down to one general servant, and
now feels happy as she hated their having two servants just to
wait on herself and Bertie; especially as he hated it also. They
really come the nearest of anybody I know to leading the simple
life." Their one servant, moreover, was usually an unmarried
mother or some other beneficiary of Alys's charitable efforts—one
of her "cases", as the family used to call them. Bertie had given
away most of his inherited money in private or institutional
generosity. Among other things he paid for educating Alys's
cousin, Val Worthington; he secretly financed Evelyn Whitehead,
the wife of his friend and collaborator, in her struggles with her
husband's rash overspending, and he even made considerable
capital loans to his mother-in-law. Hannah wrote to Mary in 1910,
"Tell B.B. that I am more grateful than ever that he so very

kindly enabled me to pay Bertie the money I owed him, for Alys tells me that he took it out of his principal to lend it, and that they have been largely living on principal for the last few years."

In all this Alys was a more than willing disciple. She had capitulated slowly to the idea of marriage, but her capitulation, when it came, was total. She adored Bertie and thought him perfect in every way, finding in her care and love for him the full satisfaction of all her previous ideals of unselfishness. As Mary had noticed from the start, she adopted all his ideas and ways of life with enthusiasm, walking or taking buses instead of taxis, for example, and putting the money so saved to some virtuous use, and wearing Mary's cast-off clothes. They even reacted against the Smith love of good food.

In July 1900 Bertie and Alys travelled to Paris with Alfred and Evelyn Whitehead to attend the International Congress of Philosophy. "Alys and Bertie", wrote Mary to Bernhard, "have been having a great time at the Mathematical and Ethical Congresses in Paris. Alys made a speech against family life, which was translated and received great applause. *Il y a du vrai dans ses idées*— but of what isn't this true? . . . I fear she is philanthropical at heart."

Back at Fernhurst in September, Bertie, casting off the bonds of Idealist philosophy, which he found hard to combine with symbolic logic, and excited by the new ideas he had absorbed at the Congress, reached a moment of what he called "intellectual intoxication". The Whiteheads were still with them, and the discussions with Alfred sparked off a burst of energy and clarity which enabled him to bring his book, *The Principles of Mathematics*, almost to completion by the end of the year.

At the beginning of 1901, he and Alys moved to Cambridge again, to share a house with the Whiteheads. The two men were working in the same field of mathematical logic, and were gradually drawing towards the collaboration which was to produce *Principia Mathematica* a few years later. Evelyn Whitehead was an intelligent, elegant woman, somewhat given to over-dramatization and invalidism. One night in February, Alys and Bertie went out to a reading by Gilbert Murray, and came home to find that Evelyn had suffered a heart attack and was in severe pain. Alys coped with the resulting household problems, and Bertie's sudden appreciation of Evelyn's pain and of the loneliness of her relations with her difficult husband brought him a second "intoxicating" experience, half mystical and half emotional. He emerged from this, he said later, entirely changed in his whole outlook on life, abandoning Imperialism for pro-Boer and Pacifist beliefs, and experiencing a great upsurge of love for all humanity.

He wrote to Alys, who had to rush off to Manchester two days later on her Temperance work: "The day before yesterday seems to me such a remote epoch that it might be two months ago. I have to assure myself that it is not. Since the time of our engagement I have felt nothing so poignantly as the last two days." It was probably inevitable, in his newly uplifted state, that he should fall in love with Evelyn, though he never specifically admitted it. It was also probably inevitable that Alys should soon sense the fact, though she, too, never admitted it. "The Whiteheads have always been the best and truest of friends to us," she wrote to Mary after Bertie finally left her in 1911, "quite the contrary to that silly rumour about her flirting with Bertie 9 years ago which had absolutely no foundation." Alys never at any time found it easy to confide in anyone, even her dearly-loved mother, and she would certainly never have told Mary anything confidential. So she kept silence, while Bertie's intimacy with Evelyn throve.

Hannah deplored Alys's involvement on practical grounds, and wrote to Mary: "Alys says poor Mrs Whitehead is, they fear, gradually dying. She is a regular invalid now, with a trained nurse. . . . Poor Alys has the whole family on her hands, and I fear will have for the rest of her life." Her view of the cause of the collapse was typical. "Poor thing, she has literally thrown her life away with her tight lacing, and her absolutely unhygienic way of living, and she sees it now and is filled with remorse, but it is too late to remedy it."

Evelyn did not die, but the Russells stayed on in the Cambridge house for six weeks, and then moved with them to the Mill House at Grantchester, to look after the Whiteheads and their two small children. It was not until May that they were able to return to Fernhurst. Although Alys was depressed and exhausted, all was superficially peaceful and Hannah told her: "It is one of my greatest joys to see thee happy in thy married life, and I often feel like thanking Bertie for making thee happy."

Beneath the surface, however, all was not well. Looking back ten years later, Bertie maintained that the happiness he and Alys had hitherto enjoyed was false, and that the awakening was bound to come. Later still he admitted—in a passage he deleted from the draft of his *Autobiography*—"I now believe that it is not in my nature to remain physically fond of any woman for more than seven or eight years. As I view it now, this was the basis of the matter, and the rest was humbug."

In 1901, however, he had not yet entirely put humbug aside, and claimed many other reasons for his change of heart. He had come to loathe all Alys's relations, particularly Hannah, whom he regarded as one of the wickedest people he had ever known, and incapable of honesty or mercy. He saw many similar flaws in Alys, and with a conjugal frankness he was later to admit might have been unwise, he told her so, Alys adored her mother, and was made miserable by his growing dislike of her; but she still saw no flaws in Bertie, and continued to love him as before.

Bertie's moral training was still dominant. He would not have considered it possible to open his heart to Evelyn—a married woman with children, and the wife of his friend—and he freely acknowledged his continuing duty to Alys. The resulting unhappiness, however, gradually made it impossible for him to banish the problem from his conscious mind any longer. He tried to revive his flagging feelings for Alys, and spent an apparently affectionate summer with her. He was to give a course of lectures at Cambridge in the two winter terms of 1901-2 and in the autumn he returned to the Whiteheads at Grantchester, while Alys followed a little later.

His letters were most loving. He wrote to her on 6 November:

Dearest, thee gives me more happiness than I can say—all the happiness I have, in fact. . . . I love the absolute certainty that all thy thoughts will be magnanimous and free from all pettiness. Since last winter I have known that life without thee would not be possible. . . . I am fairly longing to see thee again. Separations grow more and more unendurable. I feel as tho' I could spend my life making love to thee and never work any more.

But when she joined him a few days later, Alys found life with the Whiteheads unaccountably depressing, and one November day when she and Bertie went bicycling to Newmarket, she gave way to her feelings of despair. Bertie suggested a doctor, but Alys refused, for fear that he would recommend a separation. By January Bertie was aware that his love for Alys was dying. He recalled in his journal, a few months later, a certain January day when he had made one final gesture of affection. He described it somewhat over-lyrically:

Anguish lay behind, sorrow and difficulty ahead. . . . But out of the snow two pale untimely primroses raised their struggling heads giving an earnest of better days to come. . . . Surely I thought, with the flowers and the nightingales, joy too will return, again love will gladden our hearts, and discord will be forgotten. . . . I took the two primroses from their bed of snow and offered them to her as a little token of love. Both of us were touched, deeply touched; but in our hearts we knew that they were lies, we knew that spring was gone and youth was dead . . . the pathos of her life lived in my imagination in that moment, and I longed with an infinite tenderness, to revivify my dying love. Almost I succeeded, but it was too late.

This poetic melancholy soon merged into a more down-to-earth frame of mind. A week or two later, as he described briskly in his *Autobiography*, "I went out bicycling one afternoon and suddenly I realized that I no longer loved Alys. I had had no idea until this moment that my love for her was even lessening."

Clearly his claim of total ignorance was unjustified, as, no doubt, was Alys's, but while Bertie was able to face his state of mind, Alys could not. She felt increasingly ill, and it became clear

that she was having a total breakdown. She went to Brighton to
stay with a lady doctor friend, while Bertie worked with terrifying concentration on the difficult final stages of his book. He
wrote to Alys:

> I am thankful thee is really going to have some treatment at
> last. I am terribly exhausted by the strain, and . . . my nerves
> are for the present completely shattered. . . . It will be a comfort
> during this terrible separation, to feel that thee is doing what is
> best for thee—especially as, for my sake, this separation, terrible
> as it is, is absolutely necessary.

This depressed Alys more than ever, and added guilt to her
other troubles: "I have been a brute of selfishness to weigh thee
down like this and shatter thy poor nerves . . . but when that
blank despair overwhelms me I cannot exercise any unselfishness
or self-control or fortitude. . . . I have tried so hard always to
keep thee well, that I cannot believe that it is I and only I who am
making thee ill."

She was still desperately clinging to illusion. In May she wrote:
"It is funny how my depression suddenly appears and disappears
for no reason at all. . . . I was growing very near to developing
the ridiculous delusion that thee no longer cared for me." But to
this Bertie made no reply. At her request they met for an hour or
two in early June—when, of course, she wept abundantly—and
then Bertie's letters suddenly became cold and impersonal. This
was a deliberate move on his part, with the conscious intention of
destroying her affection. "I am sorry I cannot write much about
myself," he declared on 11 June. "When one is requiring a great
deal of self-control, what Mrs Carlyle calls 'the new silent system
of the prisons' is better than 'all feelings'." And he signed himself
"Most affly Bertrand Russell" instead of his usual "Thine
devotedly, Bertie".

Alys was now seriously alarmed. When she returned to Fernhurst shortly afterwards, she asked him outright if he still loved
her; Bertie answered that love was dead. "And then in the bedroom," he wrote in his journal, "her loud heartrending sobs, while

I worked next door. . . . How she was crushed and broken! How nearly I relented and said it had all been lies! And how my soul hardened from moment to moment because I left her to sob! In the middle of the night she came to my door to say she was calmer now, and would hope—poor, poor woman."

Much later, Alys wrote her own description of the crisis:

I was very lonely at Brighton, but had had long and affectionate letters from Bertie every day, till one day in early June, when the letters became cold and formal and unloving. I could not believe it and felt very disloyal to our love to even suspect such a change. . . . I was not really prepared for his confession on my return to Friday's Hill that he had ceased to love me. . . . The shock of the statement was so terrible that I almost died, but managed to keep up outward appearances, and went off to Switzerland with Beatrice Webb for a three week aftercure. It was simply angelic of her to leave Sidney for so long, but as she was homesick for him all the time and I was utterly miserable, it was not a happy holiday. I didn't confide my trouble to her or to anyone, as I felt it was too strange and abnormal, and would injure Bertie's reputation, as well as hurt my pride. . . . I asked him to try to carry on a common life of mutual interests and pursuits and friendships, and I hoped, of course, to win back his affection.

And so they started nine terrible years of concealment and strain and bitter unhappiness for both of them. Alys would never admit that it was finished. She tried to commit suicide once, and had a number of breakdowns in the years that followed, before she could even begin to achieve real resignation. They moved away from Fernhurst, as Bertie could no longer bear to be near her family, and shifted from London to various parts of the country, and back to London, looking for some place where they could stop torturing each other. Bertie refused to live in Cambridge, although most of his friends were there. In 1903 he wrote: "Alys came to Cambridge for the night and was terribly unhappy because, being pressed and pressed as to why I wouldn't live in

Cambridge, I had to tell her . . . that she got on my nerves when she was with the Cambridge people." So they finally built a house in the middle of Bagley Wood, just outside Oxford, and there they at last achieved a sort of armistice, while Bertie worked with furious concentration on the *Principia Mathematica*, the book he was writing with Whitehead, and Alys made herself busy with her political and charitable concerns.

In 1903 Bertie came to the conclusion, supported by a doctor whom he consulted, that he ought as a last resort to try to give Alys a child—whatever its inheritance might be. It was *her* family characteristics he dreaded now, not his own. "Suppose I have a child full of Carey and Mrs Smith, and see all its faults being exaggerated! It may drive one or other of us mad, but probably it's worth trying." So he made what he called "the last possible sacrifice". Unfortunately, as he noted in his journal afterwards, it was "not adequately carried out, and failed totally. . . . I shirked my duty on that occasion. I ought to have been more self-forgetful." Since their break, as he wrote in his *Autobiography*, he had "no longer any instinctive impulse towards sex relations with her". Alys wrote: "I see that I must not tempt him to any physical thoughts, as I have finally realised a last great danger—he ought not to wish for a physical relation while he does not love me, or at least I must not allow it." "One good effect has resulted," wrote Bertie. "Her feelings won my respect, and I like her better than I have done for a long time." However he also noted: "I foresee that I shall be tempted to get into more or less flirtatious relations with women I don't respect." The question of children left a trace of unadmitted resentment on both sides. In later years, secure in the possession of three children of his own, Bertie accused Alys of being barren—scarcely a proven fact—and claimed she had told Evelyn Whitehead that he was "incapable of bearing children".

In his unhappiness Bertie was often both unjust and cruel to Alys. He accused her of jealousy, flattery, insincerity and triviality of mind—much of which was the result of her deliberately forcing herself to become the sort of person she thought he wanted, and being constantly aware of his criticism. He even accused her of stealing his friends, and when she finally did manage to confide a little in Lady Mary Murray, Gilbert's wife, he claimed that she had won her and Beatrice Webb over to what he called "the other side" by telling lies.

Hannah had brought up her family in the belief that jealousy was futile and positively sinful, and that people got as much love as they deserved, and no more; as a result Alys dared not admit her feelings of jealousy, though neither could she completely suppress them. At one time Bertie saw a good deal of a girl called Ivy Pretious, a friend of the Trevelyans. There was no explicitly amorous behaviour, but there were tête-à-tête dinners and long discussions of their emotional problems, and their friends, perceiving the danger, urged Bertie to be careful. The friendship cooled in any case when the Russells moved to Oxford, but Alys had been forced into an artificial cheerfulness which only led to more misery.

Alys behaved [wrote Bertie] under the influence of her utterly groundless jealousy, just as badly as at her worst. In this case, since her jealousy can hardly injure anyone but herself I have taken very little trouble to allay it. One day, after discovering various slanders she had been spreading, I found her so unhappy that my anger vanished, and out of mere kindness I began to assure her, quietly and seriously, that there was no reason for jealousy. Thereupon she swore she had no such feeling. . . . Her lies were so bland and so apparently candid that my heart hardened towards her again, and I have let her suffer without making any effort to comfort her.

She got more and more on his nerves:

She still says things that make me rasped through and through. . . . In some ways her illness makes things easier. When she is bouncing and metallic she is much harder to bear. Poor woman! When she is not present I am sorry for her; but when I see or hear her I become all nerves, and can think of nothing but the wish to escape. She is always bumping into furniture, treading on one's toes, and upsetting lamps; and mentally she does just the same thing.

When he could master his exasperation he realized himself that he was unfair, and as time went on he did become less unkind, and a little less self-righteous.

This journal [he wrote in 1904] gives an unduly bad view of A. I think she has improved greatly, and that I was for a time very unjust to her. She had most of the faults I attributed to her but she had many virtues that I forgot all about. She has shown great pluck, and a great desire, mainly successful, to be unselfish towards me. But she is still full of jealousy, though she never consciously acts on it. To many other people she is a great help, almost an inspiration; and she is the very soul of kindness to people who do not come into competition with her.

Alys's reaction to the long agony was far less analytical and more emotional. In 1906 she developed a lump in her breast and began to hope that it might be cancer. Six months later she wrote in her journal:

I have not written here for 6 years, but I have only been unhappy for 5 yrs and a month. Tonight it seems unbearable again after the disappointment of Dr Osler's "Nothing" yesterday. . . . Now my blissful hope of six months is destroyed —even the chance of death. I do so long to leave Bertie free to live with a woman who . . . does not bore him desperately and get on his nerves as I do. . . . Little duties keep me going from day to day. But they don't satisfy the awful craving hunger for Bertie's love. It is always there, the volcano, and at first it used to burst out very often in the most unpleasant scenes—tears, recriminations I fear—I don't know and don't like to remember, only there was always the great love at the bottom. Now I can control its expression and I have only made one scene this winter. . . . At first I couldn't live without kissing him every night and morning, and how well I remember that morning . . . after 4 miserable months, when he returned my kiss for the first time. . . . If only I could die—it's such a simple solution. And yet when I dream of it, the agony of parting from Bertie is too great. He is constantly in my thoughts in the daytime, the background of everything, and when I wake in the night I always breathe a wish for blessings on my darling. I think of him too at waking—at first, for several years, waking without him was such torture. Even now I feel frightfully jealous of the servant who sees him and often speaks to him before I do.

The next entry was two years later, in 1909:

Things are no better since I last wrote, and I wake up every morning wishing I were dead. The lump in my breast grew and began to hurt, in spite of Osler's optimism, and I was very happy . . . thinking it was certainly a cancer. Every day I felt it growing with the pang of joy a woman feels over a baby, I imagine, and it was a delicious winter of hope and hard work. I endured the pain as long as possible and finally only spoke of it thinking an operation would give temporary relief without ultimate cure.

She wrote to Mary:

I have had a pain in my side for several weeks, but I called it rheumatism and would not consult a doctor for fear he would stop my meetings and the Dance. However I finished up all my jobs and sent for Dr Brooks on Friday. He spotted the lump in my left breast (which Dr Osler said was nothing last June) and advised me to have it cut out next week, after Bertie's return. He thinks it is only a little gland pressing on a nerve, and that it will be a very slight business. I shall go into the Acland nursing home for three days, and don't mind anything except the waste of time and telling Gram. She will have me dead and buried in her imagination at once. But it really is nothing to worry over so do write cheerfully to her.

It was more serious than she made out, but her hopes of cancer were dashed again:

Then came the crushing disappointment [her journal continues] when Dr Brooks told me it was non-malignant. . . . Time drags, drags. . . . But things will seem different, I am sure, when I am old—perhaps at 50 I shan't mind so much. That is $7\frac{1}{2}$ years, like the $7\frac{1}{2}$ since May 1902. . . . Now I know that [his love] is gone, but the belief that it is there still lingers in my instinctive thoughts and in almost all my dreams—it is equally painful to wake from a dream in which he is my lover as from a dream in which he is scolding me—more painful, because more difficult to readjust myself to.

None of these feeling of Alys's were allowed expression. Bertie had been her only real intimate since the death of her cousin Madge, and lacking him she turned to no-one else, but devoted herself more and more to being what Mary stigmatized as "philanthropical". Though the family noticed that all was not well with her, she offered no explanation.

Alys made a very unfavourable impression on me the other day [wrote Mary in her diary in 1903]. She has gone back to her deadly philanthropizing and everybody is rubbed a little the wrong way. . . . The children scarcely like her at all, she has become so critical and lecturing. She says queer rude things sometimes. Altogether I feel as if she weren't all right somehow.

And she added, characteristically: "I do feel awfully sorry for Bertie."

Alys resigned from the Temperance post, as she found the Society too pious for her, and began to turn her attention more and more to Women's Suffrage. This interest Bertie shared, and for one short spell in 1907 she was able to stand by his side and speak at his meetings, when, at Wimbledon, he became the first candidate on a straightforward Women's Suffrage ticket. He thought it worthwhile to stand, though he had no chance of being elected, in order to publicize the Cause, which he supported with passion. His opponents' campaign was conducted with scornful mockery and some violence. Rats were let loose at one of his meetings; drunken women, it was said, were hired by the other side to distribute his election literature and discredit him; and Alys was hit by an egg—fresh, not rotten, she reported—which gave her a "not unbecoming lump' over one eye. This delighted her, as the opposing candidate was forced to apologize in the press.

Unfortunately, if perhaps inevitably, her continuing misery and reserve immured her in a kind of pillar of salt, driving her to become, in B.B.'s words, "a monolith". She was loved and admired by a great many people, as Bertie admitted, but the impression she made for many years on those who were closest to her was artificial and cold. Her nieces disliked her for her didactic ways and the insensitivity of her kindness. "Aunty Loo has asked me to spend this weekend at High Buildings," wrote Ray in 1903. "I was never more thunderstruck. I sent back word that I would detest it—not worded quite that way. I am afraid I was rude, but I wish to goodness she would leave me alone. There is nothing I loathe so much as that kind of thing—which is so kind but so horribly unwelcome." Mary looked on in sisterly amusement. "Alys is leaving today", she wrote to B.B. from Fernhurst, "after a very jolly visit. Ray, only, resents her activities into which she tends to drag others. Yesterday she planned 'a nice afternoon' for Val and Ray, taking them bicycling up to the top of Hindhead and sending them to tea at an inn. They both thoroughly hated it."

Part IV

THIRD GENERATION

MOTHER LOVE

Mary, Ray and Karin

MARY CAME BACK from America in 1904 full of energy and happiness. She admitted she had no great ambitions to do anything in particular, but she did "expect greatly to enjoy middle age, which as it seems to be turning out, is the best time yet". Day after day was more enjoyable than the last. "I never felt in better health," she told Hannah. "I am getting *too* jolly. Last night I woke myself up laughing so hard I had to bury my head in the pillows for fear of waking Senda [one of B.B.'s sisters]." And the following March she wrote: "I asked the doctor today if there is a name for the disease I have, which is being too happy, happier than my circumstances warrant. He said it was the first time a patient came to him with that complaint—but it is called in Asylums *Euphoria!*"

One cause of her enjoyment of life was the advent of the motor car, which both she and B.B. found an endless source of delight. Their friend Edmund Houghton owned a car, and was always ready to take anyone for a driving tour. After one ecstatic trip in June 1904, Mary wrote: "I felt 20 years younger, and as if I were perfectly new to Italy . . . that delicious *exploring* feeling we used to have . . . but even more so." B.B. also enjoyed sightseeing in this new fashion, though at first he rejected as rash and extravagant Mary's eager suggestions that they should buy a car themselves.

They therefore took every opportunity to go off with any friend who owned a car, most frequently with Carlo Placci and his nephew Louis Henraux. Placci was almost as quarrelsome as Bernhard, and by the end of these excursions the two old friends were usually not on speaking terms, but Mary's good temper and the adventures of the road carried them through. They invented a number of new Saints, whom they invoked in hilarious litanies on their way. There was Santa Cacciuccia (Saint Rubber) *ora pro rotis*, against the all too frequent punctures; Santa Clavina (Saint Keys) *ora pro portis*, to ensure that the custodians of the various churches and museums would be available to let them in; and finally Sant' Aquacloacina (Saint Watercloset) *ora pro locis*, to ensure essential hygiene.

Mary's letters were full of her affection for B.B., and how they would sit out in the garden, middle-aged though they were, holding hands like lovers. She was jovially prepared to admit her various shortcomings—that she was really too fat, and not chic enough for B.B.'s taste; that she had a managing nature, and was extravagant, untidy and apt to fall asleep in the midst of the after-dinner conversations; but life was too good, and she too confident, to worry unduly. She was still exchanging quack cures with Hannah: a deep breathing cure she tried to get Ray to adopt for her slouch; an Elixir of Youth; a magnetic Healer; and a wonder-ful new cosmetic which she described to Ray: "Grandma got a 'Wrinkle Remover' and I tried it last night. Karin came and gummed plasters all along my many wrinkles, and these I kept on all night. When I took them off—nothing had happened! Most disappointing and expected!" B.B., who was sceptical of even the most orthodox medicines, found her credulity deplorable.

The managing swirl in which she gathered up her less zestful friends, and showered her chosen benefits on them, was irresist-ible. They called her "Brunnhilde" or "Juno", and though her most flirtatious days were coming to an end she had no lack of admirers. "Fafner [Hutchins Hapgood] . . . stayed till midnight," she wrote in her diary in 1907. "He always wants to make love to me, but it bores me dreadfully." Obrist was now out of favour, and when he sent her a photograph of his latest sculptural master-piece she told Hannah: "It looks something like a potato and something like a disease; an excrescence of the tumour kind. The back of it looks exactly what they would call in the *Arabian Nights* '*un derrière de bénédiction*'."

Mary regarded people as though they were novels for her to read, or, sometimes, plays for her to direct. Like Hannah, she took her fiction "live". She could never resist an unhappy love affair, and would write all the details of the latest one she had come across in her daily letters to Hannah. All too often B.B. did not find her friends as fascinating as she did, for they tended to be lame ducks and neurotics, people with deplorable married lives or involved in some other emotional drama. She was not above stirring the pot if things were not dramatic enough for her, but she was liable to lose interest suddenly and pass on to the next fascinating set of characters, leaving the first lot in the lurch. None of her protégés, however, could promise such a fruitful field for manipulation as her own growing daughters. She was determined that each in turn should see something of "The World" under her aegis, and if possible acquire a taste for the art and "culture" which she herself found so delightful.

Ray was to come out to I Tatti for a long stay in the spring of 1905, between school and Cambridge, and her visit—providentially, in Mary's eyes—coincided with the arrival in Italy of one of the younger generation of Whitall cousins, Willie Taylor, who while too young for Mary herself, would be just right, she thought, for Ray. Both she and B.B. found the young man charming, and Mary wrote home of his intelligence, wit and general desirability with such emphasis and frequency that, in Karin's phrase, the whole family began to find the very thought of him "spuey". Undeterred, Mary built castles in the air of marrying Ray to this young American.

When she met the paragon, Ray took a much less favourable view, particularly disliking his opinions on the proper subservient function of women. She was a match for all her mother's manoeuvres. "Ray . . . is very severe," Mary wrote disconsolately to Hannah. "She does not seem to have the faintest leaning towards a flirtation. . . . It isn't IN her yet. If the old monster only held herself decently she would be stunning. But I find she has a sort of dread and horror of looking nice and attractive—I fear it is the fruit of thy preachings about Man, for she distinctly wants *not* to be attractive."

Mary swept the "Young People" off on a trip to Siena, despite B.B.'s advice to let Ray take her own time about things, and threw them alone together for hours at a time, lecturing them enthusiastically in the intervals about the works of art she wanted them to enjoy. Finally both Ray and Willie rebelled, turned on Mary together, and accused her of bullying and forcible feeding. Mary was quite unabashed, and promised to reform, but as she said, "whether with what they reveal to me is a very 'managing' and 'despotic' nature, I can control my impulses long enough to keep hands off, remains to be seen". Ray's diary shows that she found Willie comic and Mary's devotion to him abject and incomprehensible, but, she added: "I have certainly got endless fun out of Willie—far more than he liked at all."

The next treat Mary organized for Ray was much more successful. Edmund Houghton took them on a motor trip and taught Ray how to drive. She was ecstatic, and Mary lamented: "We did not stop to look at a single picture or work of art all the four days. Instead we devoted ourselves to getting swims for Ray and making her so proficient with the machine that today she carried it on all day entirely by herself. . . . She is quite motor mad." Mary rushed out and bought Ray all the necessary clothes, including "a real motor cap with the 'Eyes' sewed in, and a false nose, and all the rest of it". What Ray really liked, though, was lying in the muddy road underneath the machine trying to get it going again when it stopped—a pleasure which she had plenty of opportunity to indulge on their way to Venice. Mary's final comment on Ray's initiation was: "I am sorry she is not fonder of fun and gaiety, but still I don't see why I should force her to my ideas. Wait till I get Karin in my claws!"

Ray decided to turn the experience into a novel. She called it *The World at Eighteen*, and even Logan, the great stylist, thought it had merit. "Logan read Ray's story while she was in London," Mary wrote to B.B., "and to our intense surprise he spoke of it with real praise at dinner and said . . . that it was far above the average and had decided merit." With Logan's approval they sent it to a publisher, who found it was too long for a short story and too short for a novel. Mary, without telling Ray, put up £70, and it was published. Alys and Bertie disapproved, and Alys wrote to Mary: "I feel very strongly that that way of writing would shock

her Cambridge circle very much. . . . Though they are not *thy*
world, remember that they are hers . . . and Bertie and I both
know that they would be dreadfully shocked." Luckily no such
disaster occurred, though there were one or two awkward
moments with the American family, especially Willie's mother.
Willie himself came over to England and underwent a religious
conversion with the Cowley fathers, and this deprived him of all
interest in such mundane affairs as novels. In due course the conversion wore off, and Willie finished up, Mary noted, in the
profitable but thoroughly un-Quakerly activity of armaments
manufacture.

1906 was to be Karin's turn to "come out" in Mary's somewhat
unconventional fashion, but before the end of 1905 the girl was
struck down by the ear trouble which was to involve her in
numerous operations and leave her deaf and mildly disfigured.
Karin's character was very different from Ray's. She described
herself as "rakish", and although the conventional meaning of the
word was hardly appropriate, she certainly had a gypsy-like love
of noisy entertainments, bright colours and fancy dress parties.
She was also incurably untidy, tactless, and addicted to schoolboy
slang such as "ripping", "blubbing" and "good egg".

Her first operation, in December 1905, was entrusted to a distinguished aurist called Heath, who discovered that she had a
severe and long-standing abscess instead of the mastoid they had
expected. Mary came over to London to sit with her, and Logan
wrote her a cheering letter. "Thee will evidently be famous for
thy courage and for the operation itself. Thee will be like Uncle
Bertie whose real renown is not due to his Philosophy but to
something that was once done to his teeth, which has made him
so illustrious in the Dental world that he sometimes goes to
exhibit his mouth to amazed and admiring dentists."

Karin was indeed brave, and by Easter Mary was able to pro-
ceed with the plans for the second great social initiation. It was to
take the form of a "reading party", and to include Ray as well as
Karin, and Alys was commissioned to find two nice young undergraduates to join the party. After the first suggestion—Ellie
Rendel's uncle Lytton Strachey—had (perhaps fortunately) fallen

through, Alys came up with two highly satisfactory young men: Maynard Keynes from Cambridge and Geoffrey Scott from Oxford.

Mary took them all on a motor trip to Siena, and—for the young at least—it was all bliss. Mary wrote to Hannah:

> To them everything was fun—the scrappy lunches under trees in a drizzle, the arrival at cold carpetless inns, the horrible meals in the mud that, one day, simply covered poor Scott, penetrating even to his teeth and tongue, and covering his face with a yellow slime, the punctures (we only had two), the enforced changes of route . . . everything was the occasion for laughter and merriment.

Ray much enjoyed her mother's good spirits. "Mary was wonderful," she wrote in her diary.

> She talked all through those first days, in a perfectly delightful way, giving us . . . her views on life, youth and middle age, practical philosophy, art, love, duty of mothers and children, society, enthusiasm and standing up straight . . . with a continuous flow of conversation, all charming and often screamingly funny.

Ray found both the young men very congenial: "It is hard to say which was the nicer," she wrote, "they were utterly unflirtatious, which was an immense boon. They talked to me as if I were a reasonable being . . . [and] they behaved rationally and naturally just as if they had been clever, well-read girls." There could be no greater praise from Hannah's granddaughter.

Not that they were rational all the time. There were bathing parties where they had to wear underclothes sent across to the lake in a basket by Mary; Geoffrey and Maynard dressed themselves in ladies' knickers, and struggled over a pink-ribboned chemise. On the last night Mary provided champagne for dinner.

> They all got slightly tipsy [she wrote many years later]. Ray dressed herself up in Maynard's dress suit and Karin in an old

one of her stepfather, while Geoffrey wore a black dress of mine with a gold coronet on his head, and Maynard a gown of chiffon with a headdress of pink ribbons. . . . Ray got violently sick, and when I was putting her to bed, Geoffrey came running along stumbling in my lace dress and said: "I think you had better come to the salon as Karin is sitting on Maynard's knee and it looks as if they were going to exchange kisses."

This part of the story was not retailed to Hannah.

Karin had to go back to school, but Mary took Ray home by car and, stopping in Paris on the way, made another attempt to introduce her to "The World", this time the world of literary and artistic Lesbians. Mary came to think later that this was "a moment of peculiarly bad judgement", but Ray was merely amused—Maynard Keynes had enlightened her fully on the subject.

In 1904, when Hannah had begun to be confined to a wheelchair, the family had decided that it was essential to move her out of the tall and inconvenient house in Grosvenor Road, into a flat. Hannah found the idea of a flat a little "infra dig" at first, but succumbed cheerfully to family pressure, and once the move was over found it much more convenient. Two years later, after Bertie and Alys had built their house in Bagley Wood, a further family move was planned. The girls were now away from home most of the time, and they all felt that Hannah should not live alone. So Friday's Hill and High Buildings were given up, Hannah and Logan settled down in Court Place, a pleasant house on the banks of the Thames at Iffley, just across the river from Bagley Wood, and the large London flat was replaced by a *pied-à-terre*. Apart from Bertie—whose peaceful retreat was once again invaded by hordes of Pearsall Smiths—the only one to regret the change was Ray, who so loved the country round Fernhurst that she determined to return there to live some day—and did so. Meanwhile they still had one link with the village in Grace Worthington's cottage, Van Bridge.

Logan furnished Court Place with his usual good taste, and laid out a beautiful garden. There he finished his biography of

Wotton, which neither Hannah nor Mary found outstandingly interesting. He read widely and voraciously, but until 1912 his only output was "a slender volume" of poetry published at his own expense. He spent a lot of time sailing on the river, and interested himself in housing for the poor of the parish, and he would often stay with his friends, old and new, talking elegant scandal. He spent more time visiting than being visited, since the increasing importunities of Hannah's bladder complaint made her, she explained, a very intermittent and unsatisfactory hostess.

Despite failing health Hannah was undaunted. She discovered in 1904 that she had a County Council vote, and wrote to Aunt Lill: "I am expecting to hobble to the polls this week on Alys's arm and cast my first vote! It had been one of the dreams of my life to have a vote, and I am glad it is to be realized before I die." Her comments were as pungent as ever: she hated housekeeping; she thought fashion silly; she was always glad to see the backs of her dearest friends; and her politics became more and more revolutionary. "Yes, we did rejoice in the assassination of the Grand Duke,★" she wrote to Mary in 1905, "and we only hope there will be some more. I have always said that, Quaker or no Quaker, if I lived in Russia I should have been a Nihilist."

Despite her unorthodox views, Hannah had long been a considerable figure in the Evangelical world, and each time she published a book she received hundreds of letters and personal callers came seeking spiritual help. "My stream of company goes on streaming," she told Mary in 1906. "Somebody special for a private interview is coming every afternoon. . . . Does thee think London can possibly get along without me? But here comes another—I must close. This one is a missionary from America." They pursued her to Court Place, and she wrote to Mary in 1908:

> I had a worshipper here today. A lady who came out to see about taking Grace's cottage. She found out that I was *the* Mrs

---

★ The Grand Duke Sergei Alexandrovitch, uncle of the Tsar, was assassinated in St Petersburg on 4 February 1905 by Ivan Kalyaev, a member of the Social Revolutionary Fighting Organization; he had been notorious for his severity in implementing reactionary policies.

Pearsall Smith, and she begged so hard to be allowed just to look on my face, that Logan had to bring her in to my sitting room, and there what did she do but actually kneel down and seize my hand and kiss it, and weep, so speechless with emotion that she could only ejaculate "To think I should have this inestimable privilege." It was most embarrassing. I really began to feel a sympathy with God for the worship He has to put up with so often! Logan fled from the room.

She came in for a lot of mockery from the girls after that episode.

She began to look forward more and more eagerly to her approaching death and her welcome by her Heavenly Father. "If I should die, which of course is always possible," she wrote to Mary at the end of 1908, "what I should like is to be cremated, and no funeral and no weeping relations to gather round the bed. . . . I do not expect to make an edifying deathbed, and I would far rather no-one should 'gather round' it." And in April the following year: "I have forbidden you to mourn for me. You are not to wear mourning, nor shed any tears, or I will haunt you in the shape of a waterspout."

Alys was a tower of strength to the whole family. She went to endless trouble to find partners for Karin at dances, and chaperoned her whenever she could not accept a treat alone. Even Ray was less hostile:

> The talk at Bagley Wood is all politics and social reform and women's suffrage [she wrote in her diary in 1906]. How I hate it! I am not politically minded, Aunty Loo says. I think the phrase is a comfort to her. But we have been getting on better lately. I am less infuriated by her attacks on me, and in consequence I am better able to see her good points. And they are very good. She has a sort of audacious wit that seems to belong to her subconscious self, and she is simply made of kindness.

Ray did not keep her hatred of politics and Suffrage for long. Her friend Ellie Rendel had gone on to Newnham a year ahead of her, and Ray spent a lot of her time with the Rendels. She met

Ellie's grandmother, Lady Strachey, and her aunt Philippa Strachey, both active and impassioned Suffragists, and she was soon caught up too. The Rendel males, however, took an old-fashioned view of woman's place, and Ellie's father was very strict with her. All the ladies helped to organize the Suffrage "Mud March" in 1907, and Ray wrote to Hannah: "[The Rendel boys] were walking alongside trying to look as if they enjoyed it, and protesting that they didn't believe in Suffrage. I think they must have been rather sad at seeing a grandmother, mother, four aunts and two sisters walking in the mud for what they didn't see fit to approve of." Hannah lamented: "Had I only a Bladder that was alive to its female responsibilities I should have been in that Procession myself, being wheeled along in my Bath Chair."

Newnham was full of ferment for "The Cause", but Mary was disgusted at Ray's taking to the activities she herself had run away from with such relief, and wrote to her: "I am appalled to think of thy going in for politics in a 'serious way' . . . I am sure it will bore thee to death." She also strongly disapproved of Ray's choice of Mathematics for her degree, and indeed did not really like Cambridge itself. Ray was fascinated by the abstract nature of mathematics, though she was never particularly good at it, and only just scraped through with her degree, finishing 80th out of 86. "It is like a fairyland," she had written in her diary when she was seventeen. "It gives one a queer feeling of insignificance. . . . It is just the great solid and infinite truth standing calmly still to be realized." Mary could not come to terms with this choice. She thought it uncultivated and though of course she could never admit such a thing to Hannah—unwomanly. Above all it was disappointing. She had hoped to train Ray in art appreciation and writing, and introduce her to the kind of "cultured" society she herself would have loved at that age. She had none of Hannah's happy conviction that the young know best. However Mary hoped that once Ray had left the "dowdy, bluestocking atmosphere of Newnham" she could be softened and given social polish by a year at Bryn Mawr.

Karin meanwhile suffered one disaster after another. By June 1907, when she was eighteen, she had had five operations:

One on my right ear, one on my nose and three on my left ear. I am at present fearfully deaf, so bad, in fact, that life seems nothing but a torture unless I am to get better. I know I have just got to accept it . . . but it will be an *awful* struggle to come out happy. . . . I have always longed for a life among a lot of people, a social life with many friends and meeting strangers, and now I shun everyone I do not know well; I hate the idea of meeting people. . . . If I let myself I could cry with agony.

She followed Ray to Newnham in October 1907, but felt desperately isolated and miserable and wrote to Mary for comfort. "It is rather lonely here being unhappy without a soul to tell it to. Do you know I often feel, even when my hearing is going better for a day or two, as if I hadn't really any proper life left." Mary told Logan, when she got this, "Her letter upset me most awfully, and I am still quite ill and have to stay most of the time in bed." This, in turn, upset Hannah, who was more concerned with Mary's sufferings than with Karin's, and wrote sternly to the girl:

I am very anxious about thy mother's health and I am dreadfully afraid she will have a serious breakdown unless we can somehow manage to ward it off. . . . Now what I want thee to do is this—tell thy mother all about the ups and downs of thy hearing, for of course she must know this, but tell her as cheerfully as thee can. . . . Try and cheer her up . . . and if at any time thy depression should seem unbearable, I want thee to write all about it to *me* . . . and thy dear mother will be spared.

Karin managed to keep up her spirits remarkably well. Her hearing came and went, and unfortunately hearing aids were then not at all reliable, and awkward to use, some of them being almost as large as dog kennels. Mary was sure the climate at Cambridge was bad for her. There was much family discussion; Ray argued for the vital importance of serious education; Mary accused her of being priggish, and finally it was agreed that Karin, too, should spend a year at Bryn Mawr. Some of the best lip-reading teachers, Mary maintained, were in America.

Mary and B.B. were to go over for another client-collecting tour in the autumn of 1908. The girls went with them, and Hannah suggested, to please Ray, that Ellie should go too. Karin had no need of a friend since "Pug" Worthington, her cousin and old playmate, was already at Bryn Mawr. Aunt Carey obligingly found a scholarship for Ellie, and her father was persuaded to allow her to go. Mary was dismayed. She disliked Ellie, believing she had an anti-social effect on Ray, and now Ellie displayed a highly critical approach to all things American, particularly the educational system, and Ray could not be pried loose from her. Mary came to hate Ellie for spoiling all her hopes of making Ray into something more like a real "American Girl". The friction went on until Carey took the girls to a Suffrage Convention in Buffalo. There they enjoyed themselves in their own way, and made quite a success as speakers. They met a formidable old lady called the Rev. Anna Shaw, who had been a Methodist minister, a doctor, and a suffrage agitator; she and Ray took to each other at once, and Ray conceived the idea of joining her on a speaking tour. Carey agreed, after some reservations about the interruption of their studies, and they went off for several weeks on a trip that was both adventurous and educational, though Mary considered it a waste of time. On their return, Carey advised Ray to stick to literature for the time being, and work at her writing, since she showed signs of real talent, rather than embarking too soon on an active political career. Ray agreed to this, as she had developed a considerable admiration and affection for her strong-minded cousin.

Karin was as happy in America as Mary could wish. She was becoming reconciled to her deafness, and enjoyed the friendliness at Bryn Mawr, and the hospitality of her many cousins. She had won her mother's approval by taking enthusiastically to the Classics, and was now turning to the study of philosophy and psychology, which was taught at Bryn Mawr. "It is positively a life work," she wrote home, "and when you go into it with close attention a lot of it is very unsatisfactory and vague. Of course as yet Psychology is only at the initial stage and I suppose they can only talk vaguely about it." Ray and Ellie returned to England early in 1909, while Karin stayed on to finish the academic year.

In the intervals of her maternal preoccupations, Mary had enjoyed her visit to America. This time they made a good deal of money, with the prospect of making a great deal more. A few years earlier, in 1906, Bernhard had begun to correspond with the art dealer Joseph Duveen, and had made some tentative moves towards a professional alliance. On their return to Europe this was to take firm shape, to both Berenson's and Duveen's considerable financial advantage. B.B. and Mary also met for the first time, on this trip, a young woman who was to become very important to them: Belle Greene, secretary to Pierpont Morgan, and later curator of the Morgan Library.

The Family

AFTER THE FAMOUS reading party in 1906, Mary had kept in touch with Geoffrey Scott. Keynes she had found was too self-assured and independent, but Geoffrey had all the earmarks of her favourite kind of lame duck: he was young, handsome, highly educated, and very neurotic. She wrote to him twice a week, and invited him to Fernhurst that summer, and noted in her diary that when she went back to Italy, her "dear boy" had seen her off. He had not been a success with the family, however. Karin nicknamed him "The Quivering Freak", and Hannah was concerned lest Mary should impose him upon the girls again. Mary defended herself:

> I like him, it is the sort of mind and character that always interests me, and it interests me to see it so young, before it is grown up at all. But I see his defects and impossibilities very clearly, and am not particularly hopeful about his future. Unfortunately many of the people I like are lame ducks, sometimes I think that is why I like them.

B.B. had his doubts about the friendship, but Mary reassured him:

> I am most awfully sorry thee has had a second's uneasiness and distrust. I want never to give thee *that* kind—there are plenty of others inevitable to our two characters, but surely that is superfluous. But I entirely understand thy not trusting me, and I beg thee always to say out at once if thee thinks I'm not running straight. I told thee all there was to tell about Scott, and didn't mention him again because I didn't see him again.

Though he won the Newdigate Prize for poetry at Oxford, Scott did not do well enough in his examinations to get a Fellowship, and fell into a gloomy state. After his visit to I Tatti in 1908, B.B. never wanted to have him there again, but Mary was becoming more and more possessively attached to him and did not lose touch. Meanwhile another potential lame duck called at I Tatti: a young English architect called Cecil Pinsent. Mary's "maternal" urges took wing and she decided that it would be ideal for Geoffrey, who had exquisite taste but no practical experience, and who wanted to study architecture, to team up with Cecil and share a flat in Florence. The young men were willing enough, the more so as Mary was making it her business to find work for them. Their first job together was to be the alterations she and B.B. had decided on when they were finally able to buy I Tatti in 1907—notably the creation of a worthy library for his books. The plans were approved by B.B., who had a great desire to live "unsordidly" as he called it. He had, however, no liking whatever for practical details, and the work was put in hand while they were away.

On arriving home after spending the summer of 1909 in England, Mary's horror was great to find Cecil Pinsent in residence and the entire house in chaos. Luckily B.B. was still busy in Paris, where he was starting to work with Duveen, and he stayed away for much of that year. Luckily, too, he was now making so much money that the fact that everything turned out to cost twice as much as Cecil's estimates, while highly aggravating, was not financially disastrous.

There began a nightmare period of more than a year, when Mary struggled to get things straight and B.B. became more and more enraged. Cecil was good at planning on paper, but slipshod in execution, and hopelessly lazy about supervising the workmen. Geoffrey had excellent taste, but was even more indolent and lie-abed than Cecil. Faced with expensive workmen sitting around with nothing to do, and no instructions, Mary would literally tear Cecil from his bed at noon, and she conducted a running battle to prevent the young men sitting up late talking. Though it was the "Artichokes", as the family called them, who got all the blame, a clash between B.B.'s total perfectionism and casual Italian workmanship was inevitable.

Mary was ground between the millstones of B.B.'s fury—which rose to the point of apparent mania—and the impossibility of getting anything completed without re-doing it six or seven times. As time went on, she took to concealing disasters from B.B. to escape the ghastly "Black Serpent" days when his terrifying rages erupted. She wrote home daily as usual, and began to number her different "Woes"; these eventually reached a total of 300, and her unfeeling family used to read out each instalment as if it was a serial adventure.

Towards the summer of 1910 things appeared to be settling down. The worst disaster of all, however, was to come. B.B. had seen some water colours by a French painter called Piot, then living in Fiesole, and had bought several. Piot suggested that he should decorate the huge vaulted library Cecil had built with frescoes of Italian peasants at work in the fields. In a mad moment —supported by Mary—B.B. agreed, and even liked the sketches before the colour was put on.

Piot was left in occupation with his workmen and lapis lazuli grinders throughout the summer, and Mary, on her return, was greeted by even worse chaos than the preceding year. When she and the architects (who seemed to have taken up permanent residence in the villa) were at last allowed by Piot to see the masterpieces, Mary was appalled. "I took a furtive peep at the frescoes," she wrote. "They are so horrible that they must be destroyed." Both she and B.B. admitted that they had been rash, and after the most fearful struggles with Piot the things were finally concealed behind whitewashed canvas, and did not see the light of day for sixty-five years.

There were more absorbing matters on B.B.'s mind, however. During the summer Belle Greene, whom they had met eighteen months before in New York, came over to Europe, and B.B. fell desperately in love with her. He was overwhelmed, not so much by Belle herself as by the extraordinary strength of his own emotions. He poured out his troubles to Mary and she responded with improbable nobility. "I was really quite charmed with Miss Greene," she wrote to him at the end of August, "and wish this might be the beginning of a permanent relationship, such as our middle-aged, bourgeois souls sigh for. . . . I hope thee will make this into something lasting and agreeable. I shall certainly help thee." She went on, however, to advise him: "One thing, dear, I want to say in thy ear. Don't boast to her . . . especially not about thy own differences from and superiorities to the rest of mankind." B.B.'s replies were equally lofty: "I love you . . . fear not, dear one, and I feel so grateful to what you are and for the way you are taking this new situation—so simple, so natural, and yet from any conventional point of view so extraordinary."

He kept urging Mary to come and chaperone them in Rome, as Belle was terrified of gossip getting back to Pierpont Morgan, and he was much annoyed that she would not leave the villa until it was in order. Belle was not as much in love as Bernhard, and her return to New York left him in an emotional turmoil. Mary noted in her diary that she thought Belle an adventuress, whose pride had suffered by not being able to be "Top Dog" where B.B. was concerned. He and Mary agonized a good deal about the situation during the next year, and by August 1911 her nobility was wearing a little thin:

> I find it so extremely hard to keep genuine and profound about it [Mary wrote to Bernhard] that I am often tempted to give up trying and go back to the conventional attitude thee always took to my "affairs". . . . However I have started in that path, and I do not think it would improve things now if I turned back. But I assure thee the variations between intense sympathy and amused contempt this affair of thine has caused me to pass through have been most agitating.

And B.B. replied: "Your yesterday's letter, although far from sugar and spice, is the most hope-inspiring because by far the frankest you have ever written to me. At last you are beginning to have a glimmering conception that your copybook world of high notions corresponds but vaguely to realities."

In 1909 Karin returned from Bryn Mawr to Newnham to take her Tripos in Moral Science, the first part in 1910 and the second a year later. Although still devoted to parties and flirtations, she had really been bitten by hard intellectual work, particularly philosophy, which fascinated her. She had her moments of depression, and after one wrote to the family: "My spiritual influenza is quite gone. Helen [a college friend] says it is nothing but what is commonly known as the blues, and that many people suffer from it for weeks at a time. I cannot see how they refrain from suicide, for life is not so specially worth living even when one feels happy." For the most part, however, she was full of gusto and vitality.

In 1910 Bertie was offered a lectureship at Trinity College, which carried with it bachelor rooms in college, so he and Alys decided to sell their house at Bagley Wood and take a lease of Van Bridge, Grace's cottage in Fernhurst, where Alys could spend most of her time. When he had settled in at Cambridge, Bertie found that Karin's tutors spoke very highly of her and, to her mingled terror and excitement, he decided to coach her himself. Despite her deafness and the fact that she was doing three years' work in two, she got First Class Honours in the first Tripos in 1910.

Soon after Ray got back from America, she went to stay with Ellie at the Strachey home in Hampstead. Though she knew several of the Stracheys individually, this was the first time she got to know the family as such and she fell in love with them at once and for ever. There were ten children, of whom five had married and left home. Their father, General Sir Richard Strachey, had died the preceding year at the age of ninety-one, after a long, varied and distinguished career in India. They were a talented, eccentric and individualistic family, with somewhat farouche manners. To Ray their casual but friendly attitude seemed like heaven on earth after the well-intentioned probings of her own family. When she arrived at the house, she told Mary:

Lady Strachey was sitting by the fire warming her stockinged feet and reading the last novel by Stevenson. She hardly looked up from her book to greet me, though I had been away such a long time. She just said "Well, Ray, there you are," and went back to her book. It was the same when the two boys, James and Lytton, came in to dinner. They scarcely noticed me, but went on talking of their own affairs while Ellie and I talked of ours and Lady Strachey propped her book against the tumbler and went on reading.

Mary was horrified at such off-hand behaviour, and replied, "But Ray, *we* should have felt like hearing about your American experiences, and would have felt so glad to see you that nothing else would seem so interesting." That was just what Ray wished to escape from, and when Mary complained that she seemed to like Strachey ways better than her own, Ray admitted she did; there was no polite pretence about them. She would have liked to marry into the family, she told Hannah, but the only sons apparently available, Lytton and James, were not very hopeful prospects as husbands, and "ran away with all their legs the minute they espied a female".

However she made friends with the youngest daughter Marjorie, a wild creature and no beauty, possessed of a quite extraordinarily bawdy wit. Through her, and through Maynard Keynes (who had found Ray distinctly attractive) she got to know the Stephen family, and other members of what came to be called "Bloomsbury". These young people already had a reputation for being intellectual, unconventional and iconoclastic, but to Mary, who called them "Gloomsbury", they appeared merely boorish. Ray's description of her first "Bloomsbury party" was not, however, very alarming. She, Virginia and Adrian Stephen, their sister Vanessa Bell and Marjorie's cousin Duncan Grant made up the party. "We sat round the fire in anything but gloomy silence," wrote Ray, "in fact we talked continuously of diseases and shipwrecks and other such frivolous topics. Then we somehow fell to making noises at the dog, and this awe-inspiring company might have been seen leaping from chair to chair uttering wild growls and shrieks of laughter."

In the autumn of 1910 she invited Virginia to stay at Court Place. "Ellie and I are paralyzed at the prospect," she wrote to Mary, "and have tried to plan out every half hour of their stay. . . .

It will be exceedingly entertaining, anyhow." Virginia seems to have found them as strange—if not as alarming—as they found her.

> I am staying here with a remarkable family [she wrote to a friend], Costelloes and Pearsall Smiths. Mrs Pearsall Smith is a very spruce and practical edition of "The Quaker"* without any mysticism about her, though she, too, sheds a great light! . . . She unmasks all the hypocrites—how the Friends prophesy at dinner, out of malice, so as to cheat someone of a hot dish.

In fact Ray and Virginia got on very well, and Ray went to stay with her in her Sussex cottage, Firle, or in London, several times during the next few months. "I like Virginia exceedingly," she told Mary. "She was very friendly and told me about the way she lives and the people she meets and the things that seem important. It is a very fascinating, queer, self-absorbed, fantastic set of people. But they are very interesting, and she is also nice."

By the spring of 1910 Ray could not keep away from Suffrage any longer. She was invited to go "Suffrage-touring" with the Rev. Anna Shaw again, and wrote to Carey: "I want to go to Kansas and S. Dakota and to Boston and the South, and I want to go about listening to strange people and looking at strange books; I wish you were not so sure you thought all this a waste of time." After the tour, Anna Shaw came over to England, and Ray took her on a motor trip. She developed a passion for Ray, and urged her to come back to America as her disciple; Ray did not at all want to do this, and had a difficult time fending her off.

When she finally left, Ray once more obediently settled down to writing, practising her style with Logan's advice, and published a biography of Hannah's friend, Frances Willard. Ray lived quietly and happily with Logan and Hannah at Court Place, trying to get Hannah to tell stories of her youth, reading a lot and, when she felt the need of exercise, digging violently in the garden. She observed the other two with an affectionate eye:

* Virginia's Quaker aunt, Caroline Emelia Stephen.

Uncle Logan is very difficult to fathom, and I can't think why he takes an interest in living. He talks a great deal at meals, but it always seems to me as if he talked to fill up the silences and not because he has anything to say. Gram, on the other hand, never talks unless she has things to say. . . . We three living here make a very curious household, but as a matter of fact I know that we form a very successful household.

Much as she enjoyed writing, however, it was always to be only half her life—the other half was Suffrage. She was up in London canvassing, speaking and organizing with increasing efficiency and success during the two exciting elections of January and December 1910. Bertie still did what he could in support, and Ray reported from London: "Uncle Bertie has been here for two nights. We have had long and interesting discussions on politics and suffrage, and I *think* I agree with his views. One cannot be sure, for he puts things too clearly."

She set off enthusiastically on a caravan speaking tour with Ellie and other friends, and, to her disgust, was roped into attending a Suffrage Ball. She finally made up her mind to work for Mrs Fawcett and the law-abiding Suffragists, sure that the violent methods of the Suffragettes were not for her; she thought them "emotional, unscrupulous, unwise and dangerous". Hannah wrote to Mary:

The Militant women have decided that for the sake of "The Cause", Asquith will have to be killed, and it is all arranged who is to be the martyr to do it and to bear the consequences afterwards. Also they are going to set fire to the buildings where Liberal meetings are being held, and, I am afraid, even throw bombs. I *am* thankful Ray does not belong to that branch.

She was not Nihilistic in her views when it came to her grand-children.

In the autumn of 1910 Ray started to attend lectures on electrical engineering at Oxford—the first and only woman in the class. As with mathematics, she loved the work, although she did not think she would ever be a great success at it. "The engineering", she wrote to Mary, "is still *perfectly* fascinating—I could have stayed there contentedly for hours more. I was measuring the stresses in beams and the tensions in ropes and so on. . . . It's odd to find joy in such simple things, but I certainly do." She made friends with the demonstrator, a young bachelor from Cambridge, and went off to tea with him alone, thereby arousing fond but unfounded hopes in Mary's breast.

In February 1911 she cut off her hair, and felt much the better for it. She was still liable to childish rages when her elders tried to make her pay attention to her clothes and appearance. On one occasion, when she was forced to go to a fancy dress party, she went as—and in—a potato sack, and it was one of the charms of her new friends that they shared her lack of interest in fashionable clothes. Karin, on the other hand, adored clothes, though her taste, unless rigorously controlled by her mother, was somewhat garish and extravagantly colourful. She too had become friendly with the Stephen family, but oddly enough—in view of her total lack of interest in art—it was Vanessa and Duncan Grant whom she liked best, while Ray found Virginia more congenial.

When it was Karin's turn to attend a "Bloomsbury party" in Duncan's studio, she found it less exciting than she had been led to hope:

I felt that now indeed I was to see life [she wrote to her mother], particularly when Clive [Bell] announced that several members of the party were coming in Gauguin costumes and that our host would have practically nothing on at all. But when we got there we found our bold host amply covered in yellow cotton and buttercups in his hair, with a generous display of jaeger vest at the open neck, clutching firmly to a voluminous cloak. This was a come down, but my hopes of "life" were completely dashed when Ray and Ellie put in appearance in dirty white blouses and took up their positions in gloomy silence on the sofa. . . . Then the company settled themselves on the floor, and by the light of two dim candles and the fire, sustained a weary and wandering discussion on the relative values of belief in true and false propositions, till 2.15, when the lights were turned on and we dispersed.

Karin was now coming up to her final Tripos and was to spend the Easter vacation at Van Bridge, where she was to be intensively coached by Bertie. Alys was the hostess; Ray was to be there with her car, and they had arranged to start the vacation off with a "Philosophical" weekend with G. E. Moore and the third Strachey son, Oliver, who had been corresponding with Bertie on philosophy and who had just come back from India, where he had been working on the railways. He was now thirty-seven, divorced, with a nine-year-old daughter, and eager to return to the life of books, music and conversation from which he felt he had been too long exiled.

The party appeared to be a great success. They went for long walks during the day, and talked without ceasing. Ray wrote to Mary on the Monday (27 March 1911):

Sometimes it is philosophy, and then I sit in great amazement and my mind is pulled like an elastic string, and stretched to most unusual lengths. At other times it is books or people or mere wild speculations about life, and then I sometimes manage to utter a word. I think George Moore is one of the most charming people I have ever met. He sits curled up in attitude of prayer and puts his tongue out a long way when he makes a joke, and always speaks with the utmost sincerity and the utmost clearness, and ticks things off on his fingers, and has a perfectly charming smile. All these qualities that I have mixed up together make a charming personality, and I have quite lost my heart to him.

On Wednesday 29th she took up the story again:

Everything is going on splendidly and today even the weather is behaving well. . . . Oliver Strachey is very pleasant too, and we are a harmonious party . . . Karin and Uncle Bertie are pounding away at Hegel or Leibnitz or somebody—this feeling that work is being done adds greatly to the peacefulness of the atmosphere. As I write, Moore and Oliver Strachey are discussing Consciousness, and I am only writing with "one ear".

Both girls were much taken with the good-looking Oliver, but as usual Ray kept her own counsel, while Karin confided in Mary. After Moore left she wrote:

O.S. is a very charming person. . . . That night the talk became more personal. We got on to truth telling, and we were all very witty and Uncle Bertie was very moral. . . . Aunty Loo went to bed very early and we three found ourselves free with the evening before us. By this time Oliver . . . was no longer grown up at all, but absolutely one of us, so there was no shyness. . . . At midnight we scrambled some eggs and had an orgie [sic] with tea and toast and finally went to bed at 2 reeling with laughter at our own wonderful humour and feeling ourselves a perfect trio. He had to go in the morning, and it plunged us into gloom.

Behind this cheerful childishness and growing attraction, however, there was a quite different drama going on in the cottage. On the preceding Sunday, 19 March, Bertie had dined with Lady Ottoline Morrell in London. He stayed on after everyone else had left, and in the course of the evening they discovered that they were in love with each other. Bertie's barriers came down at last, and his eagerness alarmed even Ottoline. He urged her to leave Philip at once and come away with him, but this she refused to do, and next morning he had to travel to Paris, where he was to meet Bergson and deliver some lectures in French. He wrote sternly to Ottoline from there: "If you will tell Philip and let me tell Alys I can acquiesce in your staying with him." He also reassured her, as he had once reassured Alys, when she wondered whether she was intelligent enough for him: "You really need not trouble yourself about your exact degree of intellect. . . . No woman's intellect is really good enough to give me pleasure as intellect. But love is altogether strange."

Unlike the girls, he had not enjoyed the Van Bridge party. "It is horrible here," he wrote to Ottoline on that Saturday, 25 March, when they all assembled.

Poor Alys gets on my nerves to such an extent that I don't know how to bear it another moment. I always find her very trying after an absence, but this time naturally it is particularly bad. However I talked the whole time so that inobservant people would have supposed I had not an anxiety or a trouble in the world. Karin and Ray are both here. I don't much like Ray—I think she is exactly like Alys—kind, hardworking, insincere and treacherous. Karin is quite different.

Ottoline duly broke the news to Philip, who behaved throughout the affair with great tolerance and magnanimity. Bertie told Alys on the Monday night, and reported that she "took it very well". As the party broke up he was full of hope that she would accept the new situation. "I am sure, really, that she will be much happier when she has given up the struggle to make some sort of a life with me—otherwise I could not ask her to give it up. I mind her pain more than the pain of people I like better—it is like the pain of a wounded animal." But, reasonable as it might have seemed to expect Alys to recover, she never in fact completely did so. There was less misery than in the dreadful days of 1902, but to the end of her life she never stopped loving him.

Karin stayed on to work when the others left, and Bertie wrote: "Karin read me a paper on Leibnitz which she had done for me—a very good paper. She had given up, apparently, the Catholic practices which I am glad of. She is a nice girl—it is a pity she is so devoid of gracefulness. I had hoped to do something to take the place of a father to her, but the separation from Alys will prevent that." The next weekend Karin had some Newnham friends to stay, and he commented: "Karin and her friends make me feel terribly elderly and stupid. . . . One of them . . . is remarkably clever, but very self-centred. Why do clever people so seldom have satisfactory characters?"

Ray had gone to stay with Virginia Stephen again, at Firle. Virginia, as was her habit, cross-questioned her about matters of the heart, and Ray was unusually forthcoming.

We went out once [wrote Virginia to her sister Vanessa] and got bleached and drenched; she floundered like a calf. However the talk proved interesting. Here comes a piece of gossip which you *must* keep private. Talking of Oliver Strachey, she said: "I can imagine falling in love with him." I said "I suppose you mean you *are* in love with him." She said "No; I only see that it might be—but I don't want to be." I said: "Is he in love with you?" She said: "Oh no—not a bit. But he was very friendly." This morning, however, she had a letter from him asking her to go over some railway works. This evidently pleased her. I'm pretty sure there will be an affair in that direction, she is either in love or on the verge of it. . . . Ray told me that she is very susceptible to men, though no man has been in love with her. She always stakes out the ground, as she calls it, with a new man, and considers the possibilities. "Could you marry Adrian [their brother]?" I asked her. She said that would be impossible. She is a good satisfactory creature, as downright as a poker, and very queer in the tremors of imagined love. But perhaps one would find her a little heavy?

A day or so later she added further news. "I've had letters from Ray. . . . She says fate is interfering with her plans—can Oliver have proposed? . . . There can be no doubt, I think, about her side of it . . . but I thought there was something on his side too."

Easter in 1911 fell on 16 April, and Ottoline was spending it at Studland, in Dorset. Bertie was determined to join her, but as Logan had invited himself to the Morrells for the Easter weekend, Bertie's visit was put off until the Tuesday. By coincidence, Ray too was proposing to spend Easter with Ellie in lodgings in Studland. Everything there was full up, so they went on to the neighbouring village of Corfe Castle, where at the inn they discovered Lytton Strachey—afflicted with mumps, growing a beard, and being very incompetently nursed, first by his brother James and then by Oliver. Ellie, already depressed at having failed to get a job she had hoped for, was even more cast down by Ray's pleasure at seeing Oliver, and developed a mysterious form of temporary blindness, so that Ray had to lead her about with her eyes shut. However Ray and Oliver contrived to meet often enough to arrange to correspond, before Ray returned to Court Place.

On 18 April, the Tuesday after Easter, Philip Morrell, who was now an M.P., had to go up to London. The same day Logan left Studland for home, and Bertie arrived from Van Bridge. Philip returned on the Friday, and Bertie then left, lurking in a teashop opposite the station as Philip's train drew in. As Logan commented in his thank you letter to Ottoline: "Now I think of it, how much Studland was like the scene in a Dostoievsky novel, where everybody in the story turns up for every occasion."

Bertie and Ottoline had spent three days alone together, and were now more in love than ever. Bertie went straight to Cambridge as term began that Friday and Karin too returned to Newnham. There she saw a good deal of Oliver, who was sharing lodgings with Lytton, and she found him more and more attractive. After one party she wrote to Mary: "Oliver was there . . . but as soon as he came up I was shy. . . . I spent the following night before I went to sleep thoroughly disconcerted with myself for the foolish things nervousness had made me say. . . . I no longer feel in love, although I feel very friendly."

Logan spent the weekend after Easter at Van Bridge with Alys, and they drove back together to Court Place, inspecting a possible country house for the Morrells on the way. Alys said nothing to the family except that she was sleeping badly and needed rest, but Ray, who by now was writing to Oliver almost daily, could not help noticing her unhappiness. "Aunty Loo, I believe, is having a real breakdown," she told him, "but she says she knows all about it and wants no sympathy. She is most reasonable—but cries all night and most of the day when she gets alone."

On Wednesday 27 April Hannah had a slight stroke, and though at first it did not seem serious, it soon became clear that she would not recover. Her last note to Mary is dated 28 April. "I am not at all depressed," she wrote, almost illegibly, "but rather cheered at the prospect of paralysis." And when Logan said to her at one stage: "I really don't believe, Mother, that this was anything but an attack of indigestion," she turned on him quite fiercely and said: "Thee's not very *encouraging*, Logan." Mary was cabled for, but Hannah died just before she arrived, on 1 May, aged seventy-nine.

Ray wrote to Oliver:

There is nothing to be unhappy about for her sake, for it could not have been more exactly what she has always wanted. But for me it is dreadful. You see I have lived with her since I was 12, and had a letter from her every day I was away. She was always in the same place, always interested and always approving. She never made a claim of any sort, either for attention or affection, and we all knew that what she really wanted was for each one of us to please ourselves in every way. And all this was quite unfailing—never once even in the smallest thing was she unlike this. You can see what an awful blank she leaves. . . . It is very dreary to think I shan't be able to report to her and get her comments. They were always so entertaining as well as wise and sympathetic, and she was such tremendously good company.

Karin was, perhaps, less sorrowful; besides, her Tripos was just coming up and she soon left the mourners and returned to Cambridge. As Bertie told Ottoline: "Karin wrote to say she found herself no use at Iffley so she was coming back, and wanted her lesson tomorrow. I gathered, reading between the lines, that the family gathering was on her nerves."

Hannah's death, temporarily at least, broke down the barriers between Ray and her mother. Mary wrote to Bernhard a week later:

Ray talks to me for hours and hours and I am gradually feeling that she has a very strong and sweet and reasonable character. She says that this winter alone with Grandma and *Miss Willard*, and many hours of leisure, have liberated her mind and steadied her more than she can express. . . . She tells me that she may marry Oliver Strachey. . . . They seem to understand each other, though they had apparently not spoken of love, and Ray means to go on with her work.

Mary passed this item of news on to Karin, who answered: "I wonder whether I am really to have Oliver for a brother. I shall be satisfied of course, but I wish they would come to the point." And a few days later: "If Ray doesn't seriously want him I should like him back here in Cambridge. If she does, of course it must be hands off, I suppose, though it is jolly if he finds me attractive. Of course I wouldn't want to marry him; don't worry about that, he's too old. But I fancy he fully understands the fine art of not being very serious."

She did not have long to wait. Ray wanted Mary to meet Oliver before going back to Italy, and took her over to Cambridge where they picked him up and drove back to Court Place. There Mary's curiosity was maddened, as she told Karin:

What does it mean? Surely he would not come over at this time quite openly as Ray's guest if he had no "intentions"? I feel quite like the conventional English mother—only I daren't do anything. Except I did make Ray change her dress last night and put on that grey one, at which she said "O the devil". . . . I said "It does seem a shame for a nice looking girl not to care a bit for her appearance." She was quite cross with me and said "O no, it is an immense relief." If he can stand her appearance *now*, he is safe. Her face is spotted like the pard, and she *won't* brush her hair.

The problem was that Oliver, although by now as much in love as Ray, felt himself, as a man with no job, no prospects and a nine-year-old daughter, to be in no position to propose. So Ray took action. Mary wrote: "One evening . . . Ray and Oliver, who had gone boating on the Thames, returned very late for dinner. We laughed . . . but had to accept their explanation that they had been attacked by a swan." Oliver went into more detail to Karin: "Ray proposed to me the day before yesterday and I accepted her. This is a fact, though not put quite as I would wish. Very well. Ray's version is as follows: We were very happily situated between the sewage station and the lunatic asylum at Littlemore, and the place was so romantic that it couldn't be avoided."

There was a terrible scene with Ellie, whose emotions had been far more deeply involved with Ray than Ray's with her. Oliver told Ray that on their first meeting Ottoline had classed her with Ellie as "An Anti", that is Anti-Men. "But", he added happily, "I put her right about that." Now, however, Ray was really worried about Ellie and wrote to Oliver: "She's in a very bad state and I really don't know what is to be done. . . . She *must* see the thing straight. . . . Her letters are so tragic and it's hard to know what to say." Oliver replied briskly: "One can only hope she'll get over it. . . . I don't see how we can get away from the fact that it is me you are going to marry, not her. . . . I'm afraid if you decided to marry Ellie and live with her instead of me, *I* should feel a good deal upset." In the end Ellie was persuaded to take a rest cure and gradually came to terms with the situation and decided to train as a doctor. There were further emotional disturbances, however, when the Rev. Anna, who had proposed to come over again that summer, had to be put off, and told why.

Mary started dreaming of a white wedding, but Oliver soon exploded that.

How you could have visualized her in a wedding dress beats me [he wrote to Mary]. I have tried for hours but in vain. I can conjure up the whole scene—me in a frock coat and lavender gloves, Karin and Ellie as bridesmaids, the Rev. Anna officiating at the altar, you weeping in the front pew, Logan very much embarrassed in the background—everything except the figure

of my Ray in a wedding dress and orange blossoms. That won't
come.

So they stole away quietly to Cambridge, where they got married
by special licence on 31 May, with only Karin and Lytton for
witnesses.

When Bertie heard of Hannah's death he told Ottoline how much
he had disliked his mother-in-law. "The most sordid thing I ever
went through was the death of Alys's father—but most of the
sordidness was made by Mrs Smith's avariciousness. The only
comic relief was when she sold the old man's teeth to a second-
hand dealer." Ottoline was more charitable: "I only saw rather a
nice side of the old lady, but I can quite imagine the other. . . . She
was very nice to me and very fond of Philip, I think." To which
Bertie replied: "I believe Mrs Smith improved greatly in her last
years—I only saw her about twice a year lately. But when she was
more vigorous she was terrible." He was not quite so critical of
Logan:

> Logan has a lot of good in him, but like everybody else who has
> suffered Mrs Smith's influence, he is warped more or less, and is
> lacking in some of the elementary things that one naturally
> takes for granted. When I was young, I liked him a good deal,
> and he had a very good influence on me, then it ceased. At
> times I still like him a good deal, and then his wanton cruelty
> and his prying put me off. . . . But in many ways he is very
> likeable, and I know no one whose wit delights me more.

Alys knew well how much Bertie had hated her mother—he
had never been one to withhold critical comments—and his
conventional offer to join the family at Iffley after her death,
instead of placating Alys, aroused feelings of filial outrage, and
added intolerably to her grief.

After the busy days at Court Place, dealing with Hannah's
cremation and writing the necessary letters, and after the excitement of Ray's engagement and Mary's departure, Alys returned

alone to Van Bridge on Friday 19 May in a very depressed state. She had not seen Bertie now for a month, and when he came down the following day there was a terrible scene. Alys claimed that she had not known about the Studland visit until Logan told her; Bertie told Ottoline that he found this hard to believe, but Alys could only have heard of the visit in this way; Bertie had written to Ottoline on 8 April: "If I come after term has begun . . . she will not know I am away from Cambridge. In any case, unless from detectives, she will know nothing. I told her once for all that I would tell her nothing further."

Now Alys was tortured by jealousy, and at first furiously anxious to hit back at Bertie and Ottoline. Bertie wrote:

> It is dreadful here—much worse than I had anticipated. Alys is very wild and very miserable. She talks in a strange way— moments of terrible and heartrending sincerity, and then long times of noble sentiments. She began in great anger, threatening divorce. Gradually, however, she grew quieter. She is very anxious to tell Logan—evidently his friendship for you galled her beyond endurance. Would you mind Logan being told? . . . perhaps he had better be. . . . She refuses to live with Logan but is filled with dread of loneliness—and it does seem a very awful prospect. She asked me whether if she had a child I would acknowledge it . . . she says I am utterly unhuman and cruel, and I hardly know what is the truth. I only know it is a world of misery that she lives in, and that I feel infinitely sorry for her, and yet powerless to give her any real help. . . . If only she wouldn't say her *sole* wish is to keep me from wrong-doing.

On Sunday 21 May 1911 Alys returned to Court Place and told Logan about Ottoline. She had not wished to tell Ray, although she could not hide things entirely, for fear of disturbing her happiness. Logan rallied to her support at once, and throughout the week there was much discussion and to-ing and fro-ing between the principals and mutual friends, such as the Whiteheads. Logan, despite his taste for gossip, was, Bertie and Ottoline agreed, "old-maidish" and profoundly Victorian in his moral outlook—or

perhaps it would have been truer to say, in his respect for convention. He was shocked and disturbed by Alys's condition and, like
her, much upset by his mother's death.

On Tuesday 23 May he went up to London to talk to the
Morrells, and warned Ottoline that what she was doing was
wrong, and that she would lose his friendship and that of many
others if she persisted. On his return he wrote to her:

> It was a great grief to me to say all the things I did yesterday,
> and I fear I was too hard and bitter. . . . If I was, please forgive
> me and put it down to the feelings of a brother who has been
> the helpless witness for years of his sister's misery. . . . I am
> inclined to think that I shall advise her to make a complete
> break. . . . My hope and belief is that her love and respect will
> change . . . but I do not think . . . that with her principles she
> can be asked to connive for long at things of which she very
> much disapproves. If Bertie believes in and practises freedom in
> sexual relations, he may be perfectly right from a moral point of
> view but he cannot of course ask a person who does not share
> these beliefs to act as cloak and protection to him. . . . I hope
> that Alys will be able eventually to get entirely and perfectly
> free in some manner that will involve the least possible amount
> of suffering—there would be no thought, of course, of ever
> involving anyone we loved.

A divorce involving Ottoline would have meant a lot of publi-
city and would have damaged Bertie's academic career and
Philip's political ambitions, as well as Ottoline's reputation.
Bertie was understandably uneasy, and Logan's letter, despite its
explicit rejection of such a course, did not reassure him. "Logan's
letter is un-thought out and absurd," he wrote to Ottoline. "How
does he suppose Alys can get free without involving you? . . .
How absurd to say I believe in freedom in sexual matters—I
neither believe in it nor have practised it." He had, indeed, been
technically faithful until now, but whether he then or later
believed in "freedom in sexual matters" was, perhaps, a matter of
definition.

By the end of the week Alys had regained her self-control and her balance. On Sunday 28th Logan went over to call on the Morrells again at the house of a mutual friend where they were staying, and again warned them of scandal. Ottoline wrote: "On the whole he was very nice. . . . Alys, too, is much calmer and does not, Logan now says, wish to separate us or to damage me. But he has succeeded in alarming . . . Philip very much about scandal, and this depresses me dreadfully for at present it will make it difficult for us to meet."

Next day Alys and Logan went over to Cambridge to see Bertie, and agreed to a formal separation, but not a divorce. Alys had refused to consider a divorce with bogus evidence—which had been Logan's solution—and Bertie, in his almost paranoid state, could see no reason for this refusal other than a jealous desire to ruin Ottoline. Alys was a fundamentally generous person, with a strong sense of the need to be unselfish, but at this stage she had not yet lost all hope of recovering his love, and did not wish to close the way. As she wrote to Mary:

> I realize that the situation is impossible any longer. But it is too awful to make this change just now when I have lost Mother too—I feel as if I were cut in half. . . . Bertie cannot force his love, and I cannot live with him while he feels as he does. But he easily changes, and I do not give up all hope for the future, as I still love him very, very much.

Apart from trying to prevent Ottoline from seeing Karin, on the grounds that she would be an immoral influence, Alys did not speak or act with ill feeling towards her, and wrote dignified letters to all their friends explaining that the separation was on account of incompatibility. Logan, however, could not forgive the Morrells, and his twenty-year-old friendship with Philip, which had grown to include Ottoline, withered into an irrationally spiteful hatred.

Bertie still sometimes felt guilty about Alys, and wrote to Ottoline in July: "Being with Lion [Phillimore] whom I have known since before I became engaged to Alys, has vividly recalled to me the early days of my love for Alys, when she was young and happy and blooming and full of unself-distrustful kindness. Now she is broken, tortured, twisted, with no self-confidence, no hope, no purpose. It is all my doing." At the same time, however, he came to hate her whole family more and more savagely, and accused them of every kind of dishonesty and vice.

> Every word they utter is a lie [he wrote to Ottoline in August]. If one didn't remember that one would lose all one's friends. . . . Curiosity is with them a raging passion—what with others lust or drunkenness or morphia might be. They will do *anything* to satisfy curiosity. It is far stronger than love. If Alys had to choose between regaining my love and knowing all my movements she would choose the latter.

Apart from Alys and Logan, the rest of the family were quite prepared to remain on friendly terms. Oliver wrote a cheerful letter to Bertie announcing his marriage:

> Ray and I were married last week at Cambridge; the only amusing incident was that the clerk's republican sentiments would not allow him to enter "Sir" as part of my father's name, but when pressed he put it down as his occupation. I hope that we will see plenty of you: perhaps you won't mind my saying that I should feel very much disappointed if any of the domestic troubles which seem to be to the fore should make any difference between us. Ray agrees with me in this.

Bertie answered warmly enough, but was more concerned about Karin.

> Karin [he wrote to Ottoline] thinks she has done badly in her Tripos. I shall be greatly disappointed if she doesn't get a First. She said she would be more sorry for me than for herself if that happens. I wondered to myself whether it was the last time I should ever see her. I mind very much about her. She has more philosophical capacity than I have ever seen before in a woman,

and now will probably give up philosophy. . . . She will be left to her mother and very likely go to the dogs.

Karin did get her First, and also got the first "Star", or Distinction, in Philosophy to be given to a woman at Cambridge. And she did not lose touch with Bertie.

In later years Bertie seems to have wrongly remembered Mary as having written him a cutting letter refusing to have anything more to do with him, and quoting B.B. as feeling the same. In fact, although Mary was sorry for Alys, she did not greatly blame Bertie, and wrote in June of the same year to thank him for helping her daughter, ending: "I won't say anything about the decision you and Alys have come to, except to send you my love and sympathy in all you have suffered in it, and to assure you of B.B.'s and my continued friendliness and goodwill."

DISCORD AND HARMONY

Ray, Karin and Mary

MARY WAS NOT unreservedly enthusiastic about Ray's marriage. "There is generally a Strachey or two to lunch," she wrote in her diary just before the couple left on their honeymoon, "but I am afraid I am not greatly exhilarated thereby. . . . I think Oliver is going to be—*difficult*. I am afraid I like him less and less, but perhaps things will take a turn for the better."

Ray and Oliver paid a short visit to the villino on the I Tatti estate on their way to India, where Oliver was to clear up his affairs and finally resign his job. Mary procured a piano for him, as he was, Ray said, "like a parrot with a rug over his cage" without one, and wrote to Alys about her worries: "I find myself obliged to give R and O their tickets to Marseilles and £30 for travelling expenses besides all their shopping etc. They haven't got a penny left. It really troubles me—not the fact but the idea and the future."

They sailed in October 1911, taking Karin with them, and quite soon Ray found to her delight that she was pregnant. Karin enjoyed herself with the polo set at Oliver's station, Dinapore, and then went off to Calcutta and Burma on her own. This was the year when George V and Queen Mary visited India, and the royal Durbar train was to pass through Dinapore. Oliver, as Traffic Superintendent of the railway in his area, had to pay his respects to the King Emperor in a tail coat, and Ray wrote to her step-daughter Julia: "Your father has at last got the red cloth for the King's feet, and a wonderful tail coat for his own back. We neither of us knew what a tail coat looked like, and the native tailor didn't know either, but with the help of a picture and a great deal of imagination, we have produced the article, which is wonderful to behold." It turned out that they had omitted to

give the coat a slit up the back, so that it looked very odd indeed—
which amused them, if not the King.

Ray was not well during her pregnancy. She did not like India
at all, and was delighted to get back to Europe in February. Mary
wanted her to have the child in Rome, but Ray was adamant that
it must be England, so Alys took them in at Ford Place in Sussex,
which she and Logan had rented as soon as they managed to get
rid of the Iffley house.

Alys was already dealing with one of the more difficult problems facing Ray and Oliver: the care of his ten-year-old daughter,
Julia. Deserted by her mother, she had not won much affection
from the Rendels, who had been looking after her, and Alys
wrote hopefully to Mary: "What the child needs is a loving home
atmosphere such as Ray could give her. . . . Her fearfully careless
and heedless ways make her difficult to live with. . . . If possible
she *must* be kept from growing up like Marjorie Strachey or like
Karin in the old days." But there were problems: it would be too
much for Ray, so Oliver's sister Pippa thought, "and for Oliver
too," added Alys, "who requires a great deal of attention and
doesn't want to give much." Finally Alys agreed to adopt Julia
herself, and try to train her in good manners and consideration for
others. The arrangement satisfied both Alys's conscience and her
frustrated maternal instinct, and it provided a convenient solution
for Ray and Oliver, but for Julia herself it was less ideal. As Alys
freely admitted later: "I am afraid I have been a horrid companion
to Julia, but I feel I *must* correct her for her careless selfish ways,
and she naturally resents correction." Alys used to advise Julia to
practise cheerfulness by keeping her mouth turned up at the
corners, as she did herself, thereby making of her face, Julia wrote
in her memoirs, "a desolate rigid mask . . . on which, in reality,
there was already in those days stamped a most pitiable and barren
desolation".

Mary was greatly excited at the thought of her first grandchild,
and took it for granted that the line of family matriarchs would be
continued. "It would be too amusing," she wrote to Alys, "if
Ray's child were a boy." But there was no such slip-up; a
daughter, Barbara, was born in July 1912, and Ray was able to

write to Carey: "I was so glad to get your congratulations. I knew I had pleased you by producing a daughter."

At first Oliver tried, with no great enthusiasm and less success, to find himself a job, but he and Ray finally decided to give up the idea and to write a book on Indian history together, living on Ray's income and her allowance from B.B. Ray wrote enthusiastically about the effect of their decision on Oliver's state of mind and rather shaky health, and on their domestic arrangements: "We have agreed that he is to do all the food and food bills and everything appertaining to meals, and I am to do the rest. . . . Oliver is reading cookery books and anxiously discussing . . . how to use up scraps, and I believe he is going to make a great success of it." Unfortunately, as was all too often the case, she was being too optimistic. He could think of nothing to order but a fresh leg of mutton and rice pudding every day, and Ray soon had to take the whole thing over herself. Not unexpectedly, perhaps, their way of life met with universal family condemnation, and Ray was forced to defend her husband vigorously for not taking a paid job. Peace was finally restored, though the question of money was to remain a thorny one.

Mary could not resist showering presents of money on both her daughters. Bernhard was perfectly willing to be generous, but his goodwill was undermined by the rash and reckless way in which Mary did her giving. She would not limit herself to providing a straightforward allowance, because that gave her no continuing personal satisfaction. She would urge the girls to tell her every time they had some large expense in view—house repairs, a new car, a holiday, or whatever it might be—and she would then happily settle the bills for them. She would also think up extras to throw in when no major expenses were planned, such as theatre tickets and taxis, hams from Fortnum and Mason's, a fur coat, or over-lavish toys for the children. Neither Ray nor Karin approved of this system, but though they protested they did not refuse the money, both because they needed it and because, in any case, Mary could not be stopped. And so the gifts went on, and grew more impulsive and more frequent as her addiction grew. Finally she took to concealing her expenditure from Bernhard, running up debts that he was forced to pay, as well as spending all her own income. Her extravagance, and above all her concealment of it, drove him almost mad with fury. Nor, of course, was it very good training in economy for the recipients. Ray was in any case rash and spendthrift with money, and always in financial difficulties, though this never worried her in the least. She was always sure that things would come right in the end, and sure, not without reason, that if she had to she could earn whatever she needed by journalism.

Karin was not naturally such a spender nor so optimistic as Ray, and did not get into debt. When she got back from India she took to philosophy again, and renewed her acquaintance with Bertie Russell. He had shaved off his moustache to please Ottoline, and Karin described his new appearance to her mother: "You can't imagine how fearsome he looks clean-shaven. He looks many times over cleverer; impishly, diabolically. He has an unendingly straight upper lip which comes to a point in the middle. I can't give you any idea of it but it isn't human. . . . Strange man: what a wonderful Inquisitor he would have made."

She was elected to the Aristotelian Society, and invited to read a paper in defence of the theories of Bergson, a bold position for her to take up in view of Russell's fierce opposition to them. This was well received at a meeting chaired by Bertie, and she later expanded the paper into a book, *The Misuse of Mind*. She also went to Paris to visit Bergson himself and was much gratified by his praise for her clarity and powers of comprehension. But she was not sure that she really wanted to be a professional philosopher, and she still hankered after the study of abnormal psychology.

Staying in Forence the following year, 1913, she found herself plunged into an emotional turmoil with Geoffrey Scott. Mary's attitude to Geoffrey was theoretically maternal, and she had encouraged him in a number of somewhat neurotic love affairs which he had faithfully brought back to lay at her feet. Now he fell in love with Karin, and Mary, while protesting that it would be madness for them to marry, nevertheless could not resist encouraging the affair.

Karin did not like Geoffrey, and while she was no more mal-

leable than Ray, she was less resilient, and became really upset at
the pressure Mary was putting on her. "If one has anyone on one's
nerves and holds them almost in horror, what can one do?" she
wrote almost desperately in her diary. ". . . I do wish to goodness
Mother had never conceived this unsuitable notion that we should
be friends—he never was the kind of person I could grow fond
of." Finally she fled to Munich pursued by reproachful letters
from them both.

Back in London she began once again to meet the people Mary
still called "Gloomsbury", and to report her findings to the
family. She also described the Stracheys, among whom Ray was
so happily at home:

> I called on Lady Strachey and found the whole family gathered,
> Ray puffing at her pipe; Oliver and James playing separate
> picture puzzles, savagely repelling outside interference;
> Marjorie with an emerald green Post-Impressionist tie, gesticu-
> lating wildly; Lady Strachey sitting silent opposite Oliver's
> silent (and puzzled) friend from India, home on leave; and
> Pippa holding the floor describing at great length a National
> Union open air meeting in Hyde Park.

Unlike Ray, Karin loved parties, particularly the dressing up
and acting that was such a feature of the Bloomsbury variety.
She told Mary of one such party:

> Oliver and I went as Karsavina and Nijinsky (he in a red ballet
> costume and I in a piece of purple satin and a wreath). We
> enacted Spectre de la Rose with much success. We followed
> that by the ballet of Job, in which Keynes, as the devil, poured
> boils in the shape of cherries upon the writhing Roger Fry. . . .
> Then came Lytton's play acted by Clive, Marjorie, Vanessa and
> Duncan. It was a wildly twisted take-off of the actors them-
> selves, exquisitely finished, very witty, and not exactly
> proper. . . . I have become a Gloomsberry, there is no doubt
> of it.

This was an unduly sanguine view. Virginia and Vanessa, and above all Virginia's recently-acquired husband, Leonard Woolf, did not find her entirely congenial. Virginia wrote about Karin a few years later in her perceptive but caustic diary: "I can't help being reminded by her of one of our lost dogs. . . . She fairly races round the room, sniffs the corners of chairs and tables, wags her tail as hard as she can, and snatches any scrap of talk as if she were sharp set; and she eats a great deal of food, too, like a dog." She was no less caustic about Ray, though she liked her a good deal better: "She has the look of conscious morality which is born of perpetual testifying to the right," she wrote in 1918. "She has lost such feminine charm as she had . . . but she is made of solid stuff; and this comes through and pleases me."

Karin became aware, during the summer of 1914, that Virginia's brother, Adrian Stephen, was falling in love with her. Adrian, then thirty-one, was an intelligent but somewhat lethargic young man, who had had a difficult childhood; losing the mother who had adored him when he was twelve; deeply disliking his father; always overshadowed by his charming and favoured elder brother Thoby, and after Thoby's early death by his two gifted sisters. He was alarmingly inarticulate, ineffective and overgrown—six foot five in height—and had not managed to persevere in any line of work, trying in turn to be an actor, a doctor and a barrister. Karin was not in love with him, but was swept away on a kind of silent tide, and—while war broke out almost unheeded—found herself first engaged and then married to him by the end of October.

Their honeymoon in St Ives, where the Stephen family had been so happy in their childhood, was a total disaster. She liked him, and even admired his character, but felt guilty at not being romantically in love, while his restraint and kindness, when all she wanted was to be swept off her feet, only made things worse. It all ended in gloom and tears, and when they got back to London Adrian even offered to divorce her at once if she wished. They decided against this, however, and moved to Cambridge, where Karin had now been given a Newnham fellowship. Adrian's own rather perfunctory efforts as a barrister could, they felt, be put aside for the moment. "In the circumstances," she wrote a year later in her diary, "no place could have been worse chosen. Cambridge in wartime was the lowest circle of the Inferno, a desert of gloom, empty of undergraduates and peopled by soldiers and acrimonious dons. We saw almost no-one and there was nowhere to go and nothing to do. I wept nearly every day and Adrian was in despair."

From the outside all that was visible was mess and muddle. Alys's reaction to their household was typical. "My dear," she told Mary, "K's bedroom was like a tenement room—rough unpainted boards, dormer windows with torn curtains, beds unmade, slops unemptied, pyjamas, boots and indescribable muddle on the floor, a bag of fruit, pepperpot and confusion on the commode—it was awful."

As the sun began to shine in the spring of 1915, however, things improved, so much so that Karin and Adrian finally became as affectionate as love-birds. Ray went down to visit them in May, and found them "almost absurd the way they hold each others' hands and kiss in corners." And Oliver's sister Pernel, who was a don at Newnham, said that when they walked together, the lofty Adrian and the short, solid Karin looked like "a giraffe curling down and a young bird poking up". The outcome of their new peace and happiness was that in January 1916 they had a daughter, called Ann ("A girl, thank God," commented Mary).

Ray had wanted a second child as soon as possible, but a miscarriage brought about by her own carelessness upset her profoundly, and it was some time before she regained her usual cheerfulness. Meanwhile the war had started and Oliver, who was now forty, was taken on at the War Office to work in the Code and Cypher department. Here at last, shrouded by the Official Secrets Act, he found the sort of work he enjoyed, and which— in that pre-computer age—he was outstandingly good at.

In 1916 Ray succeeded in starting another child, and their son Christopher was born in November, while Oliver was on a duty trip to Egypt. He had been out of touch for weeks, but Ray, to Mary's disgust, seemed totally unconcerned, though she might well have worried had she known that Oliver's ship had been torpedoed off Cyprus, and he had only been saved by great good luck. They were in fact very happy together, but nothing would have made Ray, the oyster, discuss her feelings with her mother.

Meanwhile the pendulum had swung back again. Ray had become bored with Indian history, and returned to Suffrage work, in which, to her delight, Oliver joined her. On the outbreak of war she transferred her energy from Suffrage to the more urgent task, she told Mary "of placing women in various 'war works' and trying to see that they are used in such a way that they don't ruin the whole labour market by taking low wages". "Don't despair over my doing it," she urged Mary who, remembering her own impatience with Frank's work never became reconciled to Ray's taste for politics and public life, "it's not really a vice, but a satisfaction. And whatever you may say in abuse of democratic politics and all the turmoil of it, its legislation does actually affect the lives of people, and make them different."

While Ray and Oliver plunged at once into war work, Karin and Adrian, like Lytton Strachey and Bertie Russell, declared themselves Conscientious Objectors. When conscription was introduced, Adrian was summoned before a tribunal and directed to take up work of national importance. So to satisfy their consciences, he and Karin collected some friends, and took over a dairy farm producing pure milk for babies—a job for which they had, of course, no experience, no talent and, as soon became apparent, no taste. After a year of chaos and discomfort, they were permitted to transfer to agriculture proper, where they toiled on until 1917. Then Adrian had a severe breakdown, affecting his heart, and was finally allowed to take less physically-exacting clerical work.

Mary and Bernard (he now preferred to spell his name without the Germanic h) were utterly outraged by Karin and Adrian's attitude to the war, and a really bitter quarrel developed, in which B.B. was only with difficulty prevented from stopping Karin's allowance for good. Indeed he never really warmed to her after this, and objected strongly to Mary inviting them to I Tatti, at any rate when he was there himself.

Ray's work, however, he approved of, and gladly provided the money for her to buy a little car. Ray was becoming more and more effective and important in the women's movement. She was now engaged in great battles with the War Office over their attempts to inflict unequal pay and totally unsuitable conditions of employment on the vital women workers in munitions; she was conducting equally urgent negotiations with the big Trade Unions on their behalf, and also lobbying politicians of all parties on the forthcoming National Service scheme. Finally as 1917 drew on, the Suffragists turned all their energies to the new Representation of the People Bill, which in their opinion had to be steered firmly towards some inclusion of the women's vote. Ray herself was largely instrumental in persuading all the warring factions of the women's movement to combine peaceably enough to push the measure through. As she wrote to Mary: "I often thank Heaven for my equable temper, for some of them are extraordinarily trying."

All this she was enjoying enormously, and wrote to Mary:

Pippa . . . and I have wound ourselves into the very thick of the intrigues, and we found ourselves dictating the leading article of The Times one day and sitting up till 4 a.m. preparing draft schemes for Mr Neville Chamberlain the next. . . . I am packed so tight with interviews that I can hardly breathe, and find myself panting from one Cabinet Minister at dinner time only to breakfast with another the next day.

With the success of the Bill, the Suffrage campaign was effectively won, even though so far the vote was only given to women over thirty. Early in 1918 Ray watched the final scenes in Parliament:

It was a thrilling day. We hurried from the Commons to the Lords, where the final ceremonies with cocked hats and red coats and swords took place—Black Rod and the Ushers and the Clerks, with the wigs and the bowing and the walking backwards and the French words and great rolling periods: it seemed really quite impressive—perhaps only because the occasion was really a great one in its way, and we were all moved by it. . . . When the moment actually came we all caught our breath a bit, and looked at each other . . . and then I skooted [sic] off in my car to tell Mrs Fawcett. . . . She was sitting up in a dressing gown by the fire—and we couldn't either of us believe it was true.

Ray had long admired and loved Millicent Fawcett, the leader of the "law-abiding" Suffragists. She had worked closely with her since before the war, and had come to be her principal lieutenant. She wrote more openly of her pride in the great event and of her feelings about the war to her than she ever could to her mother:

I don't know why I find it hard to talk about, but that does happen with things one cares for dreadfully—and ever since I was a small child England was one of those things for me. I'm not really English, and perhaps that's why I've noticed it so much. . . . I often think to myself with a real pang of pleasure that I have married an Englishman and have English children. And of course *now* that feeling has an intensity that it's hard to combine with tolerance—except that tolerance itself is an English thing.

To the surprise of the Suffragists, who had expected a far longer delay, a further Act making women eligible to stand for Parliament was passed in November 1918, only three weeks before the first post-war election. It was a terrible rush, but sixteen candidates were put forward, and Ray was one of them. All of them, including Ray, were defeated except Countess Markiewicz who, as an Irish Republican, refused to take the oath, and therefore never took her seat.

All these activities meant that Ray needed help with the children, help which Alys was delighted to provide, and which Karin was also eager to use. There were four grandchildren: Ray's son and daughter, and Karin's two daughters, Judith, born in 1918 and a true Whitall woman from the first, fiercely energetic and formidably cheerful while Ann, the elder, was a pure Stephen, very lovely, with the same Nordic good looks as Virginia and Vanessa. She was insecure and defeatist however, and cried far too much, which the rest of the family put down to Karin's neglect. As Alys wrote to Ray: "Karin had nothing to do all day and yet only sees Ann for about 15 minutes, and has no idea of her food or habits. It is very odd. I think she is fond of her in a way, but not interested [nor] with a feeling of responsibility. Ann is at a very fascinating stage just now [she was about eighteenth months old at the time] and I could play with her for hours, but Karin is soon bored." Ray too was concerned: "It is *very odd indeed* about Karin's children," she wrote. "It seems to me that if you neglect them you must at least assure yourself of the competence of the people you leave them with. But she, while inordinately fussy in theory, is as careless as possible in fact." Ray herself was not only a far more responsible mother, but a far more loving one—not surprising perhaps, in view of Karin's own unloved childhood.

Ray's son Christopher was a complete Strachey, all sensitivity and intellect, who was heard explaining to his nurse at the age of five what a gradient of one in four meant, and who used to insist on playing imaginary three-dimensional noughts and crosses in his mother's bed in the early morning. But in the Whitall tradition it was Barbara, as the eldest girl, who was favoured by the older generation. Ray said of her when she was a baby: "Barbara . . . is a monster. She grows and grows and has the appetite of—her mother and grandmother—and a great brick red face and bellow-ing voice and stamping feet, and the energy of Uncle Horace in a 'happy' mood." This was the kind of child Hannah would have approved of, and so did they, even though she was hard to manage. Mary, happily recognizing her own image no doubt, wrote to B.B., "I find that I feel the greatest elan of instinctive love for Barbara *when she is naughtiest*, screaming 'I want, I want' and beating one with her little fists. It is such a vigorous assertion of her separate personality that it vivifies all mine." Unfortunately such approval—such fellow-feeling, perhaps—was not conducive to discipline, and Ray tried to keep the child away from Mary as far as she could, which was not very far.

Naughty or not, she was the first, the titular, grandchild. Alys wrote to Mary in 1918: "Beautiful Ann and sweet Christopher and darling Judy will be enough for thy first day, though of course no child ever quite comes up to Barbara," while Mary admitted: "There's only ONE grandchild, the first, who excites the full rapture of surprise and hope and effort. The others lag behind and are only the same thing again, more or less." It was not, of course, a real child that Mary wanted, but the affirmation of her own continuance.

Alys, on the other hand, was genuinely fond of children of all kinds, and when she and Logan moved from Ford Place to a beautiful Tudor farmhouse on the Solent, called Chilling, she would fill the house for months on end every summer with Stracheys, Stephens, the three children of their friend Desmond MacCarthy, and any others whose parents could be prevailed upon to send them, particularly when the air raids started. Logan was very tolerant of these hordes, while Alys was careful to protect his quarters, which were known as "Ogre Point" and he as "Uncle Ogre". He had bought a yacht when they lived at Ford, and one of his greatest pleasures was to sail it round the south coast with a crew of two and selected guests. Among these, Karin, who did not suffer from seasickness like the other Whitall women, was the most enthusiastic.

Logan had taken British nationality in 1913, after rejecting the idea three years earlier in disgust at the fuss over the coronation of George V. Impertinent persons suggested that the real reason for his later change of mind was a snobbish desire to become a member of the Royal Thames Yacht Club, which would enable him to fly the exclusive Blue Ensign on his yacht, instead of the Red Ensign of the Merchant Navy which was all he was permitted as an American citizen.

He still spent most of his time in seclusion, reading, assembling the anthologies in which he delighted, and producing essays on various stylistic and vocabulary points for the Society of Pure English, of which he was a prominent member. He tried to get Henry James to join him in a "Lingual Manifesto" for this body, but the Master was unwilling to sign any public pronouncement. Logan was invited to his house in Rye, however, and wrote to

Alys when he got there: "It is very neat and old-maidish and comfortable, and exactly the place Henry James ought to live in. . . . He loves talking, and if you give him time for all his parentheses and qualifications and little touches, he gives you in return portraits of people and places and incidents that are quite like his writings."

When the war broke out, Logan and Alys felt that they needed a house in London as well as their summer home in the country, both for social convenience and as a base for their work for Belgian refugees. As Aunt Lill had finally died and distributed her money among the family they were in a position to afford both, so they took a tall house in St Leonard's Terrace, Chelsea, over-looking the gardens behind the Chelsea Hospital, and lived there until Logan's death in 1946.

Logan was eager to see more of Henry James, though they never became really close, and James always referred to him as "Poor Logan", though without explaining why. A meeting was arranged, however, between Karin and James's niece, Peggy, which elicited a polite and typical note from the Master: "What I can extravagantly participate in with you is the brave fact of our having such an admirable pair of nieces, and the charming luck of their taking to each other in such evident amity."

When Henry James came to fall ill, Alys sent daily reports of his ups and downs to Mary. "He is confused most of the time," she wrote in January 1916, "but he has gleams of sense, and remarked of some American cousins, the Van Burens of Albany, that 'they loved bereavements and good cookery.'" When he died Logan declared to Mary: "I do miss Henry James very much. There is no-one to tell certain things to, no-one with whom to crunch certain bones and extract the last sweetness from them. . . . He was a most extraordinary and delightful person, and one will never see his like again."

Logan had been assembling more *Trivia*, and rewriting the old ones, and in 1917 a new edition was published, first in America and a year later in England. To his delight, this time they were a considerable if not widespread success, and he was at last able to indulge in what he liked to call a "Swim-gloat" and dine out as a literary celebrity. Indeed with this book he achieved what he had longed for and worked for all his life, a modicum of real fame. He was particularly admired by other writers, such as Christopher Morley, who called him "the most perfect Mandarin of English letters", and Desmond MacCarthy, who said that *Trivia* was "the sort of bibelot that Father Time often keeps on the mantelpiece when he changes the furniture of the house".

Alys found him very easy and undemanding to live with after Bertie. Following the break-up she had been miserable for a long time, but gradually the kindness of her family and her devotion to the new generation began to heal her. She was still tactless, and Ray and Karin still privately resented her uninvited incursions, though they were genuinely grateful for the time and affection she lavished on the children. She devoted much of her time to jumble sales, charitable work and the Labour Party. She was still compulsively economical, never, for instance, using clean note-paper if she could find the back of an old letter to write on. She tried to be economical over food, too, but neither Logan nor Mary, during her yearly summer visits, were enthusiastic. As Mary wrote in her diary on one occasion: "Alys had the inspiration of giving us some warmed-over mutton (horrible) as her farewell feast. The food is the worst any of us encounter any-where. She is *too* economical!"

In 1917 she developed another lump in the breast that had been operated on in 1908, and this time it was indeed cancer. She was resolutely cheerful, and although the breast had to be removed, the disease was caught in time, and she soon recovered. She even claimed to have enjoyed the experience and wrote to her sister: "All the affection that all of you show is a soft bed of roses for my spirits, and makes life pleasanter than it has been for fifteen years. Not that I haven't been happy for the last few years, for I have, but I always have the lurking feeling left from Bertie's lectures that nobody can really like me." In 1926 there was a recurrence, but this time she was given the new radium treatment and permanently cured.

Meanwhile, stranded at I Tatti as unwilling neutrals, Bernard and Mary became, as the war dragged on, increasingly fractious and irrational. Mary's determination to return "home" each summer was only sharpened by wartime difficulties and travel restrictions. B.B. hated to let her go, and the resulting quarrels were very wearing for both of them.

Just before the war a new character had joined the community on the Florentine hillsides that Mary used to call "Frumpignano": Lady Sybil Cutting, daughter of an Irish peer and widow of a wealthy American. She was frail, elegant and talkative, and Mary disliked her more and more violently as B.B. took to spending virtually every afternoon in her company. The oppressive shadow of Belle Greene was fading, but that of Sybil, who lived almost next door, was taking its place, and Mary's peace of mind was shattered both by this, and by unwelcome, if inevitable, developments in her possessive relationship with Geoffrey Scott. He was now falling in love right and left; it was clear that he would sooner or later get married, and Mary was deeply concerned to make sure of his marrying someone she could control and who would not come between them.

In the autumn of 1913 Geoffrey had introduced to Mary a most attractive young woman called Elizabeth (Nicky) Mariano—half Neapolitan and half Baltic aristocrat. He began to show signs of being attracted to her and Mary felt sure that Nicky would be an ideal wife for Geoffrey and an ideal addition to their circle, who would bind Geoffrey closer than ever. She therefore encouraged the match before it had even surfaced in Geoffrey's mind and, greatly to Nicky's astonishment, immediately pressed her to accompany them on a trip. Nicky, however, went off to visit her sister, Baroness Anrep, at Dorpat in the Russian Baltic provinces, and was caught there by the war and then by the Russian revolution, from which the family finally managed to escape to Switzerland. Mary did not forget her, although for the time being her plans had come to nothing.

In 1917 the Berensons had to go to Paris, where B.B. was reluctantly forced to nurse his relationship with Joseph Duveen, whom he disliked, but who was the source of the greatest part of his income. Mary, on the other hand, rather liked Duveen; she had a half-admiring fellow-feeling for his robber baron personality and B.B. needed her to act as go-between. In their absence Geoffrey unexpectedly proposed to Sybil Cutting, and was accepted, and when Mary got back to Florence in December—ostensibly to prevent the Italian army from requisitioning the villa—she found that she was too late. Her reaction was wild and violent, erupting into furious reproaches and insulting letters. Returning to Paris, swearing never to see Geoffrey again, she developed first acute cystitis, then agonizing gallstones, and finally a full-scale nervous breakdown, in the course of which she nearly succeeded in throwing herself out of the window. Her own explanation of her distress was jealousy of B.B.'s flirtations with society ladies in Paris, but the loss of Geoffrey to someone who had already proved so annoyingly successful with B.B., and with him the last of her youth (she was fifty-three) might seem to afford more convincing grounds for her breakdown.

Ray was summoned to Paris, and wrote to Alys in April 1918: "There is nothing the matter with her but the reaction after her illness, but she has utterly given way to it and sees everything black as ink. I can't leave her alone with B.B. as they have the worst possible effect on each other, though poor B.B. is a perfect saint." She finally managed to get her mother to a nursing home in England, where she remained, almost delirious with pain of body and agony of mind throughout the summer and autumn of 1918. When she came out of the nursing home, she stayed most of the time at Chilling with Alys, almost reducing her, too, to a nervous breakdown.

In Mary's low state of mind, Alys's very virtues were exasperating. Mary complained to B.B.:

Alys is cramping beyond words. . . . It is surly of me to comment on this, for she is an angel of goodness. Five happy children, a governess, myself and five servants depend absolutely on her for well-being, nor does she forget the little village here. She has classes for boys who have forgotten their schooling, she has mothers' teas, she wrings sanitary improvements to the cottages out of the grasping landlord, she carries on a vast correspondence of a useful and benevolent nature.

But, she added ". . . She seems to have no self, but acts always correctly and sensibly . . . there is no kind of intimacy possible with her. I think it is because she has made up her mind not to let her feelings influence her actions." The two sisters were, indeed, very different.

Gradually however Mary began to recover, and in November, which brought the welcome news of the Armistice, the birth of her fourth grandchild Judith, and Ray's exciting election campaign, she felt well enough to travel and departed once more for Italy, leaving the family to adjust themselves in their various ways to the new conditions of peace, public and private.

WORK AND PLAY

The Family

RELEASED FROM THEIR wartime bondage, Karin and Adrian returned to London and the agreeable prospect of exercising their brains at last. Karin's interest in abnormal psychology revived, and she carried Adrian along with her. They determined to take up the new profession of psychoanalysis, but had been advised by Ernest Jones, then more or less in control of the Psychoanalytical Society, that it would first be essential to qualify as doctors. It was late for this—Adrian was already thirty-six and Karin thirty—but they were sufficiently determined to enrol for the five-year medical course at University College. Oliver's brother James Strachey and his wife Alix were seized with the same urge, and James went to Vienna where he was analysed by Freud himself and became his translator and pupil. Though James had been forced by ill health to give up his medical studies, he and Alix were nevertheless accepted as analysts, and Karin and Adrian, who developed over the years a bitter hatred of Ernest Jones and the leaders of the Psychoanalytical Society, deeply resented this, and alleged that it was due to pure snobbery, because James had been analysed by the Master.

The training period was certainly tough, the more so as Karin was so deaf. She and Adrian sat together in the front row, and Adrian would take notes and read them aloud to her at home in the evenings. Virginia's comment was: "I suppose one'll whisper one's symptoms to Adrian, and he'll bellow them to Karin; and then they'll lay their heads together. Isn't it a surprising prospect? I see in it another of Karin's gallant attempts to roll her huge stone up the hill."

All went well, however, and they undertook at the same time the long business of being analysed themselves. Karin proved to be as brilliant a student as ever, and passed her first examination top in three out of the four subjects, and second in the fourth. Gradually, however, the strain began to tell. Her hearing became extremely uneven, and her ear began to give her constant trouble. The worst period was when she reached the stage in her training when she needed to use a stethoscope. She found it almost impossible to hear anything, and was always in the hunt for new and better hearing aids to help her. Her dependence on Adrian began to exasperate her more and more, and she finally informed the family: "Adrian and I have decided that we had better live separately, as we are making each other unhappy. We are very fond of each other and I think we shall be even fonder when we have screwed up to do this."

It certainly seemed to have the effect. As Ray commented: "K and A are *too* strange. I asked K to dinner last night and there was A coming along too. They talked almost exclusively to each other, turning their backs on me, and behaved like the newly engaged. Each one to their own form of separation. It is quite past understanding."

Karin, however, was feeling more and more ill and depressed, and her ear trouble finally became so crippling that she decided to take the surgeon's advice and have a somewhat risky operation. She had it in 1925, and although it was extremely successful in improving her hearing, it left her with a bruised facial nerve, and partial paralysis of one side of her face. This was almost the last straw, but Mary arranged for her to take a cruise in the West Indies, from which she returned still slightly lop-sided, as she remained all her life, but somewhat more cheerful.

By July 1927 both she and Adrian had qualified; Adrian at last found his true bent and a considerable measure of success as a practising analyst, while Karin dashed off to work in a mental hospital in Baltimore. This she enjoyed so much that she was unwilling to come home, as she had promised, for the children's Easter holidays. Her behaviour drew a fierce protest from Alys. "Karin *ought* to come back," she wrote to Mary. "The two children are dears, but really a *great* burden to both Ray and me. *They need their mother.*" And Ray added: "Of course if [Karin] doesn't come we *can* deal with the children . . . but I don't greatly recommend it. Children's holidays are a tremendous interruption and nuisance, but they are the only times to see them, and if one has children one has to do it, it seems to me. It is one thing," she went on, "to invite your nieces to stay when it is convenient to do so, and another to have to take them in, convenient or not. Poor little imbeciles, this sounds more grudging than it is. But I've been through a lot with Karin's carelessness with her offspring."

Both Karin's children had a good deal of serious illness. Ann had two operations for the same ear trouble as her mother, but though she nearly died after the second, it luckily did not affect her hearing. Judith had repeated attacks of pneumonia as a baby, and later caught paratyphoid. Mary, of course, was very anxious to have them out for long convalescent periods at I Tatti, but B.B. had not forgiven Karin for her Pacifism and now also claimed that she and Adrian despised him intellectually because of his dislike of psycho-analysis, and that Adrian referred to him as "the Jewish Uncle". Though both accusations were vigorously denied, he refused absolutely to let Mary invite the Stephen children. He was in fact right in believing that members of Bloomsbury and their friends disapproved of him and disliked his way of life. They had an almost Puritanical feeling that he had sold his soul to the devil for a life of luxury, and an equally strong dislike and disapproval for that luxury itself.

Mary finally persuaded him to allow Ann to go out for three months, and Judith, following her illness, for two. Ann gave no trouble. Mary found her delightful, and she was, at first, even more enthusiastic about Judith. The child's insistence on calling her pet pig Celestino after the butler was, however, not a popular move, as the butler immediately gave notice, and Mary was finally happy to see Judith go, a great deal irritated by her "obstinate nature which she inherits from her mulish father, no doubt".

She was often irritated by Karin, too. "Karin is very stimulating and ingenious," she wrote to B.B., "but I fear a real wrong-head —at least from the point of view of all the rest of us. She does things in her thoughts, and then they are finished, and her practical life goes to the devil."

Adrian and Karin had few interests in common, apart from their

work, and when they were not talking shop they were usually
reduced to playing cards together. Adrian was really devoted to
her however, and the separation lasted barely a year before
gradually fading away. They found another joint interest in small
boat sailing, going off together as often as they could in the sailing
dinghy Logan had given them, and later in a larger boat they
bought themselves. They both tried to be Captain, and were both
hopelessly incompetent, and frequently so immersed in psychoanalytical argument that they collided with other boats or found
themselves stranded on a mudbank all night. But they enjoyed it
rapturously, and finally decided to look for a cottage on the East
coast as a base for sailing weekends. They found an old inn called
The King's Head on the edge of a particularly muddy creek in
Essex, and after considering various alternatives—one called
Slaughterhouse Creek and another, appropriately enough,
Bedlam's Bottom—they first rented and ultimately bought the
place.

Ray reported on the amenities to Mary. "At high tide the outlook is lovely. Otherwise (i.e. 20 hours out of 24) there is a wide
belt of slime, tin cans and sewage between shore and really wild
mud flats. . . . The house has no water. . . . There is no drainage
(not even a kitchen sink) and slops are simply thrown from the
windows into the garden." What with the mud tracked in from
the shore, the primitive outside sanitation and the periodic
incursions of Mary's old enemies the fleas, it could not be called
luxurious or even comfortable—at least for adults. Things improved as time went on, but they did not manage to install full
running water until 1935, or electricity until the following
year.

Ray too had acquired a country cottage, on her beloved Friday's
Hill. Wildly extravagant as usual, she bought nine acres of land
and built her own house, made of rammed earth or *pisé-de-terre*,
adding a huge swimming pool—eighty foot by thirty—the
following year, a rare luxury in 1921. Mary managed to pay for a
good deal of the extras—half the pool and the electricity, for
instance—but nevertheless it took Ray many unrepentant years
to work off the overdraft she had incurred. They started by

trying to call the house "Copse Cottage", but the neighbours never called it anything but "The Mud House", after the "mud" from which it was made, and so they finally gave way. Lady Strachey had suggested "Mud Hole, pronounced Muddle" and some other wag "Corpse Cottage, Friday's Hell", but in general it was just called "Mud"—and still is.

Ray took to wearing a Land Army costume, together with top boots and a regrettable straw hat, while she was down there. "She was arrayed", as Karin told Mary, "in an amazing suit of corduroy breeches and coat which made her look like 100 elephants. Her disregard of her appearance is simply stupendous, she must be very sure of her inner worth, happy soul."

Ray adored the cottage. Like Hannah at Friday's Hill House she packed it from spring to autumn with extraordinary mixtures of people—sometimes as many as thirteen or fourteen, in which case the children had to sleep by the edge of the pond, rain or no rain. There was usually what Alys called "a cloud of Stracheys"—a selection of Oliver's nine brothers and sisters, particularly Pippa, who was her closest friend and colleague. Ray was as devoted to the Stracheys as ever, and they to her, but Mary still thought of them as "Tombstones", silent and dull, and indeed they were usually struck silent in her presence, unable (or unwilling) to conduct what she regarded as "civilized" conversation. On their own, however, or with more congenial people, they would talk without ceasing, clustered round the fire however lovely the weather outside, soaring off into witty and wildly exaggerated arguments, in different versions of the over-emphatic Strachey voice, well punctuated by awesome caws of Strachey laughter. To Ray it was heaven.

All this was made feasible by the freedom which B.B.'s allowance gave her, but she was always searching to find ways of earning extra money. At one stage she became enthusiastic for the type of building material she had used in her own house, *pisé-de-terre*, and decided to form a company with her brother-in-law Ralph Strachey, who was an engineer, to build these houses all over the country. B.B. cannily refused to invest in this scheme; it turned out that there was not enough of the requisite kind of soil in England, and this, combined with trade union opposition, finally brought her only business venture to an end.

She had been quite unperturbed by her failure in the election of 1918. She went on to stand for the same constituency twice more, in 1922 and 1923, raising money from the most improbable sources, including a subscription from Carey, but she failed again both times, finally resolving (with considerable relief she said) never to try again. At the end of 1919 Lady Astor became the first woman to take her seat in Parliament, after a by-election in her husband's constituency when he became a peer, and Ray offered her services, without pay, as part-time Parliamentary Secretary and adviser, an offer which was enthusiastically accepted. She wrote to her mother: "It is so very important that the first woman M.P. should act sensibly, and she, though full of good sense of a kind, is lamentably ignorant of everything she ought to know."

Ray was soon caught up in a mass of other activities, however: writing articles to pay off the overdraft; finishing two novels based on the American history she had found so fascinating from the tales of Hannah and Anna Shaw; fighting to open new trades and professions to women; and editing the old Suffrage paper *The Common Cause*, now renamed *The Woman's Leader*. By 1921 she was also deeply engaged in League of Nations work with Lord Robert Cecil, whom she greatly admired. Later she found time to broadcast almost weekly on public affairs; to edit and write a long biographical and historical introduction to Hannah's *Fanaticism Papers*; to write a life of her old friend and chief, Mrs Fawcett, and also to write what was perhaps her best book, the history of the women's movement, which she entitled *The Cause*.

Whatever she did, she was invariably happy; revelling in total solitude, picking mushrooms or bricklaying at Mud, or speeding round the country speaking at meetings and writing articles in the train. She wrote to Mary in 1926: "It is really ridiculous how I wish to fill my letters with shouts of joy and happiness. I am enjoying myself beyond measure, and like to say so again and again." And in her case there were no contrasting "downs".

Remembering the pressures on her in her own childhood, she tried to protect her children as far as possible from Mary's incalculable and undisciplined onslaughts. Barbara, as the eldest, had been the first of the grandchildren to visit I Tatti in 1919, and unlike the Stephen children, she returned there almost every year. She was a difficult child, however; over-vehement, obstinate, excitable and self-absorbed, and while Ray became more and more concerned about Mary's effect on her, Mary for her part began to find the reality of a grandchild somewhat less enchanting than the idea of one. Ray protested: "Do, I charge you, be careful not to overdo things. . . . B. is clearly in reaction after the holidays. Those wretched children of mine have not got 'Smith' temperaments at all, and things K. and I could stand and thrive on wear those tiresome semi-Stracheys to fiddle strings." Mary merely noted in her diary that Barbara was "a poor wilful creature".

Christopher, though suffering in Mary's eyes from the disadvantage of not being a Whitall woman, was entirely satisfactory to Ray. She was continually surprised, however, at his Strachey love of music and his passion for mathematics, though this came to him from both sides. When he was just eleven she told Mary:

On Monday night he had an acute attack of indigestion and felt too ill and sick to eat. In order to take his mind off this he insisted on my teaching him how to solve simultaneous equations graphically and quadratics by algebra. We broke off only for him to rush away and vomit—and resumed after. Did you ever know such an oddity?

He grew up to work with computers, and became the first Professor of Computation at Oxford.

Unlike Karin and Adrian who were never seen apart, although said to be separated, Ray and Oliver, although on the best of terms, were rarely seen together. Oliver was an extremely sociable man, always the last to leave a party, and as Ray loathed parties, he developed a number of friendships which caused Ray's friends more concern on her behalf than they did Ray herself, as she shared with Oliver a genuine passion for non-interference. Her only real differences with him were over his daughter Julia.

Julia had grown up to be extremely beautiful, and intelligent, but she was almost unimaginably vague, unpunctual and incompetent. This was anathema to the practical Whitall women, and Alys's strictures had finally become so stern that Julia could bear it no longer and demanded shelter from her father. By this time he and Ray had moved to Gordon Square, in the centre of Bloomsbury. There they lived, first in part of number 41, and then for many years in 42, while the Stephens and Clive Bell occupied different floors of 50, James and Alix Strachey lived at 41, Maynard Keynes at 46 and Lady Strachey at 51 with the remnant of her tribe.

Ray was almost as impatient with Julia as Alys had been, though less didactic, and when on one occasion Julia went off to Florence with some friends and proposed to call on the Berensons, Ray wrote to Mary:

Now that Julia has gone and the trail of scent, powder and fuss and telephone messages has left the house, its comfort can be fully appreciated. Poor Julia—I really think she must be half-witted in some directions. *Be sure* you don't try to be kind to her for it won't work. She'll only infuriate you and you won't be able to do any good to her. *Don't try.*

In 1924, after one near quarrel with Oliver, Ray decided to make another effort herself.

Julia was very anxious to settle down here for good [she wrote to Mary]. . . . After much tossing and turning I decided to give it a really fair, not a grunching try, and in order to make this possible I have completely reorganized the house. . . . When one doesn't get irritated she is quite an amusing companion. Oliver is perfect with her and they get on like anything. Of course she is still very silly and ignorant, but she isn't any more like a sore tooth in my head.

The new peace did not last very long. By 1926 Julia was twenty-five and still did not seem able to hold a job for more than a few

weeks, though she was lovelier than ever. Ray, echoing Hannah's
Quaker training, found her preoccupation with her appearance
and her love affairs silly and uncongenial, and finally told Oliver
that he could live with Julia or with her, but not with both; if
necessary she would go and stay in the country with the children
for the time being. As she wrote to her mother: "She remains an
insoluble problem. Oliver is—and feels—responsible for her and
is prepared to take her more or less in hand. . . . I hope she will
marry off soon. It is exceedingly unsatisfactory for her as well as
for us to have her hanging round our necks." Luckily in the
following year she married the sculptor Stephen Tomlin, who
was a great friend of both Lytton and Oliver. The wedding, at
the request of the groom's father, who was a judge, was held in a
church.

Barbara was there in great excitement [reported Alys], with
her present of an alarm clock under her arm, and she held
Julia's bag and one glove, the other glove having been lost by
Julia in her walk from Gordon Square with Oliver. . . . What a
monstrous hocus pocus it is, including the "obey"—we could
hardly stand it.

Virginia described the same scene:

A prosaic affair, though the service always fills my eyes with
tears. . . . The Strachey women were of inconceivable drabness
on one side, Aunt Loo having also an aroma of hypocrisy about
her which makes me vomit; on the other side sat the Judge in
frock coat and top hat, like a shop walker. He got locked into
his pew and could not get out, except at the last moment to
sign the register. He mistook the hinge for the handle.

Peace returned when "Tommy" and Julia went to live in the
country, where Julia was, at first, improbably domesticated and
blissfully happy.

Meanwhile it was beginning to become clear that Logan had

inherited the family manic-depressive temperament in full. In his case the "happies" led him to a somewhat undignified indulgence in practical jokes and improper stories. This tendency was probably first recognized to be a sign of illness as early as 1919, when he tried to include a highly indecent quotation in his scholarly selection of John Donne's sermons.

In 1921 he began to suffer from the other family disease, bladder trouble, and finally, when he was told that the best specialists were at the Johns Hopkins Hospital, he went off to Baltimore for the necessary operation. It was his only return to America, for which he had conceived an émigré's dislike. He wrote to Mary from the hospital: "What a lack of style and distinction there is in America. Not a breath or smell of it anywhere. I think it is a declining civilization—or rather they have invented a substitute for civilization which suits them better than the real thing. Peace be with them, and all the happiness and ice cream the world can provide."

As time went on, Logan's alternations of gloom and euphoria became more marked, but he was still able to work, except in the worst depressions, and even then he would read omnivorously. He published *Words and Idioms* in 1925, and was now recognized as an expert on the English language and invited to sit on the BBC's pronunciation and word-vetting committee, of which the Chairman was Bernard Shaw. This activity gave him the idea for another practical joke; he rang up Oliver and told him that unless he received a cheque for £5 by return of post, he would decree that henceforth the official pronunciation of the name Strachey should be STROY.

His love of social life was as great as ever, particularly for the tea and luncheon parties given by elderly lion-hunting ladies in his beloved Chelsea; he played chess with his neighbour Desmond MacCarthy several times a week, and bridge at weekends. He was becoming slow and heavy and middle-aged, and began to look around for a pupil-assistant—what he called a "milver", a word he had coined himself to denote someone truly congenial and possessed of the same interests—whom he might befriend and teach. The first person he thought might prove suitable was a young man called Cyril Connolly, just down from Oxford after exactly the kind of classical education Logan approved and with exactly the wit and sophistication he most enjoyed. He was also impecunious, and Logan was able to offer him houseroom at Chilling for the summer of 1926, and a small allowance, later, for work done for him. Cyril disappointed Logan deeply, however, by getting married—something Logan claimed was the ultimate crime in a milver. He also accused Cyril of committing the other "unforgiveable crime" of writing for money, but remained on friendly if censorious terms with him.

Two years later he found a more obedient milver in Robert Gathorne-Hardy, then an antiquarian bookseller, who shared with him a delight in old books, and the work of such writers as John Donne and Jeremy Taylor. This time it was more successful: Bob consented to come and work for him, reading, researching, annotating, correcting and listening to his stories, and their association was a mutually fruitful one for many years.

Alys cherished and pampered Logan, though she disliked his gossip and his growing taste for dubious jokes, for she was sincerely fond of him and grateful for his sensitive generosity and kindness to her. In 1920 she received yet another blow. Bertie wanted to marry Dora Black, to ensure that their coming child— who might be a son, and therefore in line for his brother's earldom —should be legitimate, though Dora herself would have preferred to remain unmarried. Alys fell once more into sleeplessness and depression, but she agreed immediately to the divorce, and also to support Bertie's plea to cut short the waiting period, since the child was soon to be born.

To cheer her up, Carey invited her to Bryn Mawr as a house-mother for the winter. On her way back she travelled alone, and was able to indulge her own peculiar tastes. "I am simply exulting in the thought of the discomfort of my steerage trip," she wrote to Mary. "As a rule my friends will never allow me to be as economical and uncomfortable as I like." This was in part a reaction against the luxurious agony of travelling with Carey, who swept up one or other of her English cousins almost every summer for a trip to Europe. Alys described her insistence on going to the theatre every single night in London and Paris—

sometimes twice in one day—and how she ate hugely ("she can digest first lobster and then pork for lunch any day"), and how she insisted on taking grotesquely large quantities of luggage wherever she went. In 1923, coming back from a trip to India, she whipped Alys straight off for a tour of Spain. On their return to Paris, Alys wrote to Mary: "I have stayed on 2 extra days here to help her sort and repack her 20 pieces of luggage . . . 1 trunk of kitchen utensils and tea, 1 of drugs, 1 of electric fans (never opened as India is well supplied), 5 of books she has never read, 1 of unanswered letters and 3 of unopened newspapers which follow her in hordes everywhere."

Mary, meanwhile, had rejoined Bernard when the war ended, and had difficulty in detaching him from Paris where he had got caught up into a strangely unreal world of aristocratic power politics. "I don't know how I can tear myself away," he wrote to her, "now at last when I am going to have a chance of bringing my own ideas home to influential people." Mary was not at all impressed, and gradually the intoxication faded and the attractions of I Tatti and his beloved library revived, and they returned to the villa. There Mary heard that Nicky Mariano and her family had managed to escape from Russia and were in Switzerland. Mary was determined not to lose her this time, and prevailed upon her to come and work for them in the library at I Tatti. Geoffrey, no less neurotic than of old, swore that this was a form of revenge on Mary's part, to prove to him how foolish he had been to marry Sybil and not wait for Nicky. He did indeed fall in love with her again, and his emotional state did his marriage little good, but that did not distress Mary. Throughout the upheaval Nicky displayed her considerable gifts of charm and modesty and before the year was out Mary was writing, "We both think Nicky is a nearly perfect human being"—an opinion they never had occasion to change.

In 1920 Mary and Bernard took one last trip to America, but Mary no longer had the gusto of her youth, and it was not a great success, except financially. "I do not think we shall ever come again," Mary wrote to Alys. "It isn't our life. It happens however, that it was *the* time for us to come from the business point of view, with many new buyers entering the field."

More rewarding was their first trip to Egypt, where Nicky began to take over Mary's task as Note-taker and Rememberer. Fortunately Mary was not in the least jealous of her, though it was not long before it became evident that her relationship with Bernard was more than a professional one. Mary, indeed, loved her unreservedly from the first, though she did sometimes feel a bit plaintive. "B.B. would be extremely happy married to Nicky," she wrote in her diary in 1922, "who would make him a more satisfactory wife than I have ever been." And she added, "It is a difficult situation for me. This continual contrast between my infirmities of body *and* character with a young woman who is an angel. Fortunately I love her very much." She did wish, however, that B.B. would give her more credit for her magnanimity. "I swear I am absolutely an *angel* about Nicky, not ferocious but gentle, not cynical but sympathetic, not mechanistic but understanding. It is really hard that he gives me no credit for this, but it is so much to his advantage that he takes it for granted." Nicky was genuinely lovable and beloved, and was also extremely useful to Mary as well as to Bernard. She soon took over all the disagreeable housekeeping tasks which had caused Mary so many "Woes" in the past and, before long, much of the research work too.

Relations with Duveen, however, were still Mary's responsibility: year after year it was she who conducted most of the negotiations with him and his lieutenant, Edward Fowles. She found it exhausting, but (in the interests of their financial well-being) she was prepared to be inconvenienced by Duveen's "galumphing", and his money-oriented way of life, while B.B. was not. As she wrote to Alys from Paris in 1926:

This life is *hideous*. . . . I hope I shan't have to put myself in this situation again. . . . This worldliness and money-greed, this worship of material success—utter blindness to real values—as I see real—this innate vulgarity and hardness . . . I have too much to do here, nearly all smelling of sordidness, yet exciting, like rum.

Life at I Tatti was still a violent switchback of quarrel and reconciliation. "Another of those devastating rages," she wrote in her diary in 1927. ". . . Fortunately I did not lose my temper even inside, but felt desperately sorry for him, it made him look so ill and old and miserable. At the end I opened my arms and he came trembling and laid his silly, furious, unkind, ungoverned, throbbing head on my shoulder."

Watching the ease with which Nicky handled his rages, however, Mary was beginning to admit that perhaps she herself didn't understand him. Nicky, she said, understood him "sympathetically, affectionately. This is a great blessing. I fear I don't altogether, I suffer too much from all the animus that is directed against me, my ways, the people I love, my desires."

Nicky was becoming invaluable on their travels, too. As Mary said: "We can only cope with him by taking him in turns . . . B.B. of course doing everything. . . . He seems to get another body when he is travelling." Mary went on travelling with them for as long as she could, but finally had to admit defeat and stay at home. Instead she wrote about the trips, first two which she had taken herself, one to Palestine and Syria and one to Algeria, and finally *A Vicarious Trip to the Barbary Coast*, based on B.B.'s and Nicky's letters. Logan took immense pains in helping her with her style and inventing titles for the books, but they were too specialized and detailed to appeal widely.

Every year she insisted on her summer visit "home", staying with Alys and Logan or in a hired house if B.B. and Nicky came too. She also visited her daughters and was an exciting if demanding guest. On one occasion at the King's Head she called for the doctor, claiming to be seriously ill and in great pain. During the night, however, she felt better, raided the larder and drank a pint of cream, and in the morning insisted on arranging a fancy dress party for lunch, with oysters and champagne. The family gladly procured these—at her expense, of course—and the doctor was somewhat startled to find his patient, white-gowned and garlanded, inviting him to join the festivities.

When she was feeling cheerful, she was full of wild and exciting notions such as a kind of horn she claimed to feel in the middle of her forehead, through which she could see imaginary landscapes of intense beauty; or a scheme for tiny balloons to fix on one's shoulders, so that one could take great leaps across the country-side. This she had read about in some paper, and spent much of her own and her family's time and energy in trying (needless to say without success) to track it down in the shops. A soon as it became feasible to fly to Paris, she insisted on doing so. In 1923 she even made old Janet Ross go with her. "I induced Aunt Janet to fly on the ground that we did not rise higher than 250 feet in the air, as Dr Giglioli had forbidden her to go for fear of heart failure. As a matter of fact they run at between 2,000 and 2,500 feet high. . . . However it all went off well and she thoroughly enjoyed it."

But for longer and longer periods she was submerged in a sea of illnesses, and her credulous and inventive mind was, for the most part, devoted to thinking of new cures: oxygen, injections for rejuvenation, new spas for gout, rheumatism, kidney trouble or just plain fat; she even meditated an operation on her ankles, which had come to look like monstrous goitres, to enable her to stop wearing frumpish long skirts.

She was finding the children too much for her. "I am vegetating along here," she wrote to B.B. from England in 1928, "in the midst of a fricassee of children. I like it less than I used to, for I haven't the energy to cope with it." She even admitted: "I dare say thee has never known how often I have bitterly regretted being a mother. Life would have been so much simpler and happier for us both if I had had no children, but not only that, *dentro di me* things would have been so very much easier." But she couldn't free herself now. "I wish I could disentangle my heart from them," she wrote to B.B. a year or two later. "They are really too far away—I mean the grandchildren. Their problems are too difficult for me, their faults too distressing. . . . Just seeing their muddle is distressing, late, careless, untidy and full of awful faults which time will no doubt cure, yet one is afraid it won't." And still she came back and back. "It is a crave, like drink, to see them sometimes," she admitted.

In 1931 disaster attacked Mary both in her inner and outer worlds. Following the great slump the Berensons lost most of the

income from Duveen, as well as some £50,000 of their invest-
ments, as Mary reckoned, while the market for pictures was
virtually killed. In the end their business adviser, Louis Levy,
managed to salvage a great deal for them, but at the time they
feared that they would have to shut I Tatti, dismiss the servants,
suppress the car, and go and live "very economically" in Rome—
at least for a few years. None of this happened, but worst of all,
from Mary's point of view, B.B. stopped his allowances to her
daughters.

Mary's reaction was to fall desperately ill. She had begun to
suffer periodically from the cystitis which plagued so many of the
family, and in 1931 she insisted, against her doctor's advice—and
B.B.'s—on having a radical operation which she hoped would
cure her and remove the persistent nagging pain. Whether it was
badly done, or whether her own self-indulgent refusal to follow
instructions during her recovery was to blame, she developed a
raging infection and very nearly died.

She wrote in her diary as she gradually recovered:

I heard one of the doctors say "She is going". I felt myself
floating on a swift smooth stream towards a precipice; but far
from being frightened, I was enchanted. I have no particular
belief in the immortality of the individual; there was no
expectation of a "better world", but simply a happy almost
blissful yielding to what presented itself as the most beautiful
experience of my life. Then suddenly I heard, as if from a
hundred miles away, B.B. sobbing and crying out "Don't
desert me! Oh Mary don't desert me." (He was kneeling at my
bedside but I had left the shore, and only distant echoes came
across the murmur of the waters.) When I heard his voice and
felt the love and despair in it, I made a great effort of will, and
said to myself: "I won't" and began to swim against the
current that was bearing me off. . . . My small bark is floating
back to shore on a beautiful lake of love. Among other things I
feel as if I could never again make a fuss about anything.

A DYING FALL

The Family

KARIN WAS NOT greatly disturbed by the drop in her income when B.B. cut her allowance, as she and Adrian were both earning well by then. The children had at first been left unusually free during their holidays, but as they reached puberty Karin considered it of vital importance that they should be analysed. They both resented this, partly because it meant their being uprooted from their schools and friends, and partly because they felt it an intrusion on their privacy. However Karin insisted, and each in turn had to spend the best part of three years in London, attending day schools and living in Gordon Square. During the time that they were living at home, Karin tried at last to get to know and understand them, but by that time it was too late, and her efforts were only partially successful.

In spite of this there were few problems about the educational side of their upbringing. Ann got an Exhibition to Newnham, and Judith got a Scholarship. She followed her mother's example by securing Bertie—who said she had an even better brain than Karin—as a tutor. Ann studied medicine, and seemed to be following in Ray's footsteps in her scorn of her appearance, although—or perhaps because—she was unusually beautiful. At Cambridge, Alys told Mary, "Ann had solved the problem of dress by discarding stockings and wearing sandwich boards advertising the Labour candidate."

Alys and the elegant I Tatti contingent were never reconciled to the girls' carelessness, and were hard put to it to fit it into their scheme of life. As Ray reported to her daughter one year, when the Berensons were in London: "Nicky said an enlightening thing the other day. She met Ann and Judy in Oxford St. . . . and she said that as they came towards her—*so* filthy and proletarian looking in dress and behaviour (even to the point of being smelly) she said to herself that perhaps it was just as well. They may have to live in a world turned Red, in which case fastidious tastes would be a curse."

Ray herself was in no position to be censorious, nor was she. Though less unwashed than the children, she was fully as careless. She herself recounted to Mary: "I dined with [Grace Worthington] last night very agreeably. But so savage have I become through ten days in solitude that I put on my dress . . . INSIDE OUT —and didn't notice it till I was in the middle of dinner! I thought I had got out of that bad habit and taught myself to look in the glass." It was not by any means the only occasion. One night when she was going to a grand party at Lady Astor's house, Barbara caught her on the way out, and drew her attention to the fact that her dress (a beautiful gold and white brocade, given her by Mary) was on inside out. "Phoo!" answered her mother, "no-one will notice," and went on her way unconcerned.

Ray had been more seriously hit by the loss of income than Karin. Oliver's job was on the Secret List, and his salary was not subject to income tax, but even so, the salary was not a very big one, and he had refused promotion rather than leave the Crypto-graphic work he so enjoyed for administration, which he loathed. He and Ray both found spending money all too easy, and the children were at their most expensive stage. So they took a lodger in their London house, and Ray sold part of her Friday's Hill land and accepted a job as Lady Astor's Political Secretary, this time on a salary and full-time.

It was not easy, after being her own boss for so long, to take orders and carry out instructions she did not always consider well-judged, but irrepressibly she enjoyed this too. She wrote to Mary soon after starting:

I enjoy it more and more so that in a way I am quite glad of the necessity of earning a salary. I have been involved in 1) The politics of the BBC, 2) the forthcoming Children's Bill, 3) Allotments for the Unemployed, 4) Nursery schools in various parts of the country, 5) Pension cases in Plymouth, 6) Scandals in the Police Force, 7) the Unemployed Anomalies Act and 8)

Civil Service Superannuation, today. And you can see that it keeps me hopping.

After four years she was able to find an even more congenial job in the field she had always considered the most important now that Suffrage was won: founding, running and raising funds for the Women's Employment Federation, which was specially dedicated to finding more and better jobs for women.

Christopher, as expected, won prizes and scholarships at every turn, which was helpful; but Barbara was in revolt against all things intellectual, and only just scraped a degree. This was followed by a trip to Australia in a windjammer, a rash and misguided marriage to a Finn, and a quick divorce, leaving her somewhat chastened, with a baby to look after. Mary had come to like her less and less. "I have a grandmotherly sympathy for her," she told B.B., "but little personal sympathy. I feel surprisingly detached, sometimes even antagonistic, though I trust she does not feel it. She must unscramble her own problems, they are not mine."

Following her disastrous operation, Mary had become virtually a permanent invalid, but she somehow always managed to recover sufficiently to make the journey to England each summer. She was still suffering a lot of pain, though whether as much as she claimed it was not possible to determine. Her belief that she would never again make a fuss was, to say the least, unfounded. All through 1934 she complained. "Such pain," she wrote in her diary, "such pain, how can I bear it?" The family expected to be summoned to Italy at any moment, and Ray reported on the situation to Christopher:

Last week there was very disquieting news of Gram, and [Karin] prepared to go out; but on Sunday Logan returned and said that there was no real need to be anxious about anything except the dreadful mental disturbance which she is creating round her. They have had more doctors, and the report is a sort of internal neuralgia, which causes her pain. Then she takes a lot of drugs and gets completely upset, and B.B. and Nicky become desperate, and the hills resound with their cries. It's an *awful* state of affairs, but there's nothing to be done. I, at any rate, can't possibly go out.

Ray was indeed too deeply involved in supervising the birth of her grandchild and in rescuing her daughter.

The only thing that succeeded in distracting Mary from her pain was the baby, Roger. Barbara took him out to I Tatti, and not only Mary, but even the child-hating Bernard himself, found him enchanting. As Mary wrote to Alys: "B.B. says he looks forward to seeing him in the morning. . . . Roger jumps on B.B.'s stomach and pulls his beard, and B.B. *loves* it!" It was a surprising change of heart. "B.B., the former President of the Herod Club, today said that a Lending Library of babies should be started . . . to bring those little joy-bringers into old people's houses. . . . This is really *true*, though inconceivable." "A child . . . of only four," he wrote in *Sketch for a Self Portrait*, "so lovely to look at, so playful, so merry, so gay that it was an animal joy as well as an aesthetic delight to have him around."

It was agreed that the baby should stay at I Tatti for the time being, while Barbara came home to find work, but even he could not entirely prevent Mary's dreadful groans and complaints. She wrote frequent postcards to the family describing in detail all the symptoms in the area she called "Clapham Junction", and spent the summer of 1935 in the Vienna Cottage Sanatorium in a further attempt to find some cure, while one after another of the family joined her there to keep her amused. Sometimes her sense of humour flickered back to life. "I could not help laughing," she wrote from Vienna to B.B., "though it was very painful and I groaned at the same time, when all the doctors, peering with mirrors into the confusion and wreckage at 'Clapham Junction' all exclaimed 'Sehr schon! Merkwurdig!!' They could not have been happier over a recently cleaned Titian." But for the most part it was a nightmare.

Alys was the only one who spoke frankly to Mary. She wrote to Nicky: "The doctors are very firm about drugs, as they say that although she undoubtedly has pain, it is not nearly as bad as she thinks—which we all knew, of course." And to Mary herself she wrote: "I am sure I am right in thinking that no-one (except family) ever wants to hear more than *one sentence* about one's sufferings, nor more than one complaint, nor what Logan's doctor calls 'an organ recital'."

Apart from Roger, Mary's greatest pleasure was still the summer visit to England, bringing her great-grandchild with her, to stay with her beloved Ray, but it became impossible to cope with her at Mud in her demanding state of health, without adding a bathroom and various other improvements. Ray explained to B.B. that she could not afford this, and B.B. paid for the work. "I am always afraid", she wrote to him, "that Mother's confusion of mind over money may . . . lead you to think that we are trying to get money from you through her. . . . I also want you to feel sure that I will do my best to restrain the extravagant spending in which Mother has such a tendency to indulge." Mary was, indeed, becoming a financial as well as a personal burden.

1938 was a bad year in every way. Oliver, though he was not allowed to speak of his sources, was profoundly pessimistic about the alarming international situation, and in addition there was a great doubt and worry in the family as to whether it was right, however much Mary wished it, to leave Roger with her in the state she was in. His physical circumstances at I Tatti were certainly ideal, but it became more and more clear that it must not go on; moreover Barbara had now married again and was anxious to have him at home all the time. Logan did not agree, and wrote to his old friend George Santayana about "Mary's fool of a granddaughter" describing the delight the baby brought to Mary, and ending: "That the child should not be allowed to remain there, but be recalled to London to live with his mother (who has married a middle-class Jew) is a view strongly held by the moral members of the family, among whom I am not numbered."

After Mary returned to Florence in 1938, Ray reported to Christopher:

> Rather gloomy letters keep coming from I Tatti, where the suicide talk is in full swing, . . . and B.B. is reduced to actual

weeping, and Mrs B. says she is suffering acute agony. It is really terrible to think of it all—for life ought not to be like that towards the end. Do, I beg of you, stamp on any tendencies I may begin to develop in similar directions. I don't feel it coming on, but one never knows.

There was one last summer visit in 1939, during which war was declared. That autumn there was a titanic, and mercifully successful struggle to get Mary back to Italy—as everyone including Mary herself, urgently wished—before the frontiers closed. When war was declared, although Oliver was within a month of his sixty-fifth birthday and retirement, he was whisked off to a secret destination. He worked there, and in Canada, where he was sent to pass on his skill and experience, until 1943, when he had a heart attack and moved into Gordon Square with his sisters. He died in 1960.

In the summer of 1940 Ray was found to need an operation. She died following this in July, aged fifty-three. Before she went into hospital she wrote to her mother for the last time, saying that in view of the threatening war situation, she thought it was the right time to tell Mary that all her descendants had had happy lives packed with interest and enjoyment, and work they loved.

Even if we are all snuffed out now we should, every one of us, have had good, worthwhile existences, and been glad to be alive. This sounds very deathbedlike, but I can assure you it is not the way we feel. Life *is* very precarious now, so you might as well be told explicitly that your descendants are grateful for being born. . . . By any and every route, roundabout or direct, here is my love.

Mary had begun to drift away from real life. Bernard and Nicky were caught up in the problem of whether an attempt should be made to leave for America, as all American nationals had been advised to do, but in the event it proved too difficult; Mary could scarcely be moved; B.B. loathed the idea; and no visa could be obtained for Nicky, without whom they would not

stir. So they stayed on. The story of Bernard and Nicky's adventures as the battle raged through Florence has been told elsewhere.*
Towards the end of 1943, since B.B. was now reckoned a "non-Aryan enemy alien", they took refuge in the house of a friend who enjoyed the somewhat improbable status of a neutral diplomat, being the Minister of the Republic of San Marino to the Court of the Vatican. Mary, however, was too ill to be moved; she stayed on at I Tatti, cared for by Nicky's sister Alda Anrep and her husband, who now also worked for the Berensons. On the strength of their Baltic origin and perfect German, the Anreps were able to negotiate fruitfully with the German officers who had requisitioned the villa, and ensure that Mary was left undisturbed in her upper room. There she stayed, solacing herself by writing a life of Ray and starting one of B.B., and sending herself to sleep, as she had done for many years, by reciting lists of people she knew who had died before her.

Early in 1944 she felt it was time to take her leave of the world, and wrote to Nicky:

> I am dying only I cannot die. The doctors will not give me receipts for the medicine that might kill me and I am too ill to go out of my room to look for anything or to die in the garden. I suffer so much that the gate is already open on the long road we have to travel alone, but I cannot start. However all this is not important. What I want to express I never could express . . . It is the love and admiration and affection of many years. There is no cloud in the thought of you. . . . All is perfectly serene and I think of you with the deepest love. If I die I hope you will marry B.B. You will have my deep sympathy, but all worldly things are fading away.

To her family she wrote: "This is to say goodbye. I have been a selfish creature but still I think I have loved you. . . . I have said goodbye to everything in this world and only hope for death to come quickly. . . . I think I shall not see B.B. and Nicky again, and who knows if any remembrances go with us beyond the grave."

* Nicky Mariano, *Forty Years with Berenson* (1966).

She did see them again, however. Throughout the year B.B. wrote her loving letters and went to great lengths to think of things that might interest her:

> I have a good bit of manuscript written in the last four years that you have never seen. I want you to polish the style and that will keep you busy for some time and perhaps interest you. We have had wonderful times together. Let us dwell on them and not on the mistakes we have made. . . . Let me add, with the utmost sincerity, that I live to a great degree with reference to you. If you left me I should feel as if the spool on which the threads of my life had been wound had disappeared leaving behind only a shapeless tangle. So I urge you to live on for my sake. . . . Do not give way to the *libido* of death. It will come soon enough without the asking.

In the autumn of 1944, when the Allied troops finally reached Florence, he and Nicky were able to return to I Tatti, where Alda had already begun to bring order into the wartime chaos. In March 1945 Mary died, and a few months later B.B. wrote to his friend, Judge Learned Hand:

> My Mary's youth was all an animal could enjoy and all a human heyday could desire. When I, a junior, had my first glimpse of her in the Harvard Yard she was a vision of "cypress-slender" beauty. . . . By the time you knew her she was no longer her physical self and she had got indolent mentally. In death she looked heroically beautiful, like the grandest tomb statues of the French 12th century.

Logan, too, had become a burden, though most of the time his writing and conversation were as lively and entertaining as ever. He read ceaselessly, annotating as he went, both old books and new. When he liked a new book he would write to the author with discernment and generosity. "You have the gift of imaginative memory," he wrote to Osbert Sitwell, "of portraying scenes, places, people, with the broad brushwork of a Rubens and

the glow of his colour and the felicity of his golden illumination."
He was, too, a tireless, if stern, friend and guide to aspiring young
writers. He wrote in one of his many notebooks:

> Now for a last word to those who may knock at my door
> and ask me to tell them how to handle their pens. There are
> two questions which I put to them. The first is . . . "Young
> man, do you read the Dictionary?" . . . "Have you a note-
> book in your pocket?" is my next query; and when as almost
> invariably happens, they cannot produce one: "Good luck—
> goodbye!"

Most of his work, however, was done in the intermediate
stages between the worst of his "downs"—his "interlunaries", as
he called them—and his "ups". Alys did not know which of the
two to prefer: the downs were worse for him, and the ups for
everyone else. The "up" of 1932 had been particularly startling.
Hilda Trevelyan, a near neighbour of theirs, and a cousin of their
old friend Bob Trevelyan, was reported as "having a horrid time
with robber innkeepers" in Italy. Logan erected on this a towering
phantasy that she had been captured by brigands, and that he had
been charged with collecting money for her ransom, which he
put at 1,200 lire—about sixty dollars. Most of his friends easily
recognized one of his japes, but one or two of the more innocent
were taken in. These included Bob himself, who was notoriously
parsimonious, in spite of having inherited an ample income. Sally
Fairchild, a friend since Friday's Hill days, who was among the
less credulous contributors, wrote to a friend:

> [Hilda's] cousin Bobby Trevelyan sent £1 at once and a letter
> of horror and grief, but when he found out that it was a hoax he
> demanded it back: Logan said no . . . so Trevelyan darted into
> 11 St Leonard's Terrace before Logan was up and "stole" 3
> volumes, each part of a set of books, as hostages. After he had
> disregarded a lawyer's letter (which cost Logan 3/6) Logan had
> to fork over the £1—for his books. Meanwhile, as most other
> people sent ha'pence or farthings (and some sent unpaid tele-

grams saying their contribution was coming by post) he finds himself poorer than when he started, and not buying a new overcoat as he expected.

Two years later Alys wrote to Mary:

This year his spirits have soared up again, but he realizes that it is a "happy" and jokes about it, and tries to control it I think. It takes the form of improper stories this year, but as I never go out with him nor attend his tea-parties here, I am generally spared listening to them. . . . I feel completely detached from him, and leave his own friends to cope with him. . . . After all he is a really distinguished literary star at present, and people must put up with his disadvantages and I am only too glad to have him out of that miserable depression. . . . So we go on as we can.

Nevertheless, much of Logan's best work was done at this time. In 1933 he published *On Reading Shakespeare*; in 1936 a collection of various essays and articles called *Reperusals and Re-collections*; and in 1938 his fascinating (if not wholly convincing) memoirs, under the title *Unforgotten Years*.

He travelled often with Bob acting as courier (Bob was Logan's Nicky, said Alys) and in 1938 they ventured as far afield as Iceland. Logan, who was now 73, fell desperately ill with pneumonia, followed by an attack of real insanity. He was taken to hospital where he became delirious and very nearly died, and although he finally recovered enough to be sent home, he was still completely irrational, and subject to delusions. Karin and Logan's witch-like maid, Hammond, together with Bob's friend, Kyrle Leng, were sent to Copenhagen to take over from the shattered and exhausted Bob, whom Logan in his madness had been reviling, and Karin in her turn found it necessary to call on Ann to take over when they reached Harwich.

Karin had been writing faithfully to Mary over the years about her children and her psychiatric work, which Mary, who loved all stories of mental abnormality, found fascinating. Karin wrote books and papers on her subject, and for a number of years lectured at Cambridge with great success. In spite of her rebellion against the psychoanalytical Establishment, both she and Adrian were highly thought of by colleagues, and although Karin suffered from an undeniable lack of human warmth and instinctive sympathy—of which she was herself aware—this did not prevent her from doing valuable work with patients in her chosen field and acquiring a very high reputation as teacher and lecturer.

She had drifted away from "Bloomsbury", preferring friends of her own making, and Adrian on his own was a more welcome figure to his family. Virginia found Karin's manner crude and rasping. She wrote once when Karin suggested herself for a visit: "I don't much like the thought of those great pillar-like legs in my bed; and all that breezy goodheartedness and immense munching, and public spirit about the house." Indeed she was prejudiced against Americans in general, and the Pearsall Smiths in particular. She admitted that Adrian had needed marriage to someone as down to earth as Karin to make him feel real and substantial, but she could not relish her company. "A good cob of a woman," she summed her up dismissively, "but so hearty and without shade or softness. Age will harden her . . . and her family will coarsen her." "I feel myself", she admitted, "frightfully superior, so refined as to be almost apologetic to Leonard; so full of fine feelings and subtle perceptions, intellectual tastes and the rest that I almost blush to sit here writing or reading Milton."

When war broke out in 1939, Karin and Adrian did not feel the least urge to be Pacifists again, and Adrian joined the Army as a psychiatric doctor. But his health was deteriorating, and he almost died of pneumonia in 1941. He recovered enough to work again, and ended the war as a Major which greatly amused Karin. She had followed him when he was posted to Glasgow, and worked in a nearby hospital where she became interested in drug, shock and surgical treatments for mental illness. When Adrian was demobilized they both returned to private practice, but he was failing fast. Karin took him on a cruise as soon as peacetime conditions allowed, but he suddenly became much worse, and they had to be put ashore in Portugal and return home. He died in 1948.

For some time it had become clear that Karin, too, was far from well and that she was beginning to suffer from the twin family demons of depression and euphoria. After Adrian's death she tried the electric shock treatment she had encountered in Scotland and had recommended for Logan, but without success. She withdrew more and more from her family and friends, particularly during her periods of depression and, being a doctor, she was able to slip almost unnoticed into over-prescribing morphine for her own use. Finally she decided to endure no longer, and took a deliberate overdose in December 1953.

Before her illness became acute she had been working on two books: one, commissioned by Leonard Woolf for the Hogarth Press, on the life and importance of Freud, and one entitled "Human Misery". She had made good progress with both, but no trace of either manuscript was found after her death.

Logan recovered from the Iceland disaster of 1938, but was never entirely himself again. Lurking animosities began to darken his friendships, particularly the closest. He had never made peace with Ottoline, and justified his continuing rancour to Bob, who was a friend of both the Morrells, by explaining that he had acted in 1911 "to protect my sister from an humiliation that would have been hard for her to bear—she had had too much to bear already, and Ottoline never forgave it. I have never told you about it, and never shall do—such things had better be forgotten, if not forgiven." But, as he reported in the same letter, in 1943 he made a gesture of reconciliation to Philip: "I am glad I wrote to Philip a few weeks ago and asked him if he would come and see me; he answered in a most friendly way, and said he would be glad to come."

He never entirely stopped work, and was still fascinated, as he always had been, by the English language. He wrote to Peter Quennell in 1943: "Nothing interests me more than the coining of new words, and if I could add one to the currency of the language I should die happy. . . . Two people I have known have added

words to the vocabulary of Europe—Austen Harrison with
'Suffragette'; and Roger Fry with 'Post-Impressionist'. Bad
formations, but indispensable in their time." Unfortunately his
own hopes of introducing the word "milver" were not crowned
with success.

His chief preoccupation, however, had always been the perfect-
ing of the one book on which he based his hopes of posthumous
fame: *Trivia*. He continually polished and re-polished this; added
new items and rewrote others, until in 1933 he allowed a collected
edition to appear as *All Trivia*. Even then he could not leave it
alone. Only three months before he died in 1946, he presented a
copy to his friend, the historian Hugh Trevor-Roper, saying:

> The friendly gift is the new revised, revived, readorned, redec-
> orated, re-alembicated edition of *Trivia*, adverbially enriched
> and full of those last gossamer touches and tendernesses. If you
> ever have occasion to write an obituary notice of me, you can
> say that, realizing in my youth that I had little or no literary
> talent, I was taken with the fantastic notion that I might write
> one little book that might live on beyond my decease. I flatter
> myself that I haven't failed altogether.

During the war he and Alys were banished from their house in
St Leonard's Terrace at one stage by an unexploded bomb, but
they returned as soon as they could and stayed there through two
more bombs, one of which brought down the door of Alys's
bedroom and draped it over the foot of the bed where she was
lying. Her only concession to the blitz was to wear a large whistle
round her neck, with which to signify that she was still alive
should she be buried in rubble, while Logan admitted to gazing at
what he called "the apocalyptic splendour" of the blitz with "just
enough fear to make it pleasant".

Alys spoiled Logan outrageously. He received two pounds of
butter a week from an Irish admirer, and throughout the worst
food shortages she and the maids saw to it that he had an egg for
breakfast every day, while they had none at all. All this intensified
his natural proclivity towards a slightly querulous self-indulgence,

and now that the American money had dwindled very considerably, he began to be obsessively concerned about his finances. He and Alys were, indeed, much poorer than before, but his books were still making money and his resources were still adequate; his fears were merely another irrational symptom. Finally he began to quarrel with Alys as well as Bob, and when the doctor forbade her to visit him in his upstairs apartment, because it disturbed her so much, Logan would send her rude notes on odd scraps of paper such as cheque stubs and lavatory paper. In the end he ordered her out of the house and altered his will to disinherit Bob. Bob and Alys both knew that it was his illness that drove him, but it was a terrible period, and Alys, herself nearly eighty, was profoundly harrowed and exhausted.

Julia—all past differences forgotten—offered Alys the ground floor of her house round the corner from St Leonard's Terrace, but in March 1946, when Alys was just about to leave, Logan mercifully died. Nevertheless, as soon as his affairs were settled, Alys did accept Julia's offer, glad to abandon the house which had become such an unhappy one.

As she recovered, she found herself the last of her generation, and this filled her with a sense of liberation and, one might almost say, triumph. All her life she had been outshone by Mary, and had devoted herself first to Bertie and then—for the last thirty-five years—to Logan. Now she had reached the unexpected and heart-warming stage when she herself was the one whom people wished to meet and to listen to, though as she said herself, the habit of listening to others was hard to break. "I suffer awfully from boredom," she wrote, "though I try to hide it, and hope I am successful. Once you begin to notice it, people's self-absorption is beyond words, or rather full of words. I have a sofa in my room where people sit and talk about themselves literally by the hour."

She made strenuous efforts to become more selfish and self-indulgent, and even if they were not entirely successful, they did impart a much greater ease and sincerity to the impression she made on others, and in these last five years of her life she made, perhaps, more new friends, and became more widely liked and admired, than in all the cramped, self-immolating years that went before.

She was discovered as a broadcaster, and made an instant success with talks on the early Fabians, on her visit to Tennyson and on her philosophy of old age. Crosby Hall, the headquarters of the International Federation of University Women, for which she had tirelessly collected sixpences and begged (or even stolen) jumbles from one friend to sell to another, paid her moving tributes, and fêted her most gratifyingly, and she glowed and expanded like a Japanese flower in water.

The last turn was the strangest of all. In 1949 she wrote to Bertie to congratulate him on receiving the Order of Merit, and he returned a friendly reply. "I have been wondering," he wrote, "whether thee would care to see me some time. For my part I should like it—at least once before we die." He lunched with her in February 1950, and Alys wrote a month later in her diary:

> Meeting again after 39 years was an extraordinary experience, but though our conversation was not intimate, it was friendly and cheerful, and to me blissful. . . . I was awfully excited and quite ill for a week afterwards, but am now settled down and very happy. . . . For the first time since June 1902 I want to live. . . . Now I feel that I shall freely see him again, and to love him freely is too wonderful.

She sent him a brief account of their marriage, which she planned to include in the memoirs she was just beginning to write, and he replied: "What thee says about our marriage is very generous, and fills me with shame. There is not a syllable in it that is wounding to me." He suggested coming again, when he moved to London, and Alys wrote: "It makes me so happy that I am crying with joy. I feel I shall burst with happiness and can hardly bear it. It is utterly overwhelming: all passion is not spent."

She nearly broke down, unable to eat or sleep, and as usual, taking refuge in tears. She gave a family party for him on his seventy-eighth birthday, inviting all her greatnephews and nieces and stretching her teetotal principles far enough to serve a small quantity of beer. From time to time, during the following weeks, he came to see her and her diary reads as though written by a girl of seventeen. "June 2. O joy, O joy, Bertie has just telephoned that he would like to dine here tomorrow night. How can I wait till then?" And she prepared for his visits with touching attention to her appearance, even wearing a pink ribbon in her hair.

Later in the month Bertie went to Australia for a ten-week lecture tour, and the diary reads:

> June 25th: one week of the ten gone more quickly than I feared. Only 63 days now till Bertie's return. . . . July 9th . . . To be defeated by one loss or even several is not something to be admired, I know, as a proof of sensibility, but something to be deplored as a failure in vitality, and if Bertie was too vital, and I was not vital enough, I cannot blame him. But I hope I shall live till he returns.

As time went on she became a little calmer—but not a great deal. "July 25: I must have reread his letter 100 times, though I know it by heart of course. Still losing weight—from love, I suppose, and inward excitement."

He was back by the end of August, and came to see her again a fortnight later, but inevitably the reality was not as her heart desired. Indeed, though he was now much kinder than in his youth, and genuinely anxious to add a peaceful postscript to their story, he was in fact already meditating a fourth marriage, and though Alys was unaware of this, the situation threatened to end in embarrassment and unhappiness.

By the end of the year, however, Alys's recurrent bronchitis was becoming worse daily:

> Dec 3rd: I so often feel too poorly nowadays to read or write that I am thankful to find so much occupation in just thinking about Bertie. I can remember happily our engagement and the eight years of our happy married life, and of his changing from an unhappy morbid boy to a happy and self-confident man; first

my tenderly pitied boy, like a son, and then my adored lover and teacher. I am a lucky woman, and if I have suffered it has been worthwhile.

Bertie's future wife was Edith Finch, who had been at Bryn Mawr while Alys was there in 1921, had later taught there, and had written a life of Carey Thomas. Alys knew her well and liked her, and when she arrived in England on 13 December, Alys wrote to Bertie to ask him to come and talk about "this unexpected arrival". Bertie didn't come, and on 1 January Alys wrote in her diary: "Still Bertie doesn't telephone nor come, and I feel dreadfully sad." But finally he sent a note of apology, pleading overwork, and ended "Much love, ever thine, B." The last entry in Alys's diary, on 12 January 1951 reads: "It is the first sign of affection he has shown me, and it makes me perfectly happy. It looks as if he really cares for me a little."

She was now really ill, and Edith came to visit her with concern and pity, but fate was kind to Alys at the end, and she died on 21 January 1951, with her fragile dream unbroken.

Alys had been the last of the older ones; the last to say Thee and Thy; to remember Walt Whitman and the early days in Germantown. She had always been something of an odd man out, too; a little colourless and shadowy compared with the others, but exceptional, nevertheless, in her perseverance, and moving in her predicament.

As a family it had been a small one—only seven people in three generations, five of them women; but they were remarkable for two things: the unusual detail with which they revealed their daily life for a hundred years, and the disproportionately strong impact they made—like a burst of shrapnel—on the very different worlds they chose to inhabit.

REFERENCE NOTES
SELECT BIBLIOGRAPHY

Reference Notes

The following abbreviations of names, manuscript sources and published works
are used in the notes which follow. All documents quoted are in the Smith
Archive, in the possession of the author, unless otherwise specified. Full titles
of works quoted are given in the Bibliography on page 337.

HWS	Hannah Whitall Smith
RPS	Robert Pearsall Smith
LPS	Logan Pearsall Smith
Mary	Mary Berenson (formerly Costelloe, born Pearsall Smith)
Alys	Alys Russell (born Pearsall Smith)
Frank	Frank Costelloe
Ray	Ray Strachey (born Costelloe)
Karin	Karin Stephen (born Costelloe)
BB	Bernard Berenson
BR	Bertrand Russell
Oliver	Oliver Strachey
Ottoline	Lady Ottoline Morrell
SA	Smith Archive, possession of author
RA	Russell Archive, McMaster University, Hamilton, Ontario
BA	Berenson Archive, Harvard Centre for Renaissance Studies, I Tatti, Florence
BM	Carey Thomas Archive, Bryn Mawr College, Pennsylvania
KSU	Kent State University, Ohio
UT	Humanities Research Centre, University of Texas
Vin	Papers of Mrs Igor Vinagradoff
AS	Papers of Dr Ann Synge
UG	Hannah Whitall Smith, *The Unselfishness of God*
RR	Logan Pearsall Smith (ed.) *A Religious Rebel*
WW(T)	H. Traubel (ed.), *With Walt Whitman in Camden*
VW(L)	Virginia Woolf, *Letters*
VW(D)	Virginia Woolf, *Diaries*

FOREWORD

p. 15 "Even now in the American . . . LPS, *Reperusals and Re-collections*,
p. 357

CHAPTER I

p. 19 "One time in yearly meeting . . ." HWS, Diary, 20 October 1850; **p. 20** "RPS says he never . . ." *ibid.*, 8 March 1851; **p. 20** "RPS spent an evening . . ." *ibid.*, 24 March 1851; **p. 21** "I have an inward . . ." *ibid.*, 12 November 1851; **p. 21** "I cannot hide . . ." *ibid.*, 15 March 1852; **p. 21** "Rebellious still . . ." *ibid.*, 7 September 1852; **p. 21** "I believe my diary . . ." HWS, *UG* p. 153; **p. 22** "I am very unhappy . . ." HWS, Diary, February 1854; **p. 22** "Of course I must . . ." *ibid.*, 25 October 1855; **p. 23** "Oh my Unbelief! . . ." RPS, *Holiness through Faith*; **p. 23** "Robert stood at the corner . . ." HWS to Mary, 26 October 1901; **p. 24** "Certainly I could . . ." HWS, *UG* p. 179; **p. 24** "Finding much comfort . . ." HWS, Diary, 26 May 1859; **p. 25** "I have had a sad . . ." HWS to S. Nicholson, 30 November 1859; **p. 25** "I tell them their prayers . . ." *ibid.*, 28 July 1881; **p. 26** "My objections . . ." HWS, Diary, 10 April 1862; **p. 26** "We, of course . . ." HWS, *UG* p. 195; **p. 26** "Taught me more . . ." *ibid.*, p. 213; **p. 26** "If one looks . . ." *ibid.*, p. 214; **p. 27** "It was more than I . . ." *ibid.*, p. 218

CHAPTER 2

p. 28 "Such enjoyment . . ." HWS to S. Nicholson, 1864?; **p. 28** "Millville is doleful . . ." HWS to M. Thomas, 26 August 1868; **p. 29** "I do not think Whitall . . ." HWS to S. Nicholson, Dec? 1864; **p. 29** "Well! I came home . . ." *ibid.*, 1864?; **p. 29** "Logan and I . . ." HWS to Anna Shipley, 5 February 1866; **p. 30** "Her insubordination . . ." HWS to her mother?, 1865; **p. 30** "There is little . . ." HWS to S. Nicholson, 18 January 1865; **p. 31** "Everyone who came . . ." HWS, *UG*, p. 248; **p. 31** "Oh Carrie . . ." *ibid.*, p. 248; **p. 31** "But at this meeting . . ." *ibid.*, p. 286; **p. 31** "I count them among . . ." *ibid.*, p. 284; **p. 31** "A knowledge of truth . . ." *ibid.*, p. 287; **p. 32** "By what seemed . . ." *ibid.*, p. 288; **p. 32** "One day, in a railway . . ." RPS, Address, *The Union Meeting at Oxford* 1874, p. 168; **p. 32** "I am afraid . . ." HWS to S. Nicholson, 16 December 1868; **p. 32** "Alice . . . is so fat . . ." *ibid.*, 16 December 1868; **p. 33** "He seems, more than any . . ." HWS to E. Smith, 28 April 1869; **p. 33** "Frankie Smith, the prayer meeting . . ." HWS, *Record of a Happy Life*, p. 82; **p. 33** "If all we believe . . ." HWS to Anna Shipley, 3 August 1872; **p. 34** "A sweet Christian home . . ." HWS to a friend, 6 November 1872; **p. 34** "Robert is miserable . . ." HWS to her mother-in-law, 19 October 1872; **p. 34** "Dr Foster believes . . ." HWS to S. Nicholson, 13 November 1872; **p. 34** "Some secrets of the divine life . . ." HWS, "Dr R.'s Fanaticism", in R. Strachey (ed.), *Group Movements of the Past* p. 167; **p. 34** "Never shall I forget . . ." *ibid.*, p. 167; **p. 35** "Utterly ignorant of the wiles . . ." *ibid.*, p. 169

CHAPTER 3

p. 37 "I think thee can hardly know . . ." HWS to RPS, 25 June 1873; **p. 37**

"[The Doctor] told me . . ." *ibid.*, 29 May 1873; **p. 37** "Thy last private letter
. . ." *ibid.*, 4 July 1873; **p. 37** "I wonder whether . . ." HWS to E. Smith, 15
June 1873; **p. 38** "It surely seems as if . . ." HWS to RPS, 1 August 1873; **p. 38**
"I cannot influence thee . . ." *ibid.*, 18 August 1873; **p. 38** "I suppose I used up
. . ." HWS to Anna Shipley, 2 September 1873; **p. 38** "There does seem to
be . . ." HWS to RPS 21 October 1873; **p. 39** "What thee tells me . . ." *ibid.*,
26 September 1873; **p. 39** "When I told her . . ." HWS "Miss S's Fanaticism",
Group Movements of the Past, op. cit., p. 177; **p. 39** "The thrill commences . . ."
Lizzie Lumb to RPS, 1874 (from a contemporary copy); **p. 39** "Most earnestly
I do . . ." *ibid.*, 1874?; **p. 40** "There are several . . ." HWS to M. Thomas, 10
February 1874; **p. 40** "My independent spirit . . ." HWS to friends, 13 August
1886; **p. 41** "She happened to have seen . . ." G. Mount Temple, *Memorials of
Lord Mount Temple*, p. 116; **p. 42** "She was to me . . ." Edna V. Jackson, *The
Life that was Life indeed*, p. 49; **p. 44** "I quite enjoy . . ." HWS to RPS, 27
February 1875; **p. 44** "I do not intend . . ." *ibid.*, 7 March 1875; **p. 45** "All
Europe is at my feet . . ." LPS, *Unforgotten Years*, p. 51; **p. 45** "England looks
very . . ." HWS Family Journal, 25 May 1875; **p. 45** "We went off early . . ."
ibid., 29 May 1875; **p. 46** "Just as at Oxford . . ." *ibid.*, 9 September 1875; **p. 46**
"This morning [we] left . . ." HWS to her parents, 1 July 1875; **p. 47** "He is
thoroughly . . ." *ibid.*, 2 July 1875; **p. 47** "Some weeks after . . ." Quoted in
B. J. Warfield, *Perfectionism*, p. 259; **p. 48** "The subtle doctrine . . ." HWS to
Emelia? 3 February 1889; **p. 48** "I need not tell thee . . ." HWS to Mrs Beck,
12 February 1876

CHAPTER 4

p. 50 "It makes my heart ache . . ." HWS to Mrs Barclay, 3 June 1876, *RR* p.
30; **p. 50** "A wearisome performance . . ." HWS to Anna Shipley, 8 August
1876; **p. 50** "Boole got a great . . ." HWS to M. Thomas, July 1876 BM; **p. 51**
"Do give up this . . ." HWS to RPS, 20 June 1876; **p. 51** "Aunt Rebecca Collins
. . ." *ibid.*, 28 September 1881; **p. 51** "We have wonderful . . ." HWS to Carrie
Lawrence, March? 1877; **p. 51** "I believe Heavenly Father . . ." HWS to RPS,
20 June 1877; **p. 51** "The ladies . . . at our house . . ." *ibid.*, 22 June 1877;
p. 52 "A sort of dead level . . ." HWS to Anna Shipley, 15 June 1878; **p. 52**
"What with their seven . . ." *ibid.*, 8 July 1879; **p. 52** "It seems as if . . ." *ibid.*,
20 May 1878; **p. 52** "Their story is . . ." HWS to Carrie Lawrence, 16 October
1879; **p. 52** "I must add a line . . ." HWS to M. Thomas, 28 March 1881;
p. 53 "Only the other day . . ." HWS to Anna Shipley, 11 January 1882;
p. 53 "Joshua does not like . . ." HWS to RPS, April? 1877; **p. 53** "At
Murphy's this morning . . ." *ibid.*, April? 1877; **p. 54** "On First Day morning . . ." HWS to M. Thomas, 30 April 1878; **p. 55** "The awful condition
. . ." HWS to her mother, 4 July 1879; **p. 55** "I am thoroughly roused . . ."
HWS to Mary, 29 January 1882; **p. 56** "Aunt Hannah is the most . . ."
Edith Finch, *Carey Thomas*, p. 80; **p. 56** "As father says . . ." HWS to

Mary, 7 October 1881; **p. 57** "It is a great advantage . . ." HWS to Carrie Lawrence, 26 December 1879; **p. 58** "I can always bring Robert . . ." HWS to S. Nicholson, 30 August 1881; **p. 58** "I felt my hopeless . . ." Alys, unpublished Memoirs; **p. 59** "Daughters are wonderful . . ." HWS to Mary, 11 September 1910; **p. 60** "How do I like this . . ." HWS to her mother, 22 July 1878; **p. 60** "Sealed for eternity . . ." HWS to Mrs Barclay, 23 September 1880, *RR* p. 52

CHAPTER 5

p. 63 "Potage Paysanne . . ." Mary to Albanus Smith, 6 July 1880; **p. 64** "Oscar Wilde is a 'sell' . . ." HWS to Mary, 21 January 1882; **p. 64** "Poor Oscar Wilde . . ." LPS to Mary, 12 February 1882; **p. 64** "I haven't the time . . ." Mary to LPS, 17 February 1882; **p. 64** "Now that they are dividing . . ." LPS to Mary, 12 February 1882; **p. 64** "I confess that I haven't . . ." Mary to LPS, 17 February 1882; **p. 64** "There is a great field . . ." LPS to Mary, 11 December 1882; **p. 65** "If I were in thy place . . ." Mary to LPS, 15 May 1882; **p. 65** "Miss Sanborn lent me . . ." Mary to HWS, 2 May 1882; **p. 65** "Something sublime in it . . ." *ibid.*, 2 May 1882; **p. 65** "For he is dreadful . . ." Mary to HWS, 3 May 1882; **p. 65** "Walt Whitman must be . . ." HWS to Mary, 18 April 1882; **p. 66** "Poll, Walt Whitman . . ." Mary, unpublished account of first meeting with Walt Whitman, written c. 1886; **p. 66** "My poor father . . ." *ibid.*; **p. 66** "A smallish brick house . . ." *ibid.*; **p. 66** "Once when I went out . . ." Mary to BB, 29 December 1929, BA; **p. 66** "He is 63 years old . . ." Mary, Diary, 4 January 1883, BA; **p. 67** "Somehow I feel . . ." Mary to LPS, 23 January 1883; **p. 67** "If thee knew more . . ." HWS to Mary, 21 January 1883; **p. 68** "I hope thee will not . . ." Mary to RPS, 25 January 1883; **p. 68** "I have indulged . . ." LPS to Mary, Jan? 1883; **p. 69** "I am struck dumb . . ." Carey Thomas to her mother, copied by HWS in a letter to Mary, Jan.? 1883; **p. 69** "*My* objection to W.W. . . ." HWS to Mary, Jan.? 1883; **p. 70** "Thee writes in a spirit . . ." Mary to HWS, 13 February 1883; **p. 70** "It is a trial to me . . ." HWS to Mary, 20 March 1883; **p. 70** "I love thee, my precious . . ." *ibid.*, 14 February 1883; **p. 70** "They always treated me . . ." *WW(T)*, 18 May 1888; **p. 71** "A man more or less . . ." *ibid.*, 18 May 1888; **p. 71** "She takes her doctrine . . ." *ibid.*, 18 May 1888; **p. 71** "Staunchest living woman . . ." *ibid.*, 29 April 1887; **p. 71** "Bright particular star . . ." *ibid.*, 16 December 1888; **p. 71** "Very radical indeed . . ." *ibid.*, 20 February 1889; **p. 71** "A good boy . . ." *ibid.*, 19 December 1888; **p. 71** "The most American . . ." *ibid.*, 19 April 1889; **p. 71** "I used to go from college . . ." Alys, unpublished Memoirs; **p. 71** "I fear thee is on the road . . ." HWS to Mary, 27 January 1883; **p. 71** "I see the danger . . ." Mary to HWS, 1 February 1883; **p. 72** "We were the only people . . ." Mary, *A College Friendship: A memorial for Florence Dike Reynolds* (privately printed); **p. 73** "The mine I fear . . ." HWS to S. Nicholson, 15 July 1883; **p. 73** "There was some trouble . . ." *WW(T)*, 19 April 1889; **p. 74** "I told Mrs Hunt . . ." HWS to RPS, 9 August 1883; **p. 74** "I will try to be . . ." Mary to RPS, 21 May 1883; **p. 74** "The groans I have repressed . . ." HWS to her sisters, 18 August 1883

CHAPTER 6

p. 76 "It kills me with laughter . . ." Mary to HWS, 2 February 1884; **p. 76** "Mother has devised . . ." Mary to LPS, 13 February 1884; **p. 77** "Oh Mary, these children . . ." HWS to M. Thomas, 10 January 1884, BM; **p. 77** "It was a most interesting . . ." Mary to a friend, 1 November 1884; **p. 78** "Follow in my father's . . ." Mary, Diary 1889/1890; **p. 78** "I was convinced . . ." Mary, unpublished life of BB, BA; **p. 78** "When he mentioned . . ." *ibid.*; **p. 79** "Tall, golden-haired . . ." Flexner, *A Quaker Childhood*, p. 208; **p. 79** "Who will be next . . ." Mary to HWS, 9 October 1884; **p. 79** "Prof. Palmer has been . . ." *ibid.*, 7 December 1884; **p. 79** "Mr Palmer is very anxious . . ." Mary to RPS, 20 December 1884; **p. 80** "I believe motherhood . . ." HWS, document on marriage (1884); **p. 80** "From the first moment . . ." HWS to Mary, 21 January 1885; **p. 81** "Only when thee is older . . ." *ibid.*, 5 March 1885; **p. 81** "Find out whether . . ." *ibid.*, 6 March 1885; **p. 81** "We are getting very good . . ." HWS to S. Nicholson, 8 April 1885; **p. 82** "I never had anything . . ." HWS to Priscilla Mounsey, 29 May 1885; **p. 82** "I find that it is a foregone . . ." HWS to S. Nicholson, 30 June 1885; **p. 82** "Blossomed out into . . ." HWS, Circular letter, 3 July 1885; **p. 82** "They are both dreadfully . . ." HWS to S. Nicholson, 13 July 1885; **p. 83** "Were overwhelmed . . ." HWS, Circular letter, 9 August 1885; **p. 83** "All the arrangements . . ." *ibid.*, 5 September 1885; **p. 83** "The curious sensation . . ." Mary to friends, 14 September 1885; **p. 83** "I did not shed a single . . ." HWS, Circular letter, 5 September 1885

CHAPTER 7

p. 85 "I enjoyed my four years . . ." Alys, unpublished Memoirs; **p. 86** "Count Stenbock—who is taken . . ." Mary to friends, 7 January 1886; **p. 87** "[Mr Cowper] dresses . . ." HWS, Circular letter, 8 January 1886; **p. 87** "Robert is having quite . . ." *ibid.*, 8 January 1886; **p. 87** "Last Monday the unemployed . . ." *ibid.*, 14 February 1886; **p. 88** "On Tuesday Mary and I . . ." *ibid.*, 19 February 1886; **p. 89** "There are so many things . . ." Mary to E. Smith, 31 January 1886; **p. 89** "For a wonder Frank . . ." Mary to HWS, 10 May 1887; **p. 89** "Thee is a precious daughter . . ." HWS to Alys, 7 March 1886; **p. 90** "The music was very fine . . ." HWS, Circular letter, 2 April 1886; **p. 90** "I may as well tell . . ." *ibid.*, 2 April 1886; **p. 90** "Gathered up her skirts . . ." LPS to Mary, 14 March 1886, LC; **p. 90** "I saw the Sistine Madonna . . ." HWS, Circular letter, 10 March 1886; **p. 90** "I have not even had . . ." *ibid.*, 10 March 1886; **p. 91** "Heart ached for . . ." *ibid.*, 26 March 1886; **p. 91** "In a Sedan chair . . ." HWS to Alys, 3 April 1886; **p. 91** "Their women *do not lace*

..." HWS, Circular letter, 3 April 1886; **p. 91** "That *hateful* notion ..."
HWS to Alys, 5 May 1886; **p. 91** "Frank thinks he would be *sure* ..." HWS
to RPS, 21 May 1886; **p. 91** "I am not sorry ..." HWS, Circular letter, 14
July 1886; **p. 91** "We were all eager ..." HWS to Mary, 5 October 1886;
p. 92 "The most startling fact ..." LPS to Mary, 2 November 1886, quoted in
John Russell, *Logan Pearsall Smith* p. 39; **p. 92** "Every one of the employees ..."
LPS, *Unforgotten Years*, p. 135; **p. 92** "I am living in dread ..." LPS to Alys, 14
November 1886, quoted in John Russell, *op. cit.*, p. 40; **p. 92** "I have no doubt
..." HWS to Mary, 22 October 1886; **p. 93** "Thee is mistaken ..." *ibid.*, 22
October 1886; **p. 93** "As to thy ignorance ..." *ibid.*, 17 November 1886; **p. 94**
"Edith was leaning ..." Flexner, *op. cit.*, p. 205; **p. 94** "A most wickedly immoral
man ..." HWS to Mary, 25 December 1886; **p. 94** "He is buying things ..."
ibid., 15 January 1887; **p. 95** "I got Alys and Logan ..." *ibid.*, 18 March 1887;
p. 95 "Frank ... never left Mary ..." HWS to Carrie Lawrence, 11 June 1887;
p. 95 "I object to infants ..." LPS to Mary, 4 June 1887; **p. 96** "There certainly
is a charm ..." HWS, Circular letter, 9 August 1887; **p. 96** "It is very hard for
me ..." HWS to Priscilla Mounsey, 27 August 1887; **p. 96** "In my secret
heart ..." HWS to Mary, 5 October 1887; **p. 96** "After dinner we settled ..."
Alys to Mary, 10 September 1887, Library of Congress; **p. 97** "It is an unspeakable comfort ..." HWS to Mary, 3 November 1887; **p. 98** "Delighted at the
prospect ..." *ibid.*, 26 November 1887; **p. 98** "The one great grief ..." HWS
to Priscilla Mounsey, Dec. 1887; **p. 98** "Aunt Mary sends thee ..." HWS to
Alys, 30 April 1888; **p. 98** "Dr Bucke ... thinks Walt Whitman ..." HWS to
Mary, 1 February 1888; **p. 99** "Our children are the comet ..." *ibid.*, 29
February 1888

CHAPTER 8

p. 100 "When I tell thee ..." HWS, Circular letter, 22 May 1888; **p. 100** "As
thee sees, I am ..." LPS to Alys, 14 May 1888, quoted in John Russell, *op. cit.*,
p. 43; **p. 101** "It is a very interesting ..." HWS, Circular letter, 12 September
1888; **p. 101** "I wish you would pay off ..." HWS to her daughters, Aug.
1888; **p. 101** "He had finished his magnificent ..." Mary, Diary 1889–90;
p. 102 "We can run in and out ..." HWS, Circular letter, 22 May 1888;
p. 102 "I do not feel myself ..." *ibid.*, 22 May 1888; **p. 102** "I must say that
English politics ..." *ibid.*, 1 December 1888; **p. 103** "Father is certainly astray
..." HWS to Mary, 13 January 1889; **p. 103** "[Dr Garrett Anderson] asked
me ..." Mary to HWS, 18 January 1888; **p. 103** "It was wicked beyond words
..." Mary, Diary 1889–90; **p. 104** "Pure unadulterated trash ..." HWS,
Circular letter, 1 August 1886; **p. 104** "Mrs Oliphant ..." HWS to Emelia?,
3 February 1889; **p. 105** "Rome is full of priests ..." HWS, Circular letter, 7
February 1889; **p. 105** "The Rector has already ..." *ibid.*, 1 August 1889; **p. 105**
"Yesterday Lady Russell ..." *ibid.*, 17 August 1889; **p. 106** "She was very
beautiful ..." BR, *Autobiography*, vol. I, p. 75; **p. 106** "It was a busy day ..."

HWS, Circular letter, 17 August 1889; **p. 106** "The girls numbered about . . ."
ibid., 7 August 1891; **p. 107** "Logan said they had . . ." *ibid.*, 17 August 1889;
p. 107 "Fallen completely . . ." *ibid.*, 6 September 1889; **p. 107** "I go up
sometimes . . ." *ibid.*, 7 September 1891; **p. 107** "Her story is a sad one . . ."
ibid., 14 February 1890; **p. 109** "With all his certainty . . ." Mary, Diary
1889–90; **p. 109** "How I long for a Soul . . ." Mary, Diary, April 1890;
p. 109 "I went to Lady Victoria's . . ." Mary to HWS, 29 March 1890;
p. 110 "We found at home . . ." HWS, Circular letter, 4 August 1890; **p. 111**
"He has since confessed . . ." Mary, unpublished Life of BB, BA; **p. 111** "When
this beautiful . . ." *ibid.*

CHAPTER 9

p. 112 "Nor you did no wrong . . ." BB to Mary, 22 September 1890, BA;
p. 112 "I do feel that he ought . . ." Mary to Gertrude Hitz Burton, 5 December
1890, BA; **p. 113** "Mr Shaw's attempt . . ." BB to Mary, 29 October 1890, BA;
p. 113 "Mr Webb is probably . . ." *ibid.*, undated, BA; **p. 113** "Of course it
didn't happen . . ." Mary, unpublished Life of BB, BA; **p. 113** "About this
time . . ." *ibid.*; **p. 113** "I want so much to talk . . ." BB to Mary, 17 October
1890, BA; **p. 114** "No later experience . . ." Mary, unpublished Life of BB,
BA; **p. 115** "The vaccination, if I may . . ." *ibid.*; **p. 115** "It is a great comfort
. . ." HWS to Mary, 15 August 1891; **p. 116** "Frank is really behaving . . ."
Mary to HWS, 29 October 1891; **p. 116** "I want to be always now . . ." *ibid.*,
29 October 1891; **p. 116** "I seem to be getting . . ." *ibid.*, 28 September 1891;
p. 116 "Thy idea of right . . ." *ibid.*, 10 October 1891; **p. 117** "We attacked
church after church . . ." Mary, unpublished Life of BB, BA; **p. 117**
"Bernhard detested . . ." *ibid.*; **p. 118** "I am very glad to be here . . ." HWS to
RPS, 14 January 1892; **p. 118** "Sister is well chaperoned . . ." HWS to LPS, 26
January 1892; **p. 118** "I should only say . . ." LPS to Mary, 2 November 1892;
p. 119 "Tell Logan that after reading . . ." Mary to HWS, 11 January 1892;
p. 119 "(1) Divorce with Ray . . ." Mary, Undated paper; **p. 120** "I have been
simply tortured . . ." Mary to HWS, 8 September 1892; **p. 120** "I trust it will
all . . ." HWS to Mary, 3 January 1893; **p. 121** "It is a struggle . . ." Mary to
HWS, 20 March 1893; **p. 121** "I am sorry darling . . ." HWS to Mary, 9
January 1893; **p. 122** "During the conversation . . ." *ibid.*, 17 January 1893;
p. 122 "I am sure if thee . . ." *ibid.*, 17 January 1893; **p. 122** "Frank (naturally)
. . ." *ibid.*, 20 January 1893; **p. 122** "Oh my darling daughter . . ." *ibid.*, 27
January 1893; **p. 123** "As to your remarks . . ." Mary to Frank, 10 October
1893; **p. 123** "I have sometimes thought . . ." Frank to HWS, 20 August 1893;
p. 123 "If thy mother has . . ." Frank to Mary, 20 August 1893; **p. 123** "A
stroke of great good luck . . ." Quoted in Sylvia Sprigge, *Berenson*, p. 162;
p. 123 "Give up Berenson . . ." HWS to Mary, 26 April 1894; **p. 124** "A
curious mind . . ." Mary to HWS, 5 February 1892; **p. 124** "Miss Cruttwell
said . . ." Mary, Diary, 14 November 1902, BA; **p. 125** "They think they are

. . ." Mary to HWS, 15 May 1895; **p. 126** "(1) Really personally . . ." Mary, Diary over several years, BA

CHAPTER 10

p. 127 "Never did a mother . . ." HWS to Alys, 11 October 1893; **p. 128** "I dreamed last night . . ." BR, Journal, 21 July 1893; **p. 128** "I think of A all day . . ." *ibid.*, 21 July 1893; **p. 129** "The greatest day in my life . . ." *ibid.*, 12 August 1893; **p. 129** "I have come to the conclusion . . ." BR to Alys, 5 September 1893; **p. 130** "All is accomplished . . ." BR, Journal, 16 September 1893; **p. 131** "It is a mutual alliance . . ." Alys to BR, 27 September 1893; **p. 131** "I cannot imagine now . . ." BR to Alys, 28 September 1893; **p. 131** "I don't believe that it is . . ." Alys to BR, 5 October 1893; **p. 131** "I have at times thought . . ." BR to Alys, 7 October 1893; **p. 131** "I am afraid it is . . ." *ibid.*, 29 October 1893; **p. 132** "It is a temptation . . ." Alys to BR, 15 December 1893; **p. 132** "I assure you it is not . . ." BR to Alys, 19 December 1893; **p. 132** "It was on this occasion . . ." BR, *Autobiography*, vol. I, p. 82; **p. 132** "I feel as if there were . . ." Alys to BR, 7 January 1894; **p. 133** "I thought the difference . . ." *ibid.*, 15 January 1894; **p. 133** "I think the difference . . ." BR to Alys, 16 January 1894; **p. 133** "I have suddenly realized the fact . . ." Alys to BR, 15 January 1894; **p. 133** "I am not of a sociable . . ." BR to Alys, 16 January 1894; **p. 134** "[It] would only become . . ." *ibid.*, 28 January 1894; **p. 135** "I have indeed thought . . ." Alys to BR, 29 January 1894; **p. 135** "If I lose my belief . . ." *ibid.*, 15 February 1894; **p. 135** "Thee has all the qualities . . ." *ibid.*, 4 February 1894; **p. 135** "Reached Pembridge Lodge . . ." Alys, Journal, 20 March 1894; **p. 135** "She was no lady . . ." BR, *Autobiography*, vol. I, p. 82; **p. 135** "[I said that] I couldn't . . ." BR to Alys, 8 April 1894; **p. 136** "Nothing must be . . ." HWS to Mary, April 1894; **p. 136** "[Alys] and Bertie have been . . ." HWS to Mary, 31 May 1894; **p. 136** "I think thee and thy mother . . ." BR to Alys, 12 November 1894, RA; **p. 136** "Objected to his marrying . . ." Alys, Journal, 30 May 1894; **p. 137** "The 'solemn betrothal kiss' . . ." *ibid.*, 5 June 1894; **p. 137** "I have analysed it out . . ." Alys to BR, 10 June 1894; **p. 137** "I do not wonder thy uncle . . ." *ibid.*, 24 April 1894; **p. 138** "Were I arranging . . ." Dr Tuke, quoted by BR to Alys, 21 June 1894; **p. 138** "B. came up and said . . ." Alys, Journal, 22 June 1894; **p. 138** "B. felt that if the risk . . ." *ibid.*, 23 June 1894; **p. 138** "The more I reflect upon . . ." Dr Anderson to Alys, quoted to BR, 5 July 1894; **p. 138** "I was perfectly furious . . ." Alys to BR, 7 July 1894; **p. 139** "A physician with his wide . . ." BR to Dr Anderson, quoted to Alys, 13 July 1894; **p. 139** "We had foolishly given up . . ." Alys to BR, 23 August 1894; **p. 140** "Thee stood for me . . ." BR to Alys, 12 October 1894, RA; **p. 140** "I am sure thy former views . . ." *ibid.*, 4 October 1894; **p. 140** "I'm too egotistic to mind . . ." *ibid.*, 1 October 1894; **p. 140** "Thee *must* think for thyself . . ." *ibid.*, 22 October 1894, RA; **p. 141** "I am very annoyed with [M] . . ." Alys to BR, 4 November

1894; **p. 141** "I think thee is always a little . . ." BR to Alys, 1 November 1894, RA; **p. 142** "She seems genuinely interested . . ." *ibid.*, 6 November 1894, RA; **p. 142** "She is a *perfectly* charming . . ." *ibid.*, 13 November 1894, RA; **p. 142** "She is really, as she says . . ." *ibid.*, 10 November 1894, RA; **p. 142** "She is so nice and emotional . . ." *ibid.*, 8 November 1894, RA; **p. 142** "It *is* nice for thee . . ." Alys to BR, 6 November 1894; **p. 142** "I am *so* glad . . ." *ibid.*, 7 November 1894; **p. 142** "Why should I mind . . ." *ibid.*, 12 November 1894; **p. 142** "For some reason . . ." Alys, Journal, 9 November 1894; **p. 142** "Felt depressed and teary . . ." *ibid.*, 12 November 1894; **p. 142** "Cried most of the morning . . ." *ibid.*, 15 November 1894; **p. 143** "I found thy letter . . ." Alys to BR, 14 November 1894; **p. 143** "It has made me really . . ." *ibid.*, 14 November 1894; **p. 144** "Abandoned [himself] too recklessly . . ." BR to Alys, 15 November 1894, RA; **p. 144** "Mother and I called . . ." Alys, Journal, 24 November 1894; **p. 144** "It was brutal of my people . . ." BR to Alys, 26 November 1894; **p. 144** "I never expect thee . . ." *ibid.*, 27 November 1894; **p. 145** "Of course where different . . ." Lady Russell to HWS, 29 November 1894; **p. 145** "Rollo reminds us . . ." Lady Agatha Russell to BR, 19 November 1894, quoted in BR, *Autobiography*, vol. I, p. 121; **p. 145** "Lovely little sermonettes . . ." HWS to Mary, 13 December 1894

CHAPTER 11

p. 149 "No immediate prospect . . ." Alys to HWS, 16 December 1894; **p. 149** "And now do write to me . . ." HWS to Alys, 13 January 1895; **p. 149** "I may tell thee . . ." *ibid.*, 5 March 1895; **p. 149** "She gets it at once . . ." HWS to Mary, 9 February 1893; **p. 150** "I always wear loose Turkish . . ." *The Wheelwoman*, 3 October 1896; **p. 150** "I called on Lady Gatacre . . ." Alys, Journal, 6 January 1900; **p. 150** "With or without . . ." *The Wheelwoman*, no date; **p. 150** "Bertie and Alys seem . . ." Mary to HWS, 25 March 1895; **p. 151** "Bertie's idea is to have the State . . ." Mary to BB, 5 October 1894, BA; **p. 151** "Bertie read aloud the Book . . ." Mary, Diary, 26 March 1895, BA; **p. 151** "We call her 'Conventionality' . . ." Mary to Obrist, 24 March 1895; **p. 152** "We shall be very glad . . ." Alys, unpublished Memoirs; **p. 152** "We were confessing . . ." Mary, Diary, 17 April 1896, BA; **p. 152** "There was a time . . ." BR to Alys, 12 September 1896; **p. 153** "I am getting very anxious . . ." *ibid.*, 16 April 1897; **p. 153** "I only realize when I am away . . ." *ibid.*, 17 April 1897; **p. 153** "Cleopatra was really fine . . ." Alys to BR, 27 May 1897; **p. 153** "I am . . . much amused . . ." BR to Alys, 28 May 1897; **p. 153** "I read my paper last night . . ." *ibid.*, 12 March 1898; **p. 154** "I prepared a number . . ." Alys, unpublished Memoirs; **p. 154** "[Mary and I] had a jolly . . ." BR to Alys, 28 September 1897; **p. 154** "Last night I elicited . . ." *ibid.*, 27 September 1897; **p. 154** "Bertie was *very* affectionate . . ." Mary to BB, 26 September 1897, BA; **p. 155** "An aristocratic Bostonian . . ." BR, *Autobiography*, vol. I, p. 135; **p. 155** "Poor Mother is dreadfully . . ." Mary to BB, 9

August 1899, BA; **p. 155** "She and Bertie stayed out . . ." *ibid.*, 15 August 1899, BA; **p. 155** "I had an amusing talk with Alys . . ." Mary, Diary, 26 August 1898, BA

CHAPTER 12

p. 157 "I think I was best known . . ." LPS, *Unforgotten Years*, p. 177; **p. 157** "If I have to any degree . . ." *ibid.*, p. 162; **p. 158** "One sister paints . . ." LPS to Alys, 22 February 1892, Library of Congress; **p. 159** "Logan declares he is *not* . . ." HWS to Mary, 28 March 1894; **p. 159** "He is a little . . ." LPS to HWS, 18 June 1894; **p. 159** "One young Englishman named . . ." HWS, Circular letter, 9 August 1893; **p. 159** "Bear in mind, dear Poll . . ." RPS to Mary, 22 January 1892; **p. 160** "Uncle Horace, without telling . . ." LPS to HWS, 31 March 1893; **p. 160** "Poor Uncle H[orace] . . ." HWS to Mary, 8 September 1893; **p. 160** "I am pleased . . ." LPS to Mary, 8 September 1895; **p. 160** "These stories tell us . . ." Unsigned review in *London Chronicle*, 12 March 1895, SA; **p. 161** "I more or less expected . . ." LPS to Mary, 23 November 1895; **p. 161** "Henry James was kind . . ." LPS, Journal, 10 March 1896, KSU; **p. 161** "I shall soon . . ." *ibid.*, 1896, KSU; **p. 161** "I have really come abroad . . ." LPS to Mary, 17 December 1895; **p. 162** "What has become of thee . . ." LPS to Philip Morrell, 5 November 1896, Vin; **p. 162** "I have been pursuing . . ." *ibid.*, 11 May 1896, Vin; **p. 162** "I am trying to read . . ." *ibid.*, 13 March 1900, Vin; **p. 163** "Summer days, with all . . ." LPS, Journal, 1900, KSU; **p. 163** "I am in despair about writing . . ." LPS to P. Morrell, 6 May 1900, Vin; **p. 163** "This morning when I woke . . ." LPS, Journal, 18 November 1895, KSU; **p. 163** "He has a passion to be . . ." BR to Alys, 31 March 1898; **p. 163** "Rather mildly disgusting . . ." LPS, Journal, 1894, KSU; **p. 163** "My idea of a happy ending . . ." LPS, quoted by John Russell, *op. cit.* p. 13; **p. 165** "Everybody thinks that Oscar Wilde . . ." HWS to Mary, 4 May 1895; **p. 165** "Oscar Wilde is imprisoned . . ." Mary, Diary, 25 September 1895, BA; **p. 166** "But it is perfectly simple . . ." Family Tradition; **p. 166** "Her creed about grandmothers . . ." Ray, *A Quaker Grandmother*, p. 12; **p. 167** "We had set our hearts on . . ." *ibid.*, p. 20

CHAPTER 13

p. 168 "I am literally devoured . . ." Mary to Alys, 16 September 1891; **p. 169** "Do make enquiries . . ." Mary to HWS, 22 October 1892; **p. 169** "Aunt M. says . . . she has found . . ." HWS to Mary, 7 October 1899; **p. 169** "For the first time yesterday . . ." Mary to Alys, 24 November 1898; **p. 170** "Where another person . . ." Mary to HWS, 2 December 1893; **p. 170** "Thee remembers the essay . . ." Mary to RPS, 24 November 1893; **p. 171** "A number of papers . . ." Mary to HWS, 19 April 1894; **p. 172** "Gutekunst knows of a Velasquez . . ." BB to Mary, 10 January 1896, BA; **p. 173** "Back of all you said . . ." *ibid.*, 17 September 1894, BA; **p. 173** "I wonder whether . . ." *ibid.*, 21 September 1894, BA; **p. 173** "Poor Mariechen got bored . . ." LPS to Alys, 10

January 1895, LC; **p. 173** "In the evening Bernhard . . ." Mary, Diary, 1 November 1895, BA; **p. 173** "Very very angry . . ." *ibid.*, 7 November 1895, BA; **p. 174** "All I ask of you is . . ." BB to Mary, 31 January 1896, BA; **p. 174** "Do not think I am irritated . . ." *ibid.*, 6 January 1896, BA; **p. 174** "I beg of thee, dear artist . . ." Mary to Obrist, 30 June 1895; **p. 174** "All this time at Fiesole . . ." Mary, Diary, 7 June 1895, BA; **p. 175** "Bertie and I are at it . . ." Mary to BB, 1 August 1895, BA; **p. 175** "I am sorry to hear . . ." BB to Mary, 31 July 1895, BA; **p. 175** "I think it inadvisable . . ." *ibid.*, 3 August 1895, BA; **p. 175** "I have been simply overwhelmed . . ." Mary, Diary, 13 July 1895, BA; **p. 175** "Bernhard cannot endure . . ." *ibid.*, 2 December 1895, BA; **p. 176** "A man who cannot bear . . ." *ibid.*, 9 June 1896, BA; **p. 176** "It would be a mistake . . ." Mary to BB, 20 August 1897, BA; **p. 176** "These maiden ladies . . ." Mary, Diary, 26 November 1897, BA; **p. 176** "Bernhard seems so nervous . . ." *ibid.*, 18 October 1896, BA; **p. 177** "As tyrannical and wilful . . ." BB to Mary, 1897, BA; **p. 177** "I rejoiced at the thought . . ." Mary, Diary, 28 November 1898, BA; **p. 178** "My only excuse . . ." Mary to BB, 29 July 1897, BA; **p. 179** "You can practise a great deal . . ." BB to Mary, 30 July 1897, BA; **p. 179** "I had such a dreadful night . . ." Mary to BB, 22 August 1897, BA; **p. 179** "A telegram came from W.B. . . ." Mary, Diary, 14 November 1897, BA; **p. 179** "A person who, left to herself . . ." BB to Mary, July 1898, BA; **p. 180** "Uncle Logan and I had . . ." Mary to the family, 11 October 1900; **p. 180** "We called on the Antiquario . . ." Mary, Diary, 8 June 1899, BA; **p. 181** "Uncle Logan wanted us to look . . ." Mary to the children, 27 October 1900; **p. 181** "The great excitement of the day . . ." *ibid.*, 12 November 1899; **p. 182** "The great excitement of yesterday . . ." *ibid.*, 14 November 1899; **p. 182** "The night they stole . . ." *ibid.*, 23 November 1899; **p. 182** "Is it safe for thee . . ." HWS to Mary, 15 November 1899; **p. 182** "I shan't be happy till . . ." Mary to the family, 17 November 1899; **p. 182** "Did I tell you . . ." *ibid.*, 15 March 1900

CHAPTER 14

p. 184 "I do *hope* thee kept . . ." HWS to Mary, 31 October 1895; **p. 185** "I fear father is going . . ." *ibid.*, 15 October 1896; **p. 185** "I wrote to reassure her . . ." LPS to Mary, 15 October 1896, Library of Congress; **p. 185** "These poor little motherless . . ." HWS to RPS, 5 March 1897; **p. 185** "Poor father has *cancer* . . ." HWS to Alys, 28 January 1895; **p. 185** "I remember Mother Smith . . ." HWS to RPS, 1 April 1897; **p. 186** "He really has been very ill . . ." LPS to Mary, 23 January 1897; **p. 186** "Uncle Horace is determined . . ." HWS to her daughters, 31 October 1898; **p. 186** "Uncle Horace is still . . ." *ibid.*, 13 November 1898; **p. 186** "Father has had another . . ." HWS to Mary, 23 January 1895; **p. 187** "What a burden . . ." HWS to Alys, 8 February 1898; **p. 187** "Father's death appeared . . ." Mary to BB, 20 April 1898, BA; **p. 187** "Poor Father! . . ." Mary to HWS, 17 April 1898; **p. 188** "Blossoming forth

. . ." Mary to BB, Aug. 1898, BA; **p. 188** "Whenever she passes a public house . . ." *ibid.*, 28 April 1900, BA; **p. 189** "I confess my Quaker . . ." HWS, Circular letter, 5 April 1897; **p. 189** "I am just off to attend . . ." HWS to Alys, 7 March 1897; **p. 189** "Even your wrinkles . . ." HWS Circular, 15 December 1896; **p. 189** "Children, dear as they are . . ." Mary to BB, 11 September 1897; **p. 189** "Of course it isn't a life . . ." *ibid.*, Jan. 1897, BA; **p. 189** "[Karin] is a little angel . . ." *ibid.*, 4 August 1896, BA; **p. 190** "I could not help feeling . . ." *ibid.*, 18 July 1899, BA; **p. 190** "After much trouble I got it . . ." *ibid.*, 27 April 1900, BA; **p. 190** "The difficulty he has . . ." HWS to Mary, 22 October 1899; **p. 191** "DON'T THEE SAY A WORD . . ." Alys to Mary, 25 October 1899; **p. 191** "Thee is really a fiend . . ." *ibid.*, 31 October 1899; **p. 191** "The doctors were afraid . . ." HWS to Mary, 10 October 1899; **p. 191** "I give all these directions . . ." Frank Costelloe's Will, 5 October 1899 (copy SA); **p. 192** "I think it is wise for thee . . ." HWS to Mary, 28 October 1899; **p. 192** "Mary will have told you . . ." Alys to BB, 21 December 1899; **p. 192** "I have just been summoned . . ." Mary to BB, 14 December 1899, BA; **p. 192** "When I see him it is . . ." *ibid.*, 17 December 1899, BA; **p. 193** "[He] was so angry . . ." *ibid.*, 22 December 1899, BA; **p. 193** "It is an awfully sad thing . . ." Mary to E. Smith, 26 December 1899; **p. 194** "The sign is down . . ." HWS to Mary, 16 May 1900; **p. 194** "I had no idea . . ." *ibid.*, 12 June 1900; **p. 194** "I think the main objection . . ." LPS to Mary, 6 August 1900; **p. 194** "She doesn't seem to have . . ." *ibid.*, 13 June 1900; **p. 195** "I should laugh to see . . ." Mary to HWS, 19 May 1900; **p. 195** "Thee needn't think [that] Logan . . ." *ibid.*, 26 October 1900; **p. 195** "Thee will be relieved to hear . . ." *ibid.*, 3 October 1900; **p. 195** "Poor BB! He is so miserable . . ." *ibid.*, 3 October 1900; **p. 195** "I want thee once to see . . ." Mary to BB, 25 July 1900, BA; **p. 196** "To be really frank with you . . ." BB to Mary, 21 July 1900, BA; **p. 196** "More talks with Jephson . . ." Mary, Diary, 28 November 1900, BA; **p. 196** "To the children it was all . . ." HWS to Alys, 27 December 1900; **p. 196** "Don't this remind thee . . ." *ibid.*, 23 December 1900

CHAPTER 15

p. 197 "How life renews itself . . ." LPS, Journal, 28 January 1903, KSU; **p. 197** "'An overwhelming sense of failure' . . ." *ibid.*, 1905, KSU; **p. 197** "Who should get into our carriage . . ." Mary to HWS, 25 March 1902; **p. 198** "Philip and Lady Ottoline . . ." HWS to Alys, 11 August 1902; **p. 198** "I dreamt last night . . ." LPS, Journal, 10 August 1896, KSU; **p. 198** "Logan gave me his little . . ." HWS to Mary, 8 Sept 1900; **p. 199** "I wish Gram would not pet me . . ." Ray, Diary, 25 May 1902; **p. 199** "Karin has certainly inherited . . ." HWS to Mary, 19 November 1902; **p. 200** "It is only the personal things . . ." Ray, Diary, 19 March 1904; **p. 200** "Ray sniffs at the idea . . ." HWS to Mary, 14 June 1901; **p. 200** "I am quite amused to find . . ." HWS, Circular letter, 28 January 1902; **p. 201** "Ray is in all the glory . . ." HWS to

Mary, 17 May 1901; **p. 201** "A little too full . . ." HWS to Alys, 12 July 1902; **p. 201** "Tell Bertie the widow Boole . . ." *ibid.*, 6 February 1902; **p. 202** "My sprees are over . . ." HWS to Mary, 25 February 1903; **p. 202** "I sit and chuckle . . ." *ibid.*, 9 October 1904; **p. 202** "I found it most satisfactory . . ." HWS, Circular letter, 18 August 1903; **p. 202** "Mother had some new little steps . . ." Alys to Logan (on a letter from HWS), 12 April 1903; **p. 202** "I had to let Rose . . ." HWS to Alys, 17 September 1903; **p. 202** "Remember if I die . . ." Alys to Logan (on a letter from HWS) 27.4.1903; **p. 203** "I have heard of a cure . . ." Mary to HWS, 3 May 1899; **p. 203** "Please send me at once . . ." *ibid.*, 17 May 1899; **p. 203** "I am happier than I have ever . . ." Mary, Diary, 28 April 1901, BA; **p. 203** "I think our future . . ." Mary to BB, 27 August 1901, BA; **p. 203** "Even a jealous husband . . ." *ibid.*, 3 September 1901, BA; **p. 204** "I am so tired of addressing . . ." BB to Mary, December 1901, BA; **p. 204** "Thee could make me even more . . ." Mary to BB, September 1901, BA; **p. 204** "You were to be away . . ." BB to Mary, 20 April 1903, BA; **p. 204** "I *could not predict* . . ." Mary to BB, 24 March 1903, BA; **p. 205** "So beautiful, so brilliant . . ." Mary, Diary, 26 March 1902, BA; **p. 205** "What will become of her . . ." *ibid.*, 8 May 1902, BA; **p. 205** "Women, especially certain . . ." BB, *Sketch for a Self Portrait*, p. 15; **p. 205** "It is a great deception . . ." Mary to HWS, 22 September 1901; **p. 206** "Various princesses . . ." *ibid.*, 25 October 1904; **p. 207** "For God and the Absolute . . ." Mary, Notes for Life of BB, BA; **p. 207** "We are enchanted with . . ." Mary to HWS, 1 March 1903; **p. 207** "Last night . . . a fearful gulf . . ." *ibid.*, 16 March 1903; **p. 208** "This book of BB's . . ." *ibid.*, 10 May 1902; **p. 208** "Came home to an awful . . ." Mary, Diary, 25 January 1903, BA; **p. 209** "BB received a letter . . ." *ibid.*, 8 March 1903, BA; **p. 209** "I found him in bed . . ." Mary to HWS, 25 February 1902; **p. 210** "Mrs Gardner came to lunch . . ." Mary to the Family, 19 November 1903; **p. 210** "Mrs G's pet hobby . . ." *ibid.*, 27 October 1903; **p. 210** "We find that [Mrs G] . . ." *ibid.*, 4 January 1904; **p. 210** "We went out to a grand . . ." *ibid.*, 10 January 1904; **p. 211** "I daresay our heads . . ." *ibid.*, 10 December 1903; **p. 211** "It seems like a game . . ." Mary to HWS, 13 November 1903; **p. 211** "The Berensons began to get . . ." Mary, Journal, 2 November 1903, BA; **p. 211** "I think he is really enjoying . . ." Mary to the Family, 22 November 1903; **p. 211** "It was a great disillusion . . ." *ibid.*, 28 December 1903; **p. 212** "The best he had heard . . ." *ibid.*, 10 January 1904; **p. 212** "There is talk of their offering . . ." Mary to HWS, 20 December 1903; **p. 212** "It has been an exploring . . ." Mary to the Family, 4 March 1904

CHAPTER 16

p. 213 "Returned yesterday from Florence . . ." BR, Journal, 14 January 1903, UT; **p. 213** "If only he would not permit himself . . ." BR to Alys, 27 June 1902; **p. 213** "Alys herself has come down . . ." HWS to the Family, 25 September 1908; **p. 213** "Tell BB that I am . . ." HWS to Mary, 7 June 1910 ;

p. 214 "Alys and Bertie have been . . ." Mary to BB, 7 August 1900, BA; **p. 215** "The day before yesterday . . ." BR to Alys, 12 February 1901; **p. 215** "The Whiteheads have always been . . ." Alys to Mary, 14 June 1911; **p. 215** "Alys says poor Mrs Whitehead . . ." HWS to Mary, 9 March 1901; **p. 215** "Poor thing, she has . . ." *ibid.*, 11 March 1901; **p. 216** "It is one of my greatest joys . . ." HWS to Alys, 29 September 1901; **p. 216** "I now believe that it is not . . ." BR, Draft of *Autobiography*, RA; **p. 216** "Dearest, thee gives me . . ." BR to Alys, 6 November 1902, RA; **p. 217** "Anguish lay behind . . ." BR, Journal, 2 December 1902, UT; **p. 217** "I went out bicycling . . ." BR, *Autobiography*, vol. I, p. 147; **p. 218** "I am thankful thee is . . ." BR to Alys, 19 April 1902; **p. 218** "I have been a brute . . ." Alys to BR, 20 April 1902; **p. 218** "It is funny how my depression . . ." *ibid.*, 10 May 1902; **p. 218** "I am sorry I cannot write . . ." BR to Alys, 11 June 1902; **p. 218** "And then in the bedroom . . ." BR, Journal, 18 May 1903, UT; **p. 219** "I was very lonely at Brighton . . ." Alys, Account of the separation, May 1948; **p. 219** "Alys came to Cambridge . . ." BR, Journal, 27 January 1903, UT; **p. 220** "Suppose I have a child . . ." *ibid.*, 8 March 1903, UT; **p. 220** "Not adequately carried out . . ." *ibid.*, 8 April 1903, UT; **p. 220** "No longer any instinctive impulse . . ." BR, *Autobiography*, vol. I, p. 148; **p. 220** "I see that I must not tempt him . . ." Alys, Journal, 29 June 1907; **p. 220** "One good effect has resulted . . ." BR, Journal, 8 April 1903, UT; **p. 220** "I foresee that I shall be tempted . . ." *ibid.*, 9 March 1905, UT; **p. 221** "Alys behaved under the influence . . ." *ibid.*, 3 May 1905, UT; **p. 221** "She still says things . . ." *ibid.*, 26 July 1903, UT; **p. 222** "This journal gives an unduly bad . . ." *ibid.*, 6 April 1904, UT; **p. 222** "I have not written in here . . ." Alys, Journal, 29 June 1907; **p. 223** "Things are no better . . ." *ibid.*, 8 September 1909; **p. 223** "I have had a pain . . ." Alys to Mary (on a letter from Karin), 24 April 1908; **p. 224** "Then came the crushing . . ." Alys, Journal, 8 September 1909; **p. 224** "Alys made a very unfavourable . . ." Mary, Diary, Easter 1903, BA; **p. 225** "Auntie Loo has asked me . . ." Ray, Diary, 31 October 1903; **p. 225** "Alys is leaving today . . ." Mary to BB, 22 August 1909, BA

CHAPTER 17

p. 229 "Expect greatly to enjoy middle age . . ." Mary to HWS, 22 November 1904; **p. 229** "I never felt in better health . . ." *ibid.*, 29 November 1904; **p. 229** "I felt 20 years younger . . ." Mary to HWS, 25 June 1904; **p. 230** "Grandma got a 'Wrinkle Remover' . . ." Mary to Ray, 30 March 1908; **p. 230** "Fafner . . . stayed . . ." Mary, Diary, 15 January 1907, BA; **p. 230** "It looks something like . . ." Mary to HWS, 29 November 1907; **p. 231** "Ray is very severe . . ." Mary to HWS, 24 April 1905; **p. 231** "If the old monster . . ." *ibid.*, 24 April 1905; **p. 232** "Whether with what they reveal . . ." *ibid.*, 11 May 1905; **p. 232** "We did not stop to look . . ." *ibid.*, 7 June 1905; **p. 232** "A real motor cap . . ." *ibid.*, 11 June 1905; **p. 232** "I am sorry she is not fonder . . ." *ibid.*, 14 June 1905; **p. 232** "Logan read Ray's story . . ." Mary to BB, 16 August 1905, BA; **p. 232**

"I feel strongly . . ." Alys to Mary, 30 November 1905; **p. 233** "Thee will evidently be famous . . ." LPS to Karin, 22 December 1905; **p. 234** "To them everything was fun . . ." Mary to HWS, 1 April 1906; **p. 234** "She talked all through . . ." Ray, Diary, 21 June 1906; **p. 234** "It is hard to say which . . ." *ibid.*, 21 June 1906; **p. 234** "They all got slightly tipsy . . ." Mary, unpublished life of Ray; **p. 236** "I am expecting to hobble . . ." HWS to E. Smith, 28 February 1906; **p. 236** "Yes, we did rejoice . . ." HWS to Mary, 22 February 1905; **p. 236** "My stream of company . . ." *ibid.*, 23 July 1906; **p. 236** "I had a worshipper here . . ." *ibid.*, 6 February 1908; **p. 237** "If I should die . . ." HWS to her children, 13 November 1908; **p. 237** "I have forbidden you to mourn . . ." *ibid.*, 22 April 1909; **p. 237** "The talk at Bagley Wood . . ." Ray, Diary, 26 December 1906; **p. 238** "[The Rendel boys] were walking . . ." Ray to HWS, 10 February 1907; **p. 238** "Had I only a Bladder . . ." HWS to Mary, 13 June 1908; **p. 238** "I am appalled to think . . ." Mary to Ray, 1 February 1907; **p. 238** "It is like a fairyland . . ." Ray, Diary, 20 November 1904; **p. 239** "One on my right ear . . ." Karin, Diary, 21 July 1907, AS; **p. 239** "It is rather lonely here . . ." Karin to Mary, 7 October 1907; **p. 239** "Her letter upset me dreadfully . . ." Mary to LPS, 17 October 1907; **p. 239** "I am very anxious about thy mother's . . ." HWS to Karin, 19 October 1907; **p. 240** "It is positively a life-work . . ." Karin to Family, 21 May 1909

CHAPTER 18

p. 242 "I like him . . ." Mary to HWS, 16 January 1907; **p. 242** "I am most awfully sorry . . ." Mary to BB, 8 February 1910, BA; **p. 244** "I took a furtive peep . . ." *ibid.*, 15 October 1910, BA; **p. 244** "I was really quite charmed . . ." *ibid.*, 21 August 1910, BA; **p. 245** "I love you . . . fear not . . ." BB to Mary, 10 October 1910, BA; **p. 245** "I find it so extremely hard . . ." Mary to BB, 9 July 1911, BA; **p. 245** "Your yesterday's letter . . ." BB to Mary, 10 July 1911, BA; **p. 246** "My spiritual influenza . . ." Karin to the Family, Feb? 1910, AS; **p. 246** "Lady Strachey was sitting . . ." Mary, life of Ray; **p. 247** "Ran away with all their legs . . ." HWS to Mary (on a letter from Karin), 20 March 1910; **p. 247** "We sat round the fire . . ." Ray to Mary, 11 November 1909; **p. 247** "Ellie and I are paralyzed . . ." *ibid.*, 14 October 1910; **p. 248** "I am staying here . . ." Virginia Stephen to Violet Dickinson, 17 October 1910, *VW(L)*, vol. I, p. 436; **p. 248** "I like Virginia exceedingly . . ." Ray to Mary, 15 November 1909; **p. 248** "I want to go to Kansas . . ." Ray to Carey Thomas, 27 October 1909, BM; **p. 249** "Uncle Logan is very difficult . . ." Ray, Diary, 8 November 1910; **p. 249** "Uncle Bertie has been here . . ." Ray to the Family, 2 December 1909; **p. 249** "Emotional, unscrupulous . . ." Ray, Diary, 16 October 1909; **p. 249** "The Militant women . . ." HWS to Mary (on a letter from Ray), 12 October 1909; **p. 250** "The engineering is still . . ." Ray to Mary, 20 October 1910; **p. 250** "I felt that now indeed . . ." Karin to Mary, 19 March 1911; **p. 251** "Sometimes it is philosophy . . ." Ray to Mary, 27 March 1911,

quoted in Mary's unpublished Life of Ray; **p. 251** "Everything is going . . ."
Ray to Mary, 29 March 1911; **p. 252** "O.S. is a very charming . . ." Karin to
Mary, 29 March 1911; **p. 252** "If you will tell Philip . . ." BR to Ottoline, 25
March 1911, UT; **p. 252** "You really need not trouble . . ." *ibid.*, 25 March
1911, UT; **p. 252** "It is horrible here . . ." *ibid.*, 25 March 1911, UT; **p. 253** "I
am sure, really . . ." *ibid.*, 2 April 1911, UT; **p. 253** "Karin read me a paper . . ."
ibid., 1 April 1911, UT; **p. 253** "Karin and her friends . . ." *ibid.*, 9 April 1911,
UT; **p. 254** "We went out once . . ." Virginia Stephen to Vanessa Bell, 6
April 1911, *VW(L)*, vol. I, p. 456; **p. 254** "I've had letters from Ray . . ." *ibid.*,
8 April 1911; **p. 255** "Now I think of it . . ." LPS to Ottoline, 20 April 1911,
UT; **p. 255** "Oliver was there . . ." Karin to Mary, 27 April 1911; **p. 255**
"Auntie Loo, I believe . . ." Ray to Oliver, 27 April 1911; **p. 256** "I am not at
all depressed . . ." HWS to Mary, 28 April 1911; **p. 256** "I really don't believe
. . ." Mary to BB, 8 May 1911, BA; **p. 256** "There is nothing to be unhappy
. . ." Ray to Oliver, 5 May 1911; **p. 256** "Karin wrote to say . . ." BR to
Ottoline, 3 May 1911, UT; **p. 257** "Ray talks to me for hours . . ." Mary to
BB, 8 May 1911, BA; **p. 257** "She tells me that she may . . ." *ibid.*, 8 May 1911,
BA; **p. 257** "I wonder whether I am . . ." Karin to Mary, 16 May 1911; **p. 257**
"If Ray doesn't seriously . . ." *ibid.*, 17 May 1911; **p. 257** "What does it mean?
. . ." Mary to Karin, 15 May 1911; **p. 258** "One evening . . . Ray and Oliver . . ."
Mary, Life of Ray; **p. 258** "Ray proposed to me . . ." Oliver to Karin, 18 May
1911, quoted in Mary's Life of Ray; **p. 258** "But I soon put her right . . ."
Oliver to Ray, 29 April 1911; **p. 258** "She's in a very bad state . . ." Ray to
Oliver, 24 May 1911; **p. 258** "One can only hope . . ." Oliver to Ray, 24 May
1911; **p. 258** "How you could have visualized . . ." Oliver to Mary, 24 May
1911, quoted in Mary's Life of Ray; **p. 259** "The most sordid thing . . ." BR to
Ottoline, 3 May 1911, UT; **p. 259** "I only saw rather a nice . . ." Ottoline to
BR, 2 May 1911, RA; **p. 259** "I believe Mrs Smith . . ." BR to Ottoline, 2
May 1911, UT; **p. 259** "Logan has a lot of good . . ." *ibid.*, 15 April 1911,
UT; **p. 260** "If I come after term . . ." *ibid.*, 8 April 1911, UT; **p. 260** "It is
dreadful here . . ." *ibid.*, 20 May 1911, UT; **p. 261** "It was a great grief to me
. . ." LPS to Ottoline, 24 May 1911, UT; **p. 261** "Logan's letter is un-thought
. . ." BR to Ottoline, 25 May 1911, UT; **p. 262** "On the whole he was very
nice . . ." Ottoline to BR, 28 May 1911, RA; **p. 262** "I realize that the situation
. . ." Alys to Mary, 4 June 1911; **p. 262** "Being with Lion . . ." BR to Ottoline,
15 July 1911, UT; **p. 263** "Every word they utter . . ." *ibid.*, 27 August 1911,
UT; **p. 263** "Ray and I were married . . ." Oliver to BR, 10 June 1911, RA;
p. 263 "Karin thinks she has done . . ." BR to Ottoline, 5 June 1911, UT;
p. 264 "I won't say anything about . . ." Mary to BR, 17 June 1911, RA

CHAPTER 19

p. 265 "There is generally a Strachey . . ." Mary, Diary, 21 August 1911, BA;
p. 265 "Like a parrot . . ." Ray to Mary, 23 June 1922; **p. 265** "I find myself

obliged . . ." Mary to Alys, 15 October 1911; **p. 265** "Your father has at
last . . ." Ray to Julia Strachey, 13 December 1911; **p. 266** "What the child
needs . . ." Alys to Mary, 6 January 1912; **p. 266** "And for Oliver too . . ."
ibid., 18 January 1912; **p. 266** "I am afraid I have been . . ." *ibid.*, 3 May 1916;
p. 266 "A desolate rigid mask . . ." Julia Strachey, unpublished memoirs,
possession L. Gowing; **p. 266** "It would be too amusing . . ." Mary to Alys,
5 March 1912; **p. 267** "We have agreed . . ." Ray to Mary, 4 Sept 1912;
p. 267 "I was so glad to get . . ." Ray to Carey Thomas, 1 August 1912, BM;
p. 268 "You can't imagine . . ." Karin to Mary, 2 June 1912; **p. 269** "If one has
anyone . . ." Karin, Diary, 28 March 1913, AS; **p. 269** "I called on Lady
Strachey . . ." Karin to Mary, 22 May 1913, AS; **p. 269** "Oliver and I went . . ."
ibid., 28 June 1913, AS; **p. 270** "I can't help being reminded . . ." *VW(D)*,
5 February 1918, vol. I, p. 118; **p. 270** "She has the look . . ." *ibid.*, 17 June
1918; **p. 271** "In the circumstances . . ." Karin, Diary, 10 January 1916, AS;
p. 271 "My dear, K's bedroom . . ." Alys to Mary, 24 June 1915; **p. 271**
"Almost absurd . . ." Ray to Mary, 9 May 1915; **p. 271** "A giraffe curling
down . . ." Pernel Strachey, quoted in a letter from Ray to Mary, 9 May 1915;
p. 271 "A girl, thank God . . ." Mary, Diary, 25 January 1916, BA; **p. 272** "Of
placing women . . ." Ray to Mary, 28 June 1915; **p. 272** "Don't despair over
my . . ." *ibid.*, 28 June 1915; **p. 273** "I often thank Heaven . . ." *ibid.*, 4 February
1917; **p. 273** "Pippa . . . and I have wound . . ." *ibid.*, 4 February 1917; **p. 273** "It
was a thrilling day . . ." *ibid.*, 11 February 1918; **p. 274** "I don't know why I
find . . ." Ray to Mrs Fawcett, 18 February 1918; **p. 275** "Karin had nothing to
do . . ." Alys to Ray, 7 June 1917; **p. 275** "It is *very odd indeed* . . ." Ray to Alys,
3 April 1920; **p. 275** "Barbara . . . is a monster . . ." Ray to Mary, 20 February
1914; **p. 275** "I find that I feel . . ." Mary to BB, 6 August 1915, BA; **p. 276**
"Beautiful Ann . . ." Alys to Mary, 7 July 1918; **p. 276** "There's only ONE
grandchild . . ." Mary to BB, 27 July 1919, BA; **p. 277** "It is very neat and old-
maidish . . ." LPS to Alys, 21 October 1913, quoted in John Russell, *op. cit.*, p.
91; **p. 277** "What I can . . ." Henry James to LPS quoted by Alys to Mary,
16 June 1914; **p. 277** "He is confused . . ." Alys to Mary, 9 January 1916;
p. 277 "I do miss Henry James . . ." LPS to Mary, 26 March 1916; **p. 278**
"Alys had the inspiration . . ." Mary, Diary, 11 February 1916, BA; **p. 278**
"All the affection . . ." Alys to Mary, 5 April 1917; **p. 280** "There is nothing
. . ." Ray to Alys, 22 April 1918; **p. 280** "Alys is cramping . . ." Mary to
BB, 14 November 1918, BA; **p. 281** "She seems to have no self . . ." *ibid.*, 16
November 1918, BA

CHAPTER 20

p. 282 "I suppose one'll whisper . . ." V. Woolf to V. Bell, 18 June 1919,
VW(L), vol. II, p. 369; **p. 283** "Adrian and I have decided . . ." Karin to Mary,
17 November 1923; **p. 283** "K and A are *too* strange . . ." Ray to Mary, 14
December 1923; **p. 283** "Karin *ought* to come . . ." Alys to Mary (on letter

from Karin), 19 December 1927; **p. 283** "Of course if [K] doesn't come . . ."
Ray to Mary, 8 January 1928; **p. 284** "It is one thing to invite . . ." *ibid.*, 12
January 1928; **p. 284** "Obstinate nature which she . . ." Mary, Diary, Feb. 1926,
BA; **p. 284** "Karin is very stimulating . . ." Mary to BB, 29 July 1919, BA;
p. 285 "At high tide the outlook . . ." Ray to Mary, 25 May 1925; **p. 286** "She
was arrayed in . . ." Karin to Mary, 2 April 1924; **p. 286** "A cloud of Stracheys
. . ." Alys to Mary, 24 March 1926; **p. 287** "It is so very important . . ." Ray
to Mary, 20 November 1919; **p. 287** "It is really ridiculous . . ." *ibid.*, 20 June
1926; **p. 288** "Do, I charge you . . ." Ray to Mary, 29 January 1924; **p. 288** "A
poor wilful creature . . ." Mary, Diary 1926, BA; **p. 288** "On Monday night he
had . . ." Ray to Mary, 21 December 1927; **p. 289** "Now that Julia . . ." *ibid.*,
22 October 1922; **p. 289** "Julia was very anxious . . ." *ibid.*, 7 March 1924;
p. 290 "She remains an insoluble . . ." *ibid.*, 22 January 1926: **p. 290** "Barbara
was there . . ." Alys to Mary, 23 July 1927; **p. 290** "A prosaic affair . . ."
V. Woolf to V. Bell, 23 July 1927, *VW(L)*, vol. III, p. 401; **p. 291** "What a
lack of style . . ." LPS to Mary, 8 November 1921; **p. 292** "I am simply exulting . . ." Alys to Mary, 29 May 1922; **p. 293** "She can digest first lobster . . ."
ibid., 2 June 1923; **p. 293** "I don't know how I can . . ." BB to Mary, Feb? 1919,
BA; **p. 293** "We both think Nicky is . . ." Mary to Alys, November 1920;
p. 293 "I do not think we shall . . ." *ibid.*, 7 December 1920; **p. 294** "BB would
be extremely happy . . ." Mary, Diary, 26 April 1922, BA; **p. 294** "It is a
difficult situation . . ." *ibid.*, 28 May 1923, BA; **p. 294** "I swear I am absolutely
. . ." *ibid.*, 22 September 1922, BA; **p. 294** "This life is *hideous* . . ." Mary to
Alys, 4 September 1926; **p. 295** "Another of those devastating rages . . ." Mary,
Diary, 14 April 1927, BA; **p. 295** "Sympathetically, affectionately . . ." Mary
to Alys, 18 November 1926; **p. 295** "We can only cope with him . . ." *ibid.*, 7
August 1927; **p. 296** "I induced Aunt Janet . . ." Mary to BB, 5 July 1923, BA;
p. 296 "I am vegetating along here . . ." *ibid.*, Aug. 1928, BA; **p. 296** "I dare say
thee has never known . . ." *ibid.*, 30 August 1930, BA; **p. 296** "I wish I
could disentangle . . ." *ibid.*, 4 January 1931, BA; **p. 296** "It is a crave, like
drink . . ." *ibid.*, 4 January 1931, BA; **p. 297** "I heard one of the doctors say
. . ." Mary, Diary, March 1932, BA

CHAPTER 21

p. 298 "Ann had solved the problem . . ." Alys to Mary, 13 November, 1935;
p. 298 "Nicky said an enlightening thing . . ." Ray to Barbara Strachey, 22
September 1932; **p. 299** "I dined with [Grace] . . ." Ray to Mary, 5 January
1931; **p. 299** "I enjoy it more and more . . ." *ibid.*, 8 December 1931; **p. 300** "I
have a grandmotherly . . ." Mary to BB, 11 September 1933, BA; **p. 300** "Such
pain, such pain . . ." Mary, Diary, Oct. 1934, BA; **p. 300** "Last week there was
. . ." Ray to Christopher Strachey, 9 October 1934; **p. 301** "BB says he looks
forward . . ." Mary to Alys, 12 June 1935; **p. 301** "BB, the former President
. . ." *ibid.*, 30 June 1935; **p. 301** "A child . . . of only four . . ." BB, *Sketch for a*

Self Portrait, p. 123; **p. 301** "I could not help laughing . . ." Mary to BB, 2 August 1935, BA; **p. 301** "The doctors are very firm . . ." Alys to Nicky Mariano, 2 August 1935; **p. 302** "I am sure I am right . . ." Alys to Mary, 29 August 1935; **p. 302** "I am always afraid . . ." Ray to BB, 6 July 1937; **p. 302** "That the child should not be allowed . . ." LPS to George Santayana, 16 January 1938, UT; **p. 302** "Rather gloomy letters . . ." Ray to Christopher Strachey, 19 October 1938; **p. 303** "Even if we are all snuffed out . . ." Ray to Mary, quoted in Mary's Life of Ray; **p. 304** "I am dying only I cannot die . . ." Mary to Nicky Mariano, 5 February 1944, quoted in N. Mariano, *40 Years with Berenson*, p. 260; **p. 304** "This is to say goodbye . . ." Mary to the Family, 5 February 1944; **p. 305** "I have a good bit of manuscript . . ." BB to Mary, 8 February 1944, BA; **p. 305** "My Mary's youth was all . . ." BB to Judge Learned Hand, 15 July 1945; BA; **p. 305** "You have the gift . . ." LPS to Osbert Sitwell, 8 July 1943, UT; **p. 306** "Now for a last word . . ." LPS, Notebook, quoted in John Russell, *op. cit.*, p. 139; **p. 306** "[Hilda's] cousin Bobby Trevelyan . . ." Sally Fairchild to R. Hale, 10 November 1932, Houghton Library, Harvard; **p. 307** "This year his spirits . . ." Alys to Mary, 18 March 1934; **p. 308** "I don't much like the thought . . ." V. Woolf to V. Bell, 23 March 1919, *VW(L)*, vol. II, p. 340; **p. 308** "A good cob of a woman . . ." *ibid.*, 15 July 1918, p. 261; **p. 308** "I feel myself frightfully superior . . ." *VW(D)*, 24 August 1918, vol. I, p. 185; **p. 309** "To protect my sister . . ." LPS to Robert Gathorne-Hardy, 9 February 1943, UT; **p. 309** "Nothing interests me more . . ." LPS to Peter Quennell, 9 July 1943, UT; **p. 310** "The friendly gift is . . ." LPS to Hugh Trevor-Roper, 23 December 1945, papers of Lord Dacre of Glanton; **p. 310** "Just enough fear . . ." *ibid.*, 21 March 1941; **p. 311** "I suffer awfully from boredom . . ." Alys, unpublished Memoirs; **p. 312** "I have been wondering . . ." BR to Alys, 20 January 1950; **p. 312** "Meeting again after 39 years . . ." Alys, Diary, 1 March 1950; **p. 312** "What thee says about our marriage . . ." BR to Alys, 6 March 1950; **p. 312** "It makes me so happy . . ." Alys, Diary, 6 March 1950; **p. 313** "June 2: O joy . . ." *ibid.*, 2 June 1950; **p. 313** "June 25th: One week of the 10 . . ." *ibid.*, 25 June 1950; **p. 313** "July 25th: I must have reread . . ." *ibid.*, 25 July 1950; **p. 313** "Dec. 3rd: I so often feel too poorly . . ." *ibid.*, 3 December 1950; **p. 314** "This unexpected arrival . . ." *ibid.*, 13 December 1950; **p. 314** "Still Bertie doesn't . . ." *ibid.*, 1 January 1951; **p. 314** "Much love ever thine . . ." quoted in Alys's Diary, 12 January 1951; **p. 314** "It is the first sign . . ." Alys, Diary, 12 January 1951

Select Bibliography

(All books published in London unless otherwise stated)

The Family

ROBERT PEARSALL SMITH, *Holiness through Faith* (1870)

HANNAH WHITALL SMITH, *The Record of a Happy Life* (New York, 1873)
    The Christian's Secret of a Happy Life (Boston, 1875; London, 1896; reprinted)
    Bible Readings (Boston, 1875)
    John Whitall (Philadelphia, privately, 1879)
    The Way to be Holy (1880)
    The Interior Life (1886)
    The Open Secret (New York, 1885)
    The Veil Uplifted (1887)
    Being Reviled we Guess (Chicago, 1889)
    Everyday Religion (1874)
    Child Culture (New York, 1894), published as *Educate our Mothers* (1896)
    The Unselfishness of God (1903)
    The God of all Comfort (1906)

LOGAN PEARSALL SMITH, *The Youth of Parnassus* (1895)
    Trivia (1902)
    Sir Henry Wotton (Oxford, 1907)
    Songs and Sonnets (1909)
    Treasury of English Prose (1919)
    An Essay on Donne's Sermons (Oxford, 1919)
    Stories from the Old Testament Retold (1920)
    More Trivia (1922)
    Words and Idioms (1925)
    Treasury of English Aphorisms (1928)
    Afterthoughts (1931)
    On Reading Shakespeare (1933)
    All Trivia (1933)
    Reperusals and Re-collections (1936)
    Unforgotten Years (1938)
    Milton and his Modern Critics (Oxford, 1940)
    The Golden Shakespeare (1949)
    (ed.) *A Religious Rebel: Selected Letters of Hannah Whitall Smith* (1949)

MARY BERENSON, *Guide to the Italian Pictures at Hampton Court* (1894) (as Mary
    Logan)
    A Modern Pilgrimage (New York, 1933)

Across the Mediterranean (1937)

A Vicarious Trip to the Barbary Coast (1938)

(as Mary Costelloe) "With Walt Whitman in Camden", *Pall Mall Gazette*,
    23 December 1886

ALYS RUSSELL, "The Woman Question", in Bertrand Russell, *German Social
    Democracy* (1896)

"How to enjoy Life at 80", *The Listener*, 11 November 1948

"When the Fabians were Young", *The Listener*, 27 January 1949

RAY STRACHEY, *The World at Eighteen* (1907) (as Ray Costelloe)

Frances Willard: her Life and Work (1912)

A Quaker Grandmother (New York, 1914)

with Oliver Strachey, *Keigwin's Rebellion* (Oxford, 1916)

Marching On (1923)

Shaken by the Wind (1927)

The Cause (1928)

(ed.) *Religious Fanaticism: Extracts from the Papers of Hannah Whitall Smith*
    (1928), reprinted as *Group Movements of the Past* (1934)

Millicent Garrett Fawcett (1931)

Careers and Openings for Women (1937)

KARIN STEPHEN, *The Misuse of Mind: a Study of Bergson's attack on Intellectualism*
    (1922)

Psycho-analysis and Medicine: a Study of the Wish to fall Ill (Cambridge, 1933)

The American Family

FINCH, EDITH, *Carey Thomas of Bryn Mawr* (New York, 1947)

FLEXNER, HELEN THOMAS, *A Quaker Childhood* (New Haven, 1940)

FLEXNER, JAMES, "Mother's Important Cousins", *Blackwoods*, 319, January 1976

PARKER, ROBERT A., *The Transatlantic Smiths* (New York, 1959)

A Family of Friends (1960)

RISTOW, WALTER W., "The Map Publishing Career of Robert Pearsall Smith",
    Quarterly Journal of the Library of Congress, July 1969

SMITH, ELIZABETH (ed.) *J. J. Smith: Recollections* (privately printed, Philadelphia,
    1892)

R.N.T. (Bessie Taylor), *Mary Whitall: A Memoir* (privately printed, Philadelphia,
    1885)

General (works consulted or referred to)

ADLARD, JOHN, *Count Stenbock* (1969)

Anon. (Edward Clifford), *Broadlands as it was* (privately printed, 1890)

Anon. (Robert Pearsall Smith), *Account of the Union Meeting for the Promotion of
    Scriptural Holiness held at Oxford* (Boston, 1874)

Anon. *Record of the Convention for the Promotion of Scriptural Holiness held at
    Brighton* (1875)

ASKWITH, BETTY, *Two Victorian Families* (1971)

BELL, QUENTIN, *Virginia Woolf*, 2 vols (1972)

BERENSON, BERNARD, *Venetian Painters of the Renaissance* (New York, 1894)

    Lorenzo Lotto (New York, 1895)

    Florentine Painters of the Renaissance (New York, 1896)

    Central Italian Painters of the Renaissance (New York, 1897)

    North Italian Painters of the Renaissance (New York, 1907)

    Sketch for a Self-Portrait (1949)

    Rumour and Reflection (1952)

    Sunset and Twilight (New York, 1963)

    Selected Letters, ed. A. K. McComb (Boston, 1964)

BIXLER, J. S., *Religion in the Philosophy of William James* (Boston, 1926)

BOYD, E. FRENCH, *Bloomsbury Heritage* (1976)

CLARK, KENNETH, *Another Part of the Wood* (1974)

CLARK, RONALD, *Life of Bertrand Russell* (1976)

FRY, ROGER, *Letters*, ed. Denys Sutton, 2 vols (1972)

FURNAS, J. C., *The Americans* (New York, 1969)

GATHORNE-HARDY, ROBERT, *Recollections of Logan Pearsall Smith* (1949)

GRUBB, E., *The Evangelical Movement and its Impact on the Society of Friends* (New York, 1924)

HAMILTON, MARY AGNES, *Remembering my Good Friends* (1944)

HAPGOOD, HUTCHINS, *A Victorian in the Modern World* (New York, 1939)

HARRISON, BRIAN, *Drink and the Victorians* (1971)

HOLROYD, MICHAEL, *Lytton Strachey*, 2 vols (1967-8)

HILL, B., *Julia Margaret Cameron* (1973)

JACKSON, E. V., *The Life that is Life indeed* (1890)

JONES, RUFUS M., *Later Periods of Quakerism*, 2 vols (New York, 1921)

MARIANO, NICKY, *Forty Years with Berenson* (1960)

MORRA, UMBERTO, *Conversations with Berenson* (Westport, 1965)

MORRELL, OTTOLINE, *Memoirs*, ed. R. Gathorne-Hardy, 2 vols (1963-4)

MOUNT TEMPLE, LADY GEORGINA, *Memorial of William Francis Cowper, Baron Mount Temple* (privately printed, 1890)

OUIDA, *Friendship* (1878)

POLLOCK, J. C., *The Story of Keswick* (1964)

ROTHENSTEIN, WILLIAM, *Men and Memories*, 3 vols (Cambridge, 1931-9)

RUSSELL, BERTRAND, *Autobiography*, 3 vols (1967-9)

RUSSELL, DORA, *The Tamarisk Tree* (1975)

RUSSELL, JOHN, *A Portrait of Logan Pearsall Smith* (1950)

SAMUELS, ERNEST, *Bernard Berenson: the Making of a Connoisseur* (Harvard, 1979)

SECREST, MERYLE, *Being Bernard Berenson* (New York, 1979)

SILVER, ROLLO (ed.), *The Bright Particular Star: Letters of Walt Whitman to Mary Smith Costelloe* (New York, 1937)

SPEAIGHT, ROBERT, *William Rothenstein* (1962)

SPRIGGE, SYLVIA, *Berenson* (1960)

TAIT, KATHERINE, *My Father, Bertrand Russell* (1976)

TRAUBEL, HORACE (ed.) *With Walt Whitman in Camden* (Boston, 1906)

WARFIELD, B. J., *Studies in Perfectionism* (New York, 1931)

WATERFIELD, LINA, *A Castle in Italy* (1961)

WHITE, W., "Walt Whitman and the Sierra Grande Mining Company", *New Mexico Historical Review*, xliv, March 1969

WHITMAN, WALT, *Correspondence*, ed. E. H. Miller, 5 vols (New York, 1969–78)

WOOLF, VIRGINIA, *Diary of Virginia Woolf*, ed. Anne Olivier Bell, 2 vols (1977–8) *Letters*, ed. Nigel Nicolson, 3 vols (1975–7)

INDEX

Index